Constructivism and education

This international and interdisciplinary collection of chapters presents and discusses the many educational issues and practices that are touched on by constructivism. Drawing on perspectives from a range of different fields (ethics, mathematics education, philosophy, social psychology, science education, social studies), this book invites us to reposition ourselves in relation to the major currents that have influenced education in this century – namely pragmatism, genetic epistemology, and social interactionism. The chapters call for new reflection on the questions that are central to the project of education and that, in particular, involve the validity of knowledge and types of knowledge, the compartmentalization of school subjects, the mediating role of teachers, and, above all, the ends of education. In so doing, this book relaunches the discussion on constructivism's potential for socially empowering groups and individuals.

Marie Larochelle is a professor in the Department of Didactics, Psychopedagogy, and Technology, Université Laval. Dr. Larochelle is the co-author of *Autour de l'idée de science. Itinéraires cognitifs d'étudiants et d'étudiantes* (Presses de l'Université Laval & De Boeck) and *Qu'est-ce que le savoir scientifique? Points de vue d'adolescents et d'adolescentes* (Presses de l'Université Laval).

Nadine Bednarz is a professor in the Department of Mathematics, Université du Québec à Montréal. Dr. Bednarz served between 1987 and 1996 as Director of Centre Interdisciplinaire de Recherche sur l'Apprentissage et le Développement en Éducation (CIRADE). She is the co-editor of *Après Vygotski et Piaget. Perspectives sociale et constructiviste. Écoles russe et occidentale* (De Boeck) and *Construction des savoirs: obstacles et conflits* (Agence d'Arc).

Jim Garrison is a professor at Virginia Polytechnic Institute and State University. Dr. Garrison is the author of *Dewey and Eros* (Teachers College Press), *The New Scholarship on Dewey* (Kluwer), *Closing the Gap* (State University of New York Press), and *The Erotetic Logic of Teaching* (Kluwer).

Constructivism and education

Edited by

MARIE LAROCHELLE
NADINE BEDNARZ
JIM GARRISON

PUBLISHED BY THE PRESS SYNDICATE OF THE UNIVERSITY OF CAMBRIDGE
The Pitt Building, Trumpington Street, Cambridge CB2 1RP, United Kingdom

CAMBRIDGE UNIVERSITY PRESS
The Edinburgh Building, Cambridge CB2 2RU, UK http://www.cup.cam.ac.uk
40 West 20th Street, New York, NY 10011–4211, USA http://www.cup.org
10 Stamford Road, Oakleigh, Melbourne 3166, Australia

Portions of this book were originally published
in French by the *Revue des sciences de l'éducation*
First published by Cambridge University Press 1998

Printed in the United States of America

Typeset in Times Roman

Library of Congress Cataloging-in-Publication Data

Constructivism and education / edited by Marie Larochelle, Nadine
Bednarz, Jim Garrison.
p. cm.
Includes bibliographical references and index.
ISBN 0-521-62135-6 (hb)
1. Constructivism (Education). 2. Teaching. 3. Teachers.
I. Larochelle, Marie (date). II. Bednarz, Nadine.
III. Garrison, James W. (date).
LB1590.3.C662 1998
370.15'2 – dc21 97-46098
CIP

*A catalog record for this book is available from
the British Library.*

ISBN 0 521 62135 6 hardback

Contents

Preface

In the past several years, the constructivist thesis has taken on a significant role in the theorizations and practices of the international education community. One can find no better evidence of this than in the now classic works operating within the Piagetian perspective. Further illustration may be found in studies of a decidedly contextual cast, which focus on the sociocognitive modes of behavior manifested in school settings, the product of the inclusion of individuals within particular groups (Garnier, Bednarz, and Ulanovskaya, 1991). Constructivism, in other words, is an umbrella term covering theorizations which are primarily centered on either the cognitive subject; the situated subject (or social actor); or the locus of knowledge, which, as Collins has stated (1990), has now become the group: "a living reminder of what it is to think and act properly" (p. 5).

This diversity of interpretations, from Piagetian constructivism to radical constructivism, or from social constructivism to sociocultural approaches, is interesting on a number of counts. Indeed, as Kuhn (1983) so convincingly showed in his study of the "life of natural sciences," every paradigm which, at a given moment, generates the characteristic theorizations, practices, and solutions of a scholarly community also gives rise, within this same community, to a diversity of interpretations. By the same token, this absence of homogeneity constitutes one of the conditions necessary to the exercise and development of scholarly or scientific knowledge (for a telling example of this kind of exercise, see Steffe and Gale, 1995). Such diversity, however, makes it imperative to constantly redefine the conditions necessary to obtaining some sort of theoretical and empirical relevance. Moreover, in terms of education in the making, it serves to maintain a discussion of the different meanings educators attach to theory.

It is within this perspective that we felt the need to take stock of the constructivist perspective in education and, in particular, its contribution to the development of new ways of conceiving and carrying out educational action. The project first took form in a special issue of the *Revue des sciences de l'éducation* (vol. 20, no. 1, 1994), for which Marie Larochelle and Nadine Bednarz served as guest editors and which was devoted to this major school of thought in education. Further impetus for the project came from three American colleagues (Michael Bentley, Stephen Fleury, and Jim Garrison), who wished to pursue conversation over the "problematic subjects" (to quote from Bateson, 1981) represented by the integration of constructivism in education. In its current form, this book represents the outcome of these conversations, which have primarily focused on the presentation and discussion of a number of issues and practices of education touched on by constructivism. It draws on the perspectives offered by a variety of the reflections, questions, and practices which the authors have been grappling with in a range of different fields (ethics, mathematics education, philosophy, social psychology, science education, social studies, etc.). In addition, it has been enriched by the diversity of sociocultural viewpoints deriving from the different origins of the book's contributors (Belgium, Germany, Switzerland, the United States, and Québec, Canada).

As might be expected, the authors who were invited to participate in this collective publication pursue a number of differing objectives. Nevertheless, the positions they advocate share a common aim of highlighting the foundations, promises, and, indeed, limits of constructivism in the field of education, while also appraising a number of interpretations which have tended to trivialize the underlying stakes and issues of this perspective. In so doing, each author has, in his or her own way, invited us to reflect anew on the questions which are central to the project of education and which, in particular, involve the validity of knowledge and types of knowledge, the compartmentalization of classroom subjects, and, above all, the ends of education.

The first portion of this book brings out the frame of reference in which the perspectives of each of the contributors to the book take on meaning. The second section sets out a series of conceptual considerations concerning the problematics of cognition that have been generated by radical constructivism, didactic constructivism, and pragmatic social constructivism; a number of possible links with education are suggested en route. The third and fourth sections are devoted to presenting and discussing teaching episodes and practices, and the mediating role of teachers and their education and professional development within the constructivist mode and in connection with a number of different fields. Finally, the fifth and final section serves to relaunch an ongoing discussion over constructivism's potential for socially empowering groups and individuals.

There is no doubt that without the participation and "complicity" of a whole range of contributors this book would never have achieved its present form. Thus, we would like to underscore the participation of the *Revue des sciences de l'éducation*, a journal funded by the Social Sciences and Humanities Research Council of Canada, and the Québec *Fonds pour la formation de chercheurs et l'aide à la recherche* (a research grant foundation). It was the editorial board of the *Revue* which oversaw the original publication of a number of these texts in French – that is, Chapters 1, 2, 3, 5, 6, 7, 8, 9, 11, and 13. In particular, Adèle Chené, the *Revue*'s director, is to be commended for the valuable advisory role she played during preparation of this book, which included substantial revision of the previously published articles.

We should also like to express our sincere appreciation to SUNY-Oswego, which, thanks to its financial support, made possible the first encounters required for launching this project between us, Michael Bentley, Jacques Désautels, and Stephen Fleury.

Without the expertise of Donald Kellough, who translated Chapters 1, 2, 3, 6, 8, 9, and 11 and adapted Chapter 13, we would have been unable to present the constructivist thesis in as great a range of sociocultural and linguistic facets. We share with him the view that translation is in itself a powerful metaphor for constructivism and education (and vice versa). Indeed, in its way, translation represents a continuing effort at "making explicit" nuances and differences of perspective which both produce and are produced in the enactment of cultures of idiom (inclusive of scholarly and informal varieties, as well as other sociocultural modes of discourse). In addition, we are also most grateful to the following institutions which helped defray the cost of this translation project: Université Laval, the Fondation de l'Université du Québec à Montréal as well as the research center of this same university, the CIRADE (Centre interdisciplinaire de recherche sur l'apprentissage et le développement en éducation) with which two of us are associated.

We also wish to thank Anne Duclos of Université Laval, who, with her sense of professionalism and unflagging patience, oversaw preparation of the manuscript, and also Caroline Renaud of the *Revue des sciences de l'éducation*, who selflessly contributed her talents and diplomacy to this project.

Finally, without the encouragement and aid of William Grundy, Eric Newman, Pat Woodruff, and especially Julia Hough, all of Cambridge University Press, we surely would have been unable to see this venture through to its completion.

The Editors

Contributors

Heinrich Bauersfeld
Institut für Didaktik der Mathematik
Universität Bielefeld
Bielefeld, Germany

Michael L. Bentley
Department of Teaching and Learning
Virginia Polytechnic Institute and State University
Blacksburg, Virginia, USA

Nadine Bednarz
Département de mathématiques & CIRADE
Université du Québec à Montréal
Montréal, Canada

Paul Cobb
Department of Teaching and Learning
Vanderbilt University
Nashville, Tennessee, USA

Jere Confrey
Department of Curriculum & Instruction
University of Texas-Austin
Austin, Texas, USA

Jacques Désautels
Département de didactique, de psychopédagogie et de technologie éducative
Université Laval & CIRADE
Québec, Canada

Stephen Fleury
Elementary/Secondary Education Department
State University of New York
Oswego, New York, USA

Gérard Fourez
Département de Sciences, Philosophies, Sociétés
Université de Namur
Namur, Belgium

Jim Garrison
Department of Teaching and Learning
Virginia Polytechnic Institute and State University
Blacksburg, Virginia, USA

Marie Larochelle
Département de didactique, de psychopédagogie et de technologie éducative
Université Laval & CIRADE
Québec, Canada

Albert Morf
CIRADE

Université du Québec à Montréal
Montréal, Canada

Ladislas Ntamakiliro
Faculté de Psychologie et d'Éducation
Université de Genève
Geneva, Switzerland

Yvon Pépin
Département d'orientation, d'administration et d'évaluation en éducation
Université Laval
Québec, Canada

Marcela Perlwitz
Department of Mathematical Sciences
Purdue University Calumet
Hammond, Indiana, USA

Maria-Luisa Schubauer-Leoni
Faculté de Psychologie et d'Éducation
Université de Genève
Geneva, Switzerland

Kenneth Tobin
Graduate School of Education
University of Pennsylvania
Philadelphia, Pennsylvania, USA

Diana Underwood-Gregg
Department of Mathematical Sciences
Purdue University Calumet
Hammond, Indiana, USA

Ernst von Glasersfeld
Scientific Reasoning Research Institute
University of Massachusetts
Amherst, Massachusetts, USA

Part I
Introduction

Chapter 1
Constructivism and education: beyond epistemological correctness

MARIE LAROCHELLE AND
NADINE BEDNARZ

For several years now, research conducted within the perspective of epistemological constructivism has allowed us to develop other, fruitful ways of conceiving the problem of knowledge and, with this, the problem of learning. For instance, as constructivism implies that knowledge is always knowledge that a person constructs, it has prompted the development of didactic[1] situations which stress the need to encourage greater participation by students in their appropriation of scholarly knowledge. But how has this basic precept of constructivism contributed to the renewal of day-to-day teaching practices? What sort of participation, construction, and forms of knowledge are involved . . . and valued?

Most often, it is a "softer" version of constructivism which is favorably considered. Indeed, taking students' knowledge into account seems to have scarcely modified the usual teaching modus vivendi at any level of instruction one chooses to examine. No doubt students' points of view are elicited with greater frequency. That is, in fact, the major effect of so-called constructivism on educational practices, as Morf has emphasized in this book. However, such elicitation appears to obey no other end than to identify "what's wrong" with the students' points of view. Wrong, that is, from the perspective of the knowledge which is to be taught; no account is made of how potentially this sanctioned form of knowledge may present major divergences with student knowledge in terms of nature, scope, and viability. When this is the case, two major issues go by the board: the complexification of students' knowledge, and the development of a shared, reflexive kind of understanding of the subject and task at hand. What instead acquires prime importance is narrowing the gap separating what the student knows from the subject matter to be taught, as has been shown in the analyses of teaching episodes performed by Voigt

(1985). Thus, we are dealing once more with the same *schémas de docilité* (or "schemata of docility"; see Foucault, 1975) by which the primacy of preestablished knowledge in teaching practice is asserted. It is through such patterns that, more or less implicitly, student knowledge is bracketed off, thus giving rise to the reinstitutionalization of the social hierarchy of knowledge and the perpetuation of orthodoxy in the field concerned.

To some extent, this interpretation of constructivism provides an eloquent illustration of a specific principle of this approach – that is, that all forms of knowledge are inevitably reinterpreted according to the postulates, ends, and sociocognitive experiences of the person who takes an interest in them. However, the originality and promise of constructivism would not be great if it had merely this principle to offer. Such is not the case, though: Constructivism anticipates thoroughgoing questioning of basic principles and epistemological breaks of a kind that are much more disquieting than those which make do with simply affirming that, "if there is more than one way to get to Rome, all roads do eventually lead to Rome!"

The texts that have been gathered in this book provide eloquent testimony of the difficult breaks and questionings constructivism involves. Together, they will serve to go beyond the "epistemological correctness" that the approach risks becoming rutted in unless serious attention is directed to its whys and wherefores, and to the multiple interpretations which are open to construction. Their authors pursue a number of different ends, travel roads which do not all converge on Rome, and yet share an assuredly educative preoccupation – namely, to reflect, and cause others to reflect, on the question of "how we know what we know."

The remainder of this chapter will be devoted to presenting a brief overview of the perspectives set forth by the various authors, knowing full well, of course, that such an exercise brings into play *our* understanding of their viewpoints and *our* capacity for locating distinctions and particularities therein. In short, it is clear we will be presenting our own understanding of constructivism.

Our understanding of the constructivist perspective

Admittedly, in both epistemological and pedagogical terms, the constructivist perspective is, from the outset, quite unsettling. Perhaps that is why it has come in for a number of surprising, indeed, disconcerting interpretations. Constructivism breaks radically with the foundations of empirico-realism, which claims to encode reality in terms of substances and phenomena which are independent of the observers involved. So doing, it challenges age-old beliefs which maintain that facts speak for themselves, that knowledge is the reflection of ontological reality, and that language objectively refers to this reality.

In addition, constructivism reintroduces what objectivism has always sought to leave out, namely, properties of the observer within the description of his or her observations. Thus, the constructivist approach creates additional discomfort, so to speak, since, by the same token, it reintroduces the notion of responsibility for one's actions. For example, as von Foerster has emphasized (1992, p. 11), it takes a brain to write a theory of the brain; now, for this theory to be complete, it should also be able to explain the fact of its own elaboration, and, what is more, the writer of this theory ought to be able to account for his or her writing. In other words, when confronted with the essentially undecidable question of whether we are "discoverers" (in which case, according to von Foerster, we are looking as through a peephole upon an unfolding universe) or "inventors" (in which case we see ourselves as participants in a conspiracy for which we are continually inventing the customs, rules, and regulations), constructivism opts for the latter position, as might be expected.

As offshoot to this, constructivism entertains a specific project which aims not at developing a theory of the world but, rather, at elaborating a theory of the organism who creates for him- or herself a theory of the world (von Glasersfeld, 1987, p. 253). Contrary to what is maintained in one current interpretation, an option of this kind does not hail the return of the "sovereign subject" in all its might, be this in the form of idealism or solipsism. Were constructivism to advocate this position, it would scarcely merit a moment's thought. Escaping the dictatorship of the object – the position of naive empirico-realism – only to come under the rule of the subject is not a particularly innovative solution. At best it merely involves a metaphorical shift along one and the same continuum. But what is one to understand by the term *constructivism?*[2]

It should be pointed out at the outset that *epistemological constructivism* is neither a method nor a teaching model, although it may contribute to problematizing educational practices, as several chapters in this book serve to demonstrate. Drawing on a range of fields, including second-order cybernetics and contemporary linguistics and epistemology, constructivism centers on the development of a "rational'' model of cognitive activity of either an individual or collective variety, including the narratives which are devised to give shape and meaning to our actions. In so doing, constructivism radically diverges from theories and models which concentrate solely on the results of this activity and which, moreover, conceive of such results as the descriptions of ''states of the world.'' To paraphrase Callon and Latour (1991),[3] if it is possible to suggest such a miracle, there is, however, no explaining it! In effect, to claim that one can show a correspondence of any kind between some type of knowledge and the reality it supposedly explains does not admit of logical demonstration, for this amounts to assuming that one would know what reality is! Or, to take Korzybsky's metaphor, a map can never be said to ''be'' the territory – all the more so in that the territory is a question of representation as well. What the map ''refers to'' is inevitably an affair of not only the particularities decided on by its maker but also the distinctions he or she chooses to make in accordance with his or her project and the success with which his or her cognitive and deliberative experiences have met. Accordingly, if the possibility of a relationship between our knowledge and what goes under the name of reality is to be maintained, then we must speak only of a *functional fit*, to borrow von Glasersfeld's expression.

Turning now to another terrain, further satisfaction is scarcely to be had with the methodological type of miracle which partisans of traditional epistemologies are quick to invoke in which the success of some form of knowledge is equated with merely the quality of the research performed and the instrumentation adopted. Two competing theories may very well proceed from a form of research which is conducted according to the rule book, yet one will compel recognition and the other not. The history of science is informative in this regard: why Pasteur rather than Pouchet, Lavoisier rather than Priestley? The history of mathematics is equally instructive, as may be seen in the transformation occurring over many years and throughout a range of cultures which involves the criteria by which the validity of a demonstration or the solidity of a chain of reasoning is judged. For example, the notion of demonstration was conceived by the Greeks as an operation aimed at convincing one's interlocutor in the context of a certain oratorical game and a certain dialectic enjoying acceptance in the community. The same notion is, in the twentieth century, more closely associated with a kind of proof which aims primarily at achieving noncontradiction of the edifice (Barbin, 1988).

To sum up, how does knowledge develop and acquire authority in terms of having the most validity for the community of scholars or as possessing the greatest credibility for particular individuals? What paths have been taken in the process of its production and legitimation? What postulates, beliefs, concepts, and theories are brought into play? What alliances and networks arise in connection with its development? What lines of argument, refutation, and positionings accompany its elaboration? These are but a number of the preoccupations which drive the constructivist project and explain why this approach cannot make do with simply studying results and tried-and-true forms of knowledge, as is characteristic of classical epistemology. As Meyer (1979) reminds us, every result, every type of knowledge was originally a problem which, to exist as such, necessitated a theory and a language, not to mention actors,[4] who could structure and organize it so it was amenable to analysis or, depending on the circumstances, presentable in terms of convincing colleagues of the utmost promise it held for setting out the issues. In terms of elucidating cognitive activity (be this of a private nature or derived from scholarly knowledge), the constructivist project understandably draws methodological inspiration from the principle of symmetry developed by David Bloor which requires that success and failure be treated similarly, using the same concepts and the same interpretative frameworks (Callon and Latour, 1991).

When transferred into the realm of education, the dematerialization of cognition and its products (a process constructivism presupposes) and the principle of symmetry (a condition to which the implementation of constructivism is subjected) lead to major revisions in terms not only of the content matter being taught but also of the way in which form is imparted to these contents. At issue is the need to move forward from a world of facts and materialities to a world of symbols and models which take account not only of the cognitive and deliberative experiences of doers and creators but also of the social relationships which encompass experiences of either kind. A number of chapters in this book are addressed to this very problematic.

From epistemological constructivism to teaching: a variety of views (Part II)

The move from an ontological world to an experiential world is where, moreover, the *radical character of constructivism* is to be located, as von Glasersfeld makes clear in a text he developed in response to the questions of preservice teachers he met during a recent stay in Québec

(Chapter 2). Knowledge cannot be transmitted; it cannot be neutral either. Instead, it is constructed, negotiated, propelled by a project, and perpetuated for as long as it enables its creators to organize their reality in a viable fashion. In terms of daily teaching practices, von Glasersfeld's radical point of view is particularly disquieting. It challenges one of the hardiest beliefs enjoying currency in education today, which maintains the transmissibility of knowledge and upholds the (magical) efficacy of sight and language in respect to that capacity. It is as though by watching a body fall, one could see gravity, or, by using language, one could convey ideas, meanings, and conceptual structures as so many "little packages" to a receiver, as he has ironically stated. From the constructivist perspective, this in essence entails abandoning the mechanistic "channel of transmission" as metaphor of linguistic communication, in which, located at one end, there is a transmitter (the source of knowledge) and, at the other, a receiver (the student). To pursue this image, the art of teaching then consists in the skill with which messages devoid of ambiguity are transmitted, the art of learning in the ever-increasing skill with which a receiver extracts the meaning of the message picked up by his or her sensory apparatus.[5] As other authors of this book would have it, the communication involved here ought instead to be conceived of as a means serving to "orient" students' efforts at construction. That is, it should help them reflect on the processes, referents, and scope of their constructions and aid them in becoming acclimatized to the singular nature of the elements and activities from which other constructions – including those of a scholarly variety – are generated.

Actualization of the constructivist project, however, requires several other "conversions," as Morf and Garrison have suggested (Chapters 3 and 4). For constructivists, it is not enough to break with the object: one must also be careful to avoid the pitfall of the subject!

Thus, according to Morf, if epistemological constructivism is to generate a didactic theory with which a teacher may interpret and contribute to the forming of knowledge, it must also provide an analytical schema with which to approach not only a student's cognitive activity but also the ways in which this activity functions and undergoes transformation in ordinary experience as well. However, such a theory should also guard against superimposing this activity's genesis on that of the subject. But there is more. Yet another conversion is involved for it follows that knowledge can no longer be typified according to the usual semantic categories: now, instead, it must be viewed in terms of a dynamic process. And, as corollary to this, researchers and teachers must now be able to unceasingly reexamine the conceptual framework guiding their interpretation of students' solutions. They must also consider students' solutions in terms of experience-generated potentialities for action standing in relationship to one another according to the type of cognitive activities which such potentialities frame or set off. In terms of teaching practice, this way of classifying knowledge takes on particular importance. As Morf has emphasized, such a classification enables a teacher to not only "act in synergy with the particularities" of the different types of knowledge thus identified but also to recognize the implications of his or her action according to the mode of knowledge development favored. Now, where one such mode tends to involve a uniform set of operations and the other derives from a more highly developed kind of cognitive action (explaining, inventing), the latter will clearly prove crucial to a constructivist didactics.

Opting for a different angle of approach, Garrison takes up the question of the subject by way of a series of reflections by Dewey and Mead which emphasize socialization, hence interaction, as a condition for the subject's emergence. In a radical break with the temptation of the sovereign, unitary subject to which, in his opinion, constructivism is prone, Garrison follows Mead's lead in stating that "there is no me without us." Or, to borrow from Mehan (1996), all searches for sources of the self "beneath the skin and between the ears" would amount to a project as vain as to ask whether the "me" of the blind person starts at the handle of the stick, halfway up the stick, or at the tip of the stick (Bateson, 1981, p. 459). It is in action that the agent realizes him- or herself and constitutes him- or herself. More precisely, it is both in and by the discourse of the Other, in and by interactions and transactions, that his or her understanding of him- or herself and others is shaped. Garrison's position might be viewed as consecrating "the death of the subject." However, it is instead the individual, petrified subject of "folk psychology" who comes in for rough treatment – that is, the subject who was deemed to have features and an identity unto him- or herself. The subject Garrison favors is, rather, a subject in situation, a subject inclined to adopt various identities and roles in keeping with different fields of action and the narrative scripts provided by the community at large – a subject who, in situations of conflict, is also able to exercise a certain reflexive monitoring over his or her various "me's" and narratives, and who thus is capable of restructuring him or herself and the world in which he or she finds him- or herself. A number of classic notions are thus revisited, among which the particularly "charged," continually debated notion of self,[6] in addition to that of conscience and the a priori rationality of action.

Teaching within the constructivist mode: practices and promises (Part III)

In more than one respect, conceiving the knowing subject as a *situated* subject intersects with a number of preoccupations addressed by research devoted to what goes under the name of "cognition in context" (see Chaiklin and Lave, 1996). Generally speaking, the chapters in this section, and the sections following it, subscribe to this notion and bring out how the appropriation of knowledge is as much a function of the immediate context of interaction as of the surrounding representations and beliefs which serve to define "the immediately existing" (Amerio's expression, 1991).

Constructivism at work

A range of practices. The first chapters in this third section highlight teaching and investigative episodes and practices which provide "real time" illustration of the fertility of contructivism in terms of *enacting* mathematics and science education.

The research of Cobb, Perlwitz and Underwood-Gregg (Chapter 5) provides particularly clear insights into socioconstructivism in the making and, as with other contributors to this book, they accord much importance to collective activity and in-class debates. They are concerned with the tensions underlying the teaching and learning of mathematics at the primary-school level and, in particular, those which result from the obligation for the mathematical practices enjoying favor to be both meaningful for students and relevant according to established practice. They cast doubt on the viability of this dual agenda whenever it is conceived in terms of the transmission of the "cultural heritage of a society," as "sociocultural" theories propound. In their comparison of the teaching practices made use of in so-called traditional mathematics classes with those developed in so-called inquiry mathematics classes, the authors show how the former favor the strictly procedural and ritual manipulation of conventional symbols; students are encouraged to develop their capacities for reciting the expected answers much more than their abilities to reflexively participate in the argumentative play involved in mathematics. In "inquiry classes" on the other hand, the teacher is no longer the sole authority present; instead, he or she forms a "community of validation" with the students. Where such a situation prevails, the manipulation of mathematical symbols acquires an entirely different meaning. Students elaborate "meaningful mathematical entities" on the basis of action upon conventionally shared mathematical objects – hence, within the context provided by "their" mathematical activity and the problems which such activity gives rise to. What is more, this elaborative process entails their involvement in mathematical argumentation with fellow classmates. Then, the unfolding and end result of their activities are *re-presented* to them, progressively and in a more conventional manner, as a way by which their teacher may initiate them into scholarly practices.

In a certain way, the research of Cobb et al. may also be understood as involving epistemological democracy inasmuch as teaching action should serve ends opposed to the "colonization of the knowledge of students by that of scholars" (Terhart's formulation, 1988). Instead, finality resides in "an increase in potentialities" (von Foerster's expression, 1992) – the moments, in other words, when students gain awareness of the specific features of a knowledge game which is different from that with which they are familiar and develop understanding of the areas in which various knowledge games are likely to overlap.

Thus, as was previously mentioned, deriving inspiration from constructivism for reflection on educational practices requires more than simply reexamining contents. Indeed, such an exercise also ought to bear on the whys and wherefores of the combined communicational and didactic contract which imparts form to these contents and which binds teacher/researcher, student, and knowledge together within a given educational situation (Brousseau, 1986). Or, to frame the question differently, how a person pictures and conceives the knowledge being taught, his or her own capacity for calling such representations into question, and ultimately his or her participation in the process of producing knowledge – to take but these issues – bring into play another series of considerations: the "place" which is devolved upon him or her during schooling, the epistemological status which is accorded the person's knowledge, and the type of relationship to authority which he or she comes to develop.

Thus, with its fully socioconstructivist stance to approaching cognitive activity in vivo, the study by Schubauer-Leoni and Ntamakiliro

(Chapter 6) sheds interesting light on the possible conflict emerging between the rationalities brought into play by the didactic contract. Particularly noteworthy is the focus they place on the elements both private (what a person thinks to him- or herself and considers worth making apparent) and public (what that person actually makes apparent in a given situation) that compose this contract. In order to penetrate the realm of practice falling under the governance of the didactic contract, the authors set up a study context which was based on a type of contract (termed experimental) which differed from the didactic type of contract in a particular way. On the one hand, the experimental scenario comprised four steps that, if followed, made possible the progressive introduction of a break with the habitual didactic contract – progressive in that it began with problems of a classical type or which involved a range of solutions and then moved on to impossible or absurd problems. On the other hand, this scenario was broken up with questions which encouraged students to engage in a task which was scarcely legitimate within the usual didactic contract and which consisted in dealing with the relevance of a problem and not merely providing an answer to it. Making the most of this tacit (if not provocative) challenge to the expectations surrounding this new contract, the authors enquired into the ways in which students responded: Would they take the liberty of discussing the relevance of problems or, indeed, of rejecting them publicly? Or would they instead reinstitute the logic of schooling with which they were most familiar and which held that the problems being dealt with were legitimate and could be supplied with an answer? Need we add that the paths which such reinstitution takes and the extent to which they become engrained depend on the support and approval given the whole process by the teacher? As the authors remind us, the answer is not an easy one, but the "pulling and tugging" occurring between the conceptual aspects which are specific to the problems at hand and those which are specific to the presumed receivability of an answer provide interesting indications of how the representations involved are interconnected.

A similar preoccupation may be detected in Chapter 7, which was contributed by Jere Confrey. However, the angle she uses to approach her subject is somewhat different in that it focuses on the "nested epistemologies" (Lyons' expression, 1990) which arise among the various actors of a research interview or a teaching situation, most often without their knowing it. In particular, the author analyzes the fact that it is not at all unusual for card-carrying constructivists in the research and teaching community to "forget" the implications of what nevertheless is one of the key concepts of this approach, namely, the concept of viability. Such an oversight is observed whenever they claim that what a student has said is erroneous or inadequate instead of perceiving their own lack of flexibility when it comes to taking other perspectives into consideration. And so the "voices" of students often go unheard by teachers/researchers, who do not always accord legitimacy or relevance to the epistemological models, inventions, and innovations offered by the students. All too often in the course of their analyses and classroom action, teachers/researchers confine themselves to the role of observer, thereby remaining impervious to the observation they are engaging in. Confrey, however, has constructed a methodology for listening and analysis which does indeed allow for the intertwining of the student's "voice" and the teacher's "perspective." Thus equipped, she uses a number of examples to show how the conceptual asymmetry often characterizing this perspective can undergo continuous transformation thanks to interaction with students (in keeping with their constructions). At issue, says Confrey, is an essential component of the constructivist enterprise, which forces us to continually call into question our interpretations, indeed our "perspective" in the interpretation we make of the "voice" of cognitive activity among students. In short, we must recognize that the "Other" – that is, students – contributes to the development of our perspective, a conclusion which, moreover, makes learners of us too.

The study presented by Désautels (Chapter 8) concerns the in-class simulation of a scientific community within a project aimed at familiarizing young adults with the scientific enterprise. It, too, sheds light on the "epistemological innovations" of students whenever the latter are called upon not to reenact science in accordance with what is tried-and-true (i.e., the results) but, rather, to "put it (science) into action." He highlights a number of ideological and cognitive issues surrounding the prevailing type of relationship to scientific knowledge, wherein knowledge and its devoted emissaries come to acquire an indestructible immunity. A contrast is thus provided with his portrayal of how *epistemological reflection in action*, coupled with the loosening of constraints inhering to the teaching situation, increasingly enable these youths to take charge of their learning process and develop a better informed, more dynamic notion of what science is. (It is worth adding that such expansion may be said to occur whenever more than one answer is possible – a situation that requires, moreover, that it be assessed as such by the society of peers concerned.) As might be expected (and as was brought out in the study by Schubauer-Leoni and Ntamakiliro), a number of inner conflicts may be observed: All students do not demonstrate, at least in discursive terms, their usual self-assurance when the time comes to fly the cozy nest of epistemological realism or institutional certitudes, or to cast off the familiar role of model reciter in favor of that more daring role of producer. However, it would appear that the re-creation of a number of the issues and interrogations accompanying the production of knowledge and its legitimation in the form of science bore interesting fruit nonetheless. This dual process permitted students to ''revise and correct'' not only the representations they entertained of their own powers of cognition but also their conceptions of science: science is no longer equated with an exhibit room of curiosities from the sovereign realm of Reality, to which only a few (male) initiates were admitted.

Future promises and stakes. In a kind of recursive second-order cybernetics process, the next chapters bring out the potentialities of constructivism not only in terms of rethinking educational action in fields such as social studies and ethics education, but also of revitalizing the learning of formal types of knowledge by linking them to informal knowledge, a variety of knowledge which is usually endowed with minor status in school settings.

Thus, according to Fourez (Chapter 9), the constructivist approach that has proven fertile for the study of science also holds promise for the study of ethics. Moral choices are contingent and indissociable from our human ways of thinking. In this, they may be compared to scientific practices, which inevitably bring into play core values, forms of reasoning, ideologies, representations, and narratives. By the same token, it is plausible to speak of ethical paradigms in the same way we speak of scientific paradigms. As support for this conception of ethics, the author evinces the ''justificatory model'' developed by Boltanski and Thévenot (1991), which is based on a method having an anthropological cast. This conceptual framework involves an examination of the actual approaches and productive processes adopted by moralists as well as of the arguments by which discussion assumes form and ethical justification is taken as shared. In particular, Fourez dwells on a number of Western ethical and political constructions that have been submitted to this type of analysis and brings out the levels and registers of justification (the ''cities'' – that is, communities of reception and legitimation) serving to singularize them. Whether we are dealing with the city of a market and commercial variety or the city having a civic scope, we are nevertheless obliged to admit that when their underlying visions meet, clashes are likely to occur. Indeed, where, in terms of daily experience and action, such contact does occur, this invariably involves a process of compromise and thoroughgoing questioning (similar to that occurring in interdisciplinary research), in which each city comes bearing its world and typical "objects." From an educational point of view, a constructivist perspective on ethics offers numerous possibilities, among them the capacity to examine the way in which ethical positions are constructed, debated, and defended. This perspective also makes it possible to adopt a different approach to the teaching of morals. In particular, and in a parallel with other forms of knowledge, the search for a certain common good can be explicated in terms of an agreement as to what is taken for an "objective world," that is, a socially constructed paradigm.

While Fleury (Chapter 10) also recognizes the fertility of constructivism for empowering students to understand their social worlds, he nevertheless remains skeptical as to the likelihood that such potential will be realized in American-style social studies.[7] Were constructivism ever to be represented in this field, doubtless it would be in a trivial form. It scarcely could be otherwise, for by reducing to nil the idea that any sort of correspondence could exist between "the map and the territory," radical constructivism also challenges the social categories and classifications which pass themselves off as being "natural." From a political point of view, such claims may indeed represent the fifth column maneuver. For by favoring the sociohistorical contextualization of scholarly knowledge, and the ends and political options which are pursued therewith, constructivism runs counter to educational practices which are oriented toward domestication – that is, those practices in which "reality, and the world, are presented to the learner as a completed, definitive datum" (Freire in Gadotti, 1979, p. 11). Now, social studies represents a field of knowledge which is particularly important for maintaining the dominant culture. Indeed, history teaching plays a key role in consecrating this as *the* legitimate national culture (Bourdieu, 1994, p. 115). However, when the foundations of history are no longer presented as having emerged ex nihilo but, indeed, as the mouthpieces of the persons who have produced them, the project of inculcating a national image of the self is necessarily compromised. In short, there are major stakes involved if constructivism is ever to take its place in social studies education. As Fleury points out, there is no assurance that its integration will be as pronounced as in other fields such as mathematics or science, despite the promise which it holds out for a social education for democracy.

It is Pépin's point of view, however (Chapter 11), that the promise of constructivism risks becoming a dead letter if the "formal knowledge/informal knowledge" polarity characterizing educational practices is not reversed. That, at least, is one of the interpretations that can be made of the somewhat caustic approach he takes toward received educational truths, in particular concerning the vacuity of the traditional teaching project which strives to substitute the formal knowledge acquired in a school setting for the practical knowledge possessed by students. When confronted with a perspective which accords pride of place to formal knowledge and to no other, and which is subservient to the tried-and-true variants of this kind of knowledge when it comes to drawing up didactic strategies, the author adopts the opposite position: we should instead direct our attention and energies toward informal practical knowledge to shed light on our choices and practices. He reminds us that knowledge is inevitably experiential, hence, practical in nature, to the extent that it contributes to the "viability" of the producers of this knowledge "in the world." Knowledge is also purposeful, since if it is to be constructed, a certain cognitive energy must be mobilized. Now, according to Pépin, formal school education can rarely be accredited such capacities for empowerment or mobilization. In truth, were school-learned knowledge capable of becoming embodied in students' practical knowledge and demonstrating a modicum of usefulness for the pursuit or survival of students' projects, this would only rarely occur within the "disciplinary" approach which is usually favored and promoted. As apparently an inoffensive statement concerning the rule of three can, of course, generate development of practical knowledge. But it would take an exceedingly clever person to determine if such knowledge belonged to reasoning by proportions or, instead, derived from the dynamic of human relationships set in motion by instituted contexts of authority. Indeed, as the author emphasizes, it is all too often forgotten that school education takes place within a context of communication involving a variety of representations whose mastery and, indeed, manipulation by students is not merely a question of cognition. Whence the interest of using what Pépin terms "informal practical learning" to examine this context – not only in terms of the possibilities generated by the latter but also of the tensions brought into play.

The mediating role of teachers and teacher education (Part IV)

As might be imagined, conceiving of teaching in a constructivist mode implies a number of conceptual shifts and, indeed, breaks, which inevitably create repercussions for teaching practices as well as for teacher education and "professional development." The chapters in this section deal precisely with this problematic and bring out the stakes and the potentialities which constructivism implies for an initiation into the practice of teaching and the in situ actualization and institution of this practice.

Thus, as part of a reflexive ordering of his own professional commitments and experiences of cognition, Tobin (Chapter 12) elaborates on a number of issues and stakes involved in the move from a positivist to a constructivist and sociocultural perspective of science education. Adhering to a conception of science as a form of argument, hence as a social activity which presupposes particular theoretical and empirical practices, Tobin asserts that a student's introduction to the sciences in the school setting is not a mere question of acquiring theories and algorithms, but is indeed a "form of enculturation into a community of practice." Hence, we are also dealing with a social question, and, by the same token, as Rogoff has pointed out (1995), with a question of participatory appropriation – that is, the "process by which individuals transform their understanding of and responsibility for activities through their own participation" (p. 150). For teaching, such a perspective represents a daunting challenge. Indeed, it assumes that the teacher focuses on interaction and coparticipation in order to facilitate the emergence and sharing of a type of sociodiscursive cohesion within a given community of practice, while bearing in mind that this community is constituted by the very fact that its members have something to accomplish together – that is, building understandings about science. In other words, while the sociocultural perspective decenters the locus of knowledge and power, it does not exempt the teacher of all educational responsibility, as Brousseau (1996) has pointed out. Nor does such a perspective imply returning to the so-called discovery teaching approach, which maintains that the student community, if left to its own devices, cannot but eventually discover the knowledge which is to be taught. Quite the contrary, an "enculturational" conception of teaching assumes that the mediating role of the teacher is focused on how students might render their knowledge visible to themselves and others. What is more, thanks to an incessant and reflexive process of decision making, the mediating focus is also placed ''on the identification of activities that can continue the evolutionary path of the classroom community toward the attainment of agreed-upon goals'' (Tobin, this book).

However, recognizing the purposeful and contextual character of cognition, co-constructing a learning community with students which is both ''sovereign'' unto itself yet open to other possibilities – in short, playing an active, informed, and democratic role as teachers is not a matter of spontaneous generation. Such a problematic also makes evident the need for yet another series of conversions in connection with what teacher education, ''professional development'' programs as well as the usual formats of interaction between teachers and researchers, serve to bring about, particularly in terms of participatory appropriation. Indeed, here again, it cannot be a question of ''colonizing'' teachers' knowledge with knowledge that has been concocted within ''scholarly circles,'' lest one indulge in the asymmetrical relationship to knowledge which we denounced above.

Thus, Bauersfeld (Chapter 13) draws on Bourdieu's concept of *habitus*, among others, to remind us that our teaching practices – especially in mathematics teacher education – overlook the effect of the teaching and learning experiences which future teachers have gone through over the entire course of their schooling. Despite our avowed constructivist intentions, we nevertheless cling to the belief that in order to have students shed or transform their initial representations (mostly of an empirico-realistic nature, that is, embedded in the channel of transmission metaphor), we teachers need only speak the magic word. That is, it suffices to present a promising discourse on new teaching practices and learning conditions or an increasingly refined perspective on the constituents of knowledge which future teachers will eventually be responsible for familiarizing their own students with. Just so, aren't we dealing here with one of those panaceas which constructivism takes so strongly to task? Is it not a tenet of constructivism that students' representation must be engaged with? All in all, claims the author, a ''rhetorical shift'' alone will not suffice, for a ''contextual shift'' must also be effected lest the former be understood according to a setting and a mode of participation and interaction rendering it inoperative. If future teachers are to view the constructivist model of cognition and its attendant sociointeractionist practices as viable and legitimate, they must be provided the opportunity, while they are still learners, to ''try these practices out on themselves'' in our classes. They must, in other words, be given the chance to experience, in the very context of their education, a ''class culture'' of a kind which generates new potentialities within their reality and from which they are likely to draw inspiration in their future professional practice.

In a series of reflections which offer several points of comparison with the arguments put forward by Tobin and Bauersfeld, Bentley (Chapter 14) presents the potentialities of professional development of science teachers in situ. The examples he gives of different projects serve to outline the new profile which emerges from educational reforms drawing their inspiration from a constructivist conception; in addition, they provide the basis for a series of reflections on collaborative research and professional development. Bentley's view stands in opposition to a view frequently encountered in debates over standards in mathematics and science education, according to which the development of science curricula is the affair of experts, with teachers serving merely to implement the decisions of their higher-ups. He advocates instead that we move (1) from a prescriptive to a negotiated and emergent form of curriculum, and (2) from an individualistic to a collective conception of the act of teaching. The form of teaching he favors is embedded in a "Professional Practice Community" (PPC), which not only decenters the locus of knowledge and power but also the locus of risk taking. Thus, in the PPC model, in contrast with the usual top-down approach, teachers and researchers undertake a collaborative type of research based on the co-construction of knowledge and which is conducive to the deployment of teaching strategies that are meaningful not only in terms of learning per se, but of the community of which the students are themselves members. Accordingly, from an epistemological point of view, Bentley's comments may be seen as the expression of the hypothesis according to which the complexification of teachers' knowledge is indissociable from the context in which teaching practices are actualized, and inseparable from the understanding which teachers have of the risks and potentialities which underlie such practices. In other words, just as ideas no longer appear to descend from some notional firmament, the converse applies equally well: the immortal realm of standardized, "ready-made" models of teaching practice no longer answers to our supplications.

Conclusion (Part V)

As a number of the chapters of this book serve to illustrate, the constructivist thesis may be viewed as a duly formulated invitation to change the kind of questions to be entertained with respect to knowledge and to the *rapport au savoir*, or relationship to knowledge. It may also be viewed as an invitation to furthering our reflexive monitoring of our epistemological posture and commitments and to facilitating the handling of the questions and problems which may eventually come to the fore.

But there is more. By "making the order of things less peaceable, and less natural," as Amerio (1991) has stated, constructivism may also be understood as a powerful tool to question and challenge the usual power/knowledge relationship. Indeed, if thinking is reconstructing, "it is conceivable that a knowing subject eventually refuses existing reality (society), imagines an alternative reality (or society), and [consequently] begins to devise actions directed at change" (p. 100). In other words, in constructivism the knowing subject is also an acting subject: "*he or she knows* that he or she can act, do, and bring about change" (p. 111). Accordingly, constructivism may be viewed as a lever of social empowerment which goes beyond the here and now by devoting attention not only to the beliefs and social relationships which often appear "immobilized" (Amerio's expression), but also to the means precisely by which they may be "mobilized" and, potentially, transformed . . . by acting subjects.

In keeping with these considerations, the closing chapter of this book, by Désautels, Garrison, and Fleury, attempts to relaunch discussion about the issues and practices examined in each of the preceding sections. In the process, they provide a telling illustration of how what they call "critical-constructivism" stands in opposition to the unmitigated sociopolitical vaporousness only too frequently encountered nowadays.

Part II
From epistemological constructivism to teaching: a variety of views

Chapter 2

Why constructivism must be radical

ERNST VON GLASERSFELD

During the twentieth century, Jean Piaget was in the forefront of the development of constructivism and the struggle to overcome conventional ideas about the acquisition of knowledge. In the course of Western history, most philosophers tackled the following epistemological questions: "What is knowledge? How does one come to know? Can knowledge be certain?" They arrived at their answers using a logic they considered to be universal and independent of human subjects. Piaget broke with this tradition by raising a question which appeared to be simpler and more pragmatic: "How does a child manage to acquire what goes by the name of knowledge?"

In the eyes of his philosophical contemporaries, Piaget's theory of knowledge involves the "genetic fallacy" and is tainted with the sin of "psychologism." The philosophical establishment therefore feels justified in ignoring the work of that "Genevan dilettante." For the general public, given Piaget's interest in children, genetic epistemology is merely a somewhat abstract theory for explaining cognitive development – an offshoot of child psychology.

This initial misunderstanding was compounded when Piaget's term *constructivism* began to be discussed in educational circles. It gave rise to statements such as: "It's obvious, after all, the children don't simply swallow all adult knowledge whole, they have to construct it!" Even today, a good many authors are convinced that they are constructivists, yet they never questioned traditional epistemology. It was their naive interpretation that prompted me to add the qualifier *radical* to constructivism.

It was, indeed, radical to break away from the traditional way of thinking according to which all human knowledge ought or can approach a more or less "true" representation of an independently existing, or ontological, reality. In place of this notion of representation, radical constructivism introduces a new, more tangible relationship between knowledge and reality, which I have called a relationship of "viability." Simply put, the notion of viability means that an action, operation, conceptual structure, or even a theory, is considered "viable" as long as it is useful in accomplishing a task or in achieving a goal that one has set for oneself. Thus, instead of claiming that knowledge is capable of representing a world outside of our experience, we would say, as did the pragmatists, that knowledge is a tool within the realm of experience. Piaget (1967) expressed this by saying that knowledge does not attempt to produce a copy of reality but, instead, serves the purposes of adaptation.

In this connection, it is important to point out that in the case of a cognitive organism, adaptation proceeds on two levels. On the biological level, adaptation is aimed at survival; on the conceptual level, adaptation is aimed at producing coherent, noncontradictory structures.

I have explained elsewhere the reasons which appear to me to support such a radicalization, first in the domain of history of philosophy (von Glasersfeld, 1978, 1985, 1995), then in connection with the functioning of natural languages (von Glasersfeld, 1983, 1990), and then again in the field of cybernetics (von Glasersfeld, 1979, 1981). For the purposes of this presentation, I will only take up a few basic points.

To understand constructivism, it is above all necessary to be constantly aware of the ambiguity in the ordinary use of the term *reality*. On the one hand, it refers to an ontological reality that lies beyond all knowing; this reality is analogous to Kant's *Ding an sich*, which he qualified as a heuristic fiction (Kant, 1787, p. 307ff; 1881–4, p. 572ff). On the other hand, there is the lived, tangible reality of our experience, from which we derive all that we call "knowledge" – that is, not only the conceptual structures, the actions and the mental operations which are considered viable, but also the patterns of action and thought that have failed.

The term *experience* is difficult to define because it requires consciousness – and at the present we do not have a viable model for that phenomenon. It would be tempting to say that everything which reaches our consciousness becomes experience, but of course such a definition would be too narrow. Under hypnosis, for example, it is possible to locate traces of sensations and even ideas of which we had been totally unaware until then. Nevertheless, I have decided to proceed with a working hypothesis, according to which experience is made up of sensations and the empirical and reflective abstractions of which we *are* aware.[1]

Second, the cognitive subject operates within the realm of experience, and this experience is always segmented and ordered as a result of the sequential mode of functioning that is inherent in the process of attention. Segmentation is basically the product of sensory and motor organs, but then it is shaped by the concepts the individual subject has already constructed. Hence, experience is always subjective. Nevertheless, it is important to point out that this elementary sort of subjectivity in no way hinders the development of "intersubjectivity" over the course of interactions which may be termed "social."[2]

Third, rational knowledge always relates to the realm of experience and to the abstractions (concepts, relations, theories, models) which have been constructed in the attempt to create a more or less regular, predictable world. This quest for models with predictive capacity is based on the belief that future experience will be similar to past experience, at least as far as the regularities which have proven viable until now are concerned (Hume, 1758).

Giambattista Vico was the first philosopher to speak explicitly of reason as a human activity that constructs scientific knowledge (Vico, 1710). Radical constructivism builds on his insights and makes a clear distinction between this knowledge and the intuitions of poets, artists in general, and mystics. Essentially, it is the same distinction that Cardinal Bellarmine suggested in order to save Galileo from an indictment of heresy. Galileo, he said, could simply present his theories as models designed to work out his predictions, but he was never to claim that they were a true description of an absolute reality, a reality to which only the Church had access through revelation.

Fourth, from the constructivist perspective, scientific knowledge is made up of theoretical models which have proved viable within a given area of experience. Even if a particular scientific model is the best available at the moment, it should never be viewed as the only possibility of solving the problems for which it was designed. Furthermore, whenever several solutions have been found, one of them may be preferred for reasons of economy, simplicity, or "elegance," but not because it is "true" in an ontological sense. Instead of truth, constructivism speaks of viability and compatibility with previously constructed models. In other words, scientific models are tools.

Obviously a tool that works in a dozen different situations is worth more than a dozen different tools that each work in only one. However, this unification of models has not always been achieved. At the present time, the most striking example of this difficulty is the nature of light. Physicists have to approach the diverse phenomena of light with the help of two conceptually incompatible models, one based on the concept of wave and the other on the concept of particle.

My last and perhaps most important point concerns language. Once again, the constructivist point of view is diametrically opposed to the tradition according to which linguistic communication is a means of conveying knowledge. In that view, speaking suffices to transfer ideas and knowledge – that is, conceptual structures – from one person to another.

It takes but a moment of reflection to realize that this notion of transmission is illusory. Perhaps the illusion arises from the fact that language seems to work quite well in practical, concrete situations. Therefore the question is not raised of how the contents of a piece of language (which necessarily is the product of an individual consciousness) can be successfully transferred from one consciousness to another. To genuinely grasp this question, it will be necessary to examine closely how the process called ''communication'' actually functions.

When you are engaged, as you are now, in reading what I have written, communication can be said to be taking place. To be more precise, you are in the position of a receiver. Let's take a moment to observe what goes on. To begin with, you have to be able to perceive a series of black marks printed on the page and to identify these marks, first as letters and then as combinations of letters forming words of a language with which you are familiar. You are familiar with a language whenever the meanings of most of its words hold some association for you. At that point, the perception of words calls up meanings in your head and you attempt to link these meanings together in order to develop larger conceptual structures that are related to the sentences of the text. If you succeed and manage to produce structures that appear reasonable to you, you feel that you have understood what the author intended to say.

Described in this way, the process would appear to be quite simple. Indeed, it seems obvious, because we are so very accustomed to it. As a rule, however, it involves an invalid hypothesis, namely that the meanings which the author associated with the words of his text are tacitly assumed to be the same that are now called up by these words in the reader's head. This is an unwarranted assumption. The meanings of words – and this also applies to every sign and every symbol – must be constructed by each user of the language individually, and this construction is based solely on the subjective experience of the particular person. Hence it stands to reason that the interpretation of a word or a text will always remain an essentially subjective operation.

Of course, when children are learning their mother tongue through their interactions with the users of that language, they are led to modify their word-meanings so that these end up being more or less compatible with other people's usage. This creates the impression that meanings are "shared," but it cannot be emphasized strongly enough that the compatibility that is necessary to communicate satisfactorily in everyday life always remains at some remove from an exact correspondence. Moreover, we can never verify if the meaning which is associated by a given person to a particular word is absolutely the same as the meaning we have associated with it. We can only say that so far it has apparently worked. This feeling of apparent compatibility of meaning is, however, always based on the experience of a limited number of situations.

With these remarks on communication, I believe I am touching on one of the most sensitive issues of teaching. If knowledge cannot be transmitted, but must instead be constructed by each student individually, this does not imply that teaching must dispense with language. It implies only that the role of language must be conceived of differently. We can no longer justify the intention of conveying our ideas to receivers (as though ideas could be wrapped in little packages by means of words). Rather, we will have to speak in such a way as to "orient" students' efforts at construction.[3] In order to orient someone, however, you have to have a starting point. Even six-year-olds have something inside their heads. They have lived, made experiments, and they have developed ways of coping. They can interpret the actions and words of their teacher only according to the empirical and operative abstractions which they have worked out previously. This means that it is absolutely necessary for teachers to have some notion of their students' conceptual networks. We call this a model. Obviously such models are and always remain hypothetical because it is impossible to get inside someone else's head. But with experience and informed intuition, a teacher can come to make increasingly useful assessments about what is occurring in the heads of students. This ability separates individuals who are gifted for teaching from those to whom it is merely a rule-governed job like so many others.

A certain degree of interest and sympathy are needed in order to develop one's own mental model of another person. Unfortunately, the spirit prevailing in most schools springs from the notion of "transmitting'' the knowledge outlined in course programs, as though it were actually possible to funnel knowledge ''as is'' into the receptacle-like heads of students who are all the same. It is this misguided illusion of passive learning which prevents teachers from taking students' thinking into account. If a teacher is preoccupied with ''correct'' answers, he or she is unlikely to provide students with the possibility of explaining the conceptual route which *they* took to solve the given problem. Yet, analysis of the process which led a student to answer in a particular way is one of the best means available for understanding his or her concepts and mental operations.

A last point. If we repeatedly tell children that their solutions to problems are wrong, we should not be surprised that their enthusiasm for tasks involving numbers dries up. If, instead, we ask children, ''How did you go about getting this answer?'' we discover that in many cases they are capable of seeing for themselves that something did go wrong. At that point, children become aware that it is *they* who are capable of constructing solutions to problems and that they themselves can decide whether something works or does not. This is the beginning of self-regulation, of a feeling of autonomy, and, as a result, the start of a potentially active learning process.

My practical experience with applying constructivist ideas in classes is limited almost entirely to arithmetic in the first few grades of primary school. However, I have the impression that the general conclusions I have drawn from work in this area are relevant also for teaching physics and other school subjects. I am all the more convinced of this because our general approach is not a new idea. The notion of self-regulation was implemented by Maria Montessori, and it was stunningly illustrated in the book written by Ashton-Warner (1963), who described her work in a school in New Zealand. Indeed, a number of extraordinary teachers have always managed to foster their students' active understanding rather than making do with the repetition of ''correct'' answers. In order to achieve this, however, they had to rely on their intuition. Radical constructivism offers a theory of knowledge, communication, and the learning process which could serve as a point of departure for all teachers who have not been blessed with the gift of exceptional intuition.

Chapter 3
An epistemology for didactics: speculations on situating a concept

ALBERT MORF

The relationship between constructivist epistemology and teaching is uneasy, as is often evidenced by the dissatisfaction or irritation which arises in discussions over didactics. This essay has been written with a dual objective in mind: The first consists in tentatively suggesting one possible explanation for the difficulties encountered in transposing constructivism into teaching practice, the second in proposing a number of speculations as to what might constitute a more relevant, if somewhat makeshift, type of epistemology for pursuing reflection on didactics.

At the outset, however, I wish to exclude from this debate the case of specialists who have seized on constructivism to advocate respectable didactic principles which are merely compatible with this current of thought and nothing more. Take, for example, their insistence on the necessity of students' participation in the reconstruction of knowledge, a principle which has been applied in various ways from the days of the venerable Active School down to the present. It is not constructivism's duty to supply up-to-date arguments to pedagogical ideologies of even the most well-reasoned variety.

Subject, object, and knowledge

One traditional formula suggests that we consider knowledge as a particular relationship between a subject and an object; this way of viewing things lends itself well to interesting abstractions and worthwhile conceptual elaboration. But even before it was considered from the perspective of didactics, it was a source of ambiguities which the emergence of constructivism has not sufficed to clear up.

The *subject* appears at the outset as the subject encountered in the psychologist's notion of the term – that is, as a being who is endowed with the tools of knowledge (ranging from perception to reflection). Thereafter, in a theory, this real subject may be subsumed under subjects of a more abstract nature, such as groups of students or types of individuals. Finally, the epistemic subject may take on increasingly general definitions until it is ultimately identified with any cognitive system which is capable of generating meanings.

The *object* also undergoes a similar process of expansion and abstraction. The thing-object, which the subject appears to directly apprehend, gives way to other observable realities, such as event-objects or processes governed by laws, which carry over from thing-objects the appearance of reality as existing independently of the subject (even when they are admitted to be the product of induction). The epistemic object nevertheless remains malleable in the hands of theoreticians and lends itself to arbitrary classifications to the same degree as the epistemic subject.

The *particular relationship* may be understood first of all as the product of interaction between the real subject and the real object. However, it is also possible to conceive of this as a representation of the object in the subject: take, for example, the concept of empirical abstraction in Piaget, or theories of concept formation. In contrast with the subject and the object, knowledge as the relationship between the two does not lend itself well to conceptual elaboration; knowledge is treated as the *object which is known* (by the scholar or teacher), and thus it belongs either to external reality or to the subject, and its conceptual elaboration is jeopardized by this conflict at every stage.

Didactics researchers concerned with theorizing teaching practice are faced with a situation which is ambiguous from the outset. When they consider students (whatever their epistemic status), it is the students who form the first term of the subject–object relationship. When they consider didactic intervention, however, it is the researchers themselves who become knowledge-bearing subjects. For that reason, they occupy a dual position as the observers and the observed. That is, in order to theorize the problems specific to didactics, they study students and their activity (they observe), but they must, at the same time, account for the particularities of knowledge which they are portraying (they are observed). Thus, the status of subject affects students and researchers alike.

The notion of object also undergoes a similar split.

This situation renders the concept of knowledge unstable whenever it is a question of didactics. Whenever knowledge is considered as an entity to be brought out in a student, it ceases to be a relationship of subject and object and becomes an *aspect of the psychological subject*. Forming or transforming an element of knowledge always implies cognitively transforming a subject. In addition, if this same element of knowledge is considered as some entity to be transmitted or conveyed, it collapses into the didactics researcher's knowledge.

In didactics research, efforts to elaborate a basis for theorization have given rise to a perpetual conflict between, on the one hand, psychological theory, which proposes models of the student (learning processes, intellectual tools, development, motivations, etc.) and, on the other, epistemological schemata of knowledge. The latter have generated teaching principles that are occasionally naive. Such principles propose, for example, reorganizing the knowledge of specialists by proceeding from the simple to the complex or from the concrete to the abstract (believing on occasion that both approaches amount to the same thing), with the result that some didactics researchers rely on the most stripped-down axiomatics of their discipline in order to "work from the ground up" in a classroom setting.

It is tempting to think that one may avoid this conflict by founding didactics on genetic epistemology. Space will be devoted below to explaining why this way out of the problem remains unsatisfactory for the time being.

In conclusion, we must ask ourselves whether the difficulties encountered in constructing a theory of didactics are not related to the approach which considers the knowledge at issue to be either an aspect of the student (i.e., the subject), or an aspect of the objects known by the teacher. In other words, it seems as though didactics theory were lacking an object which is specific to it.

In order to provide theory with just such an object, it is necessary to perform a conversion. Just as constructivism succeeded in treating the object as an aspect of knowledge, the subject must also be successfully dealt with as an aspect of knowledge. It is on the second half of this argument that epistemological constructivism appears unprepared to undergo conversion.

The contribution of constructivism

In didactics, epistemological constructivism refigures the relationship of object to knowledge by eliminating recourse to the external object from theory. Since knowledge cannot be reduced to a direct apprehending of reality, however expanded and abstract this may be, its development in students cannot be reduced to the transmission of observed truths either. Likewise, since that which is known (knowledge) is the product of a construction, conveying such knowledge thus amounts to a reconstruction by either the interlocutor or the student.

The major effect of constructivism on teaching has been to open up new possibilities: it has justified the introduction of types of teaching practice and didactics which base the acquisition of knowledge on the elaboration of knowledge by the students themselves. The fecundity of these approaches is dependent on two conditions: First, the epistemology of teachers must be adequate – that is, their own image of knowledge must be relevant for a didactics based on reconstruction; secondly, their interpretation of students' cognitive activity must be relevant for their own didactic strategies. It is clear that at the present time these two conditions are only rarely met.

Just as theoretical science provides an engineer with models of reality and action, didactics ought too to provide teachers with models of knowledge which enable them to interpret and act. Hence, constructivism ought to generate a sui generis theory of didactics. In order to do so, however, it must first be transformed from an epistemological constructivism into a didactical constructivism.

The relationship of object to knowledge has undergone profound change, but what of the relationship of subject to knowledge? Whereas knowledge has ceased being a reflection of reality, subject and knowledge continue to be closely amalgamated. In this connection, didactic action appears first of all as a type of action on a subject (questions are put to the subject; he or she is provided with explanations; textbooks are created with the subject in mind; it is the subject who understands or makes mistakes, who is more or less motivated, etc.). Didactical thinking continually travels back and forth between the subject and knowledge, without, however, making the steps in this process clear, if indeed it recognizes that such movement is actually occurring.

This situation is an uncomfortable one: it appears that psychology, even in the case of those branches which are close to constructivism, does not supply the models which are appropriate to deducing the principles of didactic action. Now this inadequacy, which is apparent in terms of both theory and practice, rests on an illusion.

In effect, whereas constructivism dispenses with the concept of truth as existing independently of knowledge, it maintains the illusion of the knowable subject. The subject-in-itself is still referred to in every didactics, and obviously lends itself to all sorts of postulates, many of which conflict with one another.

It is possible to imagine a number of explanations for this state of things. Today, no adult would attempt to explain physical reality by identifying him- or herself with objects; to do so would border on magical thinking. In didactics, identification with the subject appears to be the rule, allowance being made for a number of adjustments which have been made possible by child psychology. The intuitions of the teachers still pass for self-evident truths.

This illusion stems from another, more theoretical source. Piaget's genetic epistemology was derived from psychology. The observation of the activity of children is considered to reveal knowledge, as much so for the states of knowledge as for their transformations.

The theoretical foundations of didactics superimpose the genesis of knowledge on the genesis of the subject from the very outset. This poses no significant problem for the orientation of Piaget's work. As long as genetic epistemology is primarily concerned with the genesis of the tools of knowledge, one may justifiably ascribe structures of action to the subject and view phenomena such as *décalages horizontaux* (i.e., lags in development) as matters of secondary importance. In this context, it is even acceptable to ignore the fact that only selected sectors of adult experience are accessible to operational treatment. In opposition to this, a focus on instruments leaves didactics theory empty-handed, since it must account for knowledge itself and the direct action specifically aimed at transforming it. The notion of founding a didactics on purely structural epistemological models appears an unlikely possibility.

For a didactical constructivism

The enterprise of preparing a theory which is relevant for didactics involves the dual requirement of choosing an object of theory and a point of view. In the case with which we are confronted, this choice is difficult because it obliges us to free ourselves from the subject – that is, from the categories taken over from psychology and genetic epistemology. A theory can take shape gradually in the form of a speculation. Such a speculation need not be arbitrary; rather, it should propose a number of tentative, open schematizations since it also ought to lend itself to ongoing interaction with observation and experimentation. The following are suggestions which could prove useful in orienting research.

(a) The main object of theory should consist in knowledge which may be ascribed to an unspecified subject. It is allowed that observable knowledge may fall within a cognitive system which could be an individual subject, a group, a culture – that it may, in other words, fall within any system capable of assigning a meaning to an object or event. The term *unspecified* implies, however, that the characteristics of this system (hence of the subject, in the broader meaning of the word), are not to be brought into any description of the knowledge in question. An analogy will serve to render the term *unspecified* somewhat less disturbing. In our everyday physical world, combining the total weight of 200 g of feathers and 100 g of glue does not give us a moment's pause. We know, however, that such an operation does not go without saying in all cultures, or at all stages of development. The validity of adding 200 plus 100 had to be worked out for unspecified quantities, as also the unit of weight had to be elaborated for unspecified materials. Hence, a process of detachment occurred among objects, their properties, and operations. This detachment has not been accomplished in all areas of knowledge; it certainly has not been accomplished in the case of didactics.

(b) Theory ought to account for the transformation of knowledge (either during interaction with external conditions or within itself); of course, development is included within these transformations, but it should not be identified with the development of a subject. By excluding the psychological subject from the body of theory, it follows that processes of ontogeny and learning shall not be introduced in any other capacity than as external conditions or factors which have an effect on the transformation of knowledge.

(c) Theory should be oriented in accordance with didactical objectives. The description and analysis of knowledge, as well as the models of its transformation, should be carried out in a way which makes it possible to derive action on knowledge (hence didactics), at least in terms of generating verifiable hypotheses.

On the other hand, theory should not automatically incorporate the constructivist orientation. Instead, it ought to account for the functioning of knowledge in a way which leaves room for constructivist conceptions without, however, imposing them to the exclusion of others. In other words, the frame of reference proposed by theory should be free of a priori judgments as to the origins of the knowledge whose observation it makes possible. To sum up, the categories of description must accord with a dual requirement: knowledge will be described as *knowledge by an unspecified subject of an unspecified object*. This requirement will also be extended to the definition of knowledge.

If we succeed in developing a suitable theoretical approach, it should be acceptable, for example, to speak of a rational type of knowledge without necessarily ascribing this to a rational subject. It should be possible, for example, to not consider knowledge of the rule of three as a rational type of knowledge only because it has a rational origin or because it is applied by a rational subject; it may well be the case that the subject is acting in blind obedience to some automatism.

(d) The definition of knowledge, it has been remarked, must remain open until such time as a serious theory takes shape. As for the definition which is advocated here, it conforms to postulates which acquire meaning above all in relation to the didactical orientation of this essay.

It is worth noting that in the French version of this text, ''knowledge,'' the collective noncount noun in English, has often been employed using the plural form: *les connaissances.* While the singular *la connaissance* has also been employed, it is not Knowledge, the philosopher's concept, of which it is a question, but rather the multiple forms of knowing.

The chief determining postulate consists in considering knowledge as potentialities for action. The choice proceeds more from an angle of observation than a definition. In this perspective, knowledge is interesting to the extent that it gives forth onto action; for the observer, knowledge appears only in action, be this material, cognitive, or discursive in nature. Finally, in a later phase of theoretical construction, I will be concerned with locating the origin of knowledge in action itself, in accordance with a circular process which has been directly inspired by genetic epistemology.

Two additional clarifications are in order here. In the first instance, every potential for cognitive action will not be considered as knowledge; thus, for example, possessing a fully functioning central nervous system certainly represents a potential for action, but it is not knowledge in and of itself. Also, it is cognitive action which is subject to emphasis, even if this entails giving it a very broad meaning: in observable action, it is the cognitive components which are of interest to us.

In the second instance, as concerns the origin of knowledge, a potential for action will be considered as knowledge if it results from the activity of the cognitive system on its objects. For example, the capacities of an infant will not be considered as knowledge (whereas without a doubt, they represent a potential for action). However, the first skills which the infant develops by means of acting on his or her environment could, even at this early stage, be considered as knowledge. In short, for the purposes of definition, I consider knowledge as *experience-generated potentialities for action.*

(e) Knowledge which is defined in this manner and which is considered from the perspective of didactics theory does not necessarily conform to the categories of classical epistemology. Above all, it is not a question of my attempting here to account for the constitution of scientific knowledge. By concentrating primarily on everyday knowledge (albeit in a school setting), room is provided for gradually constructing a theory which is capable of accounting for: the functioning of several types of knowledge in the realm of everyday experience; their transformations in various situations of adaptation; and the possibilities for intervening in the formation of knowledge.

The types of knowledge to be given form by theory will be variable in terms of inclusiveness and extensiveness. Hence, they will be resistant to all attempts to establish an inventory of semantic fields. Thus, for example, knowledge of several irregular verbs may, for the same knowing subject, represent both a set of automatized habits or a linguistic phenomenon which requires explanation. In the first instance, a parallel may be drawn with an automatism of elementary calculation, because both function and undergo transformation in a similar fashion; in the second instance, however, it matters not that the object of knowledge remains the same, for the functioning and transformations of this knowledge will be totally different (as will also the didactical approach to be adopted). Two types of knowledge, selected at random in everyday knowledge but occurring in areas at some remove from one another (such as mechanics and the cooking arts) can both give rise to evolved forms of cognitive action (explaining, inventing, correcting), or, on the contrary, impose an unvarying series of operations to be executed. Description of these types of knowledge will create relationships with one another not on the basis of fields or areas but rather on the characteristics of the activity which is conditioned by them.

Description and analysis of potentialities for action

It goes without saying that the parameters which may be used to describe knowledge are, from the outset, of an infinite variety. Choosing them depends in the first instance on the orientation of the observer. I will make do here with offering a number of examples which should serve to illustrate the variety of possible distinctions.

The first set of examples may fall outside the customary constructivist choices.

Stability/instability. This distinction corresponds to a historical concern of teachers, who venerate perpetuity and abhor oblivion. Old didactical principles such as *non multa sed multum* (''not many, but much'') have traveled down the ages without having been definitively contested.

Openness/closedness. The types of knowledge established for an identical object of knowledge may be open and tentative, ready to change in keeping with experience and to incorporate new objects – ready, as well, to disappear from the subject's stock and gear. Other types are established in their definitive form from the outset; their mode of functioning is predictable in a given situation. In all likelihood, distinct modes of formation (didactic or spontaneous) could be ascribed to each type of knowledge.

Level of organization. For a single area of reality, various levels of knowledge could be set out, such as the stages proposed in the theory of Piaget (preoperational, concrete operational, and formal), and so could levels of abstraction, and so forth. In passing, it is worth using this example to point out once again that the proposed approach implies that it is not a given subject which is said to be ''concrete operational'' but a given instance of knowledge. In addition, it is easy to allow that for a given reality, several levels of vicarious knowledge may exist in one and the same subject. For example, in the case of our own physiology and its instances of malfunctioning, we can activate various reactions such as intuitive, almost infantile, connection-making, or coherent, rational schemata, simplistic formulae or hypothetico-deductive reasoning, according to our orientation and our preparation. Teaching with consciously worked-out objectives entails defining not only the level of knowledge which is to be eventually attained but also that of the knowledge which is to be transformed by such teaching.

The following are two examples of distinctions which would be made in the framework of a constructivist-oriented didactics.

Potential for association. Certain types of knowledge are characterized by the fact that they seem to tend to undergo not only consolidation (by being confronted with a variety of cognitive objects) but also coordination with one another. Other types, on the other hand, appear to avail themselves of nothing more than application and repetition, thus remaining autonomous. This distinction is of obvious interest for didactics research, since the capacity to recognize such types of knowledge provides researchers with a theory enabling them to act in synergy with the particularities of each knowledge type.

Generativeness. As in the preceding example, this distinction serves to formulate a type of experience which is rather common among those concerned with epistemology or teaching: Certain types of knowledge which are otherwise satisfactory and effective remain sterile when confronted with new problems, whereas other types appear to contain everything required to produce new knowledge under certain conditions. A change in conditions leads the former from success to failure, whereas it sparks invention and research in the latter. Such is the very core of constructivism, as a constructivist didactics involves nothing more than mobilizing and situating knowledge of the type referred to here as generative. Accordingly, didactical constructivism should be provided with the instruments necessary for identifying such types of knowledge.

It becomes immediately apparent that there is a whole range of possible distinctions, but it is equally foreseeable that they are quite likely to intersect one another in the course of observation and hence undergo a reduction in number. It would be inappropriate, however, to attempt to establish a system of stripped-down description prior to observing and experimenting with categories of knowledge. For example, it is by overlapping system-derived observations onto one another that it will become possible to determine perhaps that generativeness may overlap openness but not necessarily levels of organization.

Thus, research should be pursued with a view to exercising the dual freedom of delimitation and selection of filters. Just as in the work of teachers themselves, in theory, one may choose objects of observation which are either limited elements (for example, a particular rule of grammar, a topical physical phenomenon) or wide-ranging wholes. Moreover, descriptive criteria may well be determined by prior choices which have nothing to do with theory per se. Hence, the choice by a teacher in favor of obtaining predictable, unchanging behavior or, on the contrary, in favor of eliciting adaptable, fluid knowledge is not a choice which a theoretically oriented didactics is going to decide; such a choice has, rather, cultural and ideological sources. Nevertheless, theory can enable teachers to better define their objectives and to recognize the implications of them.

Didactical choices

A framework of observation centering on the concept of knowledge/potential for action is, however, insufficient for guiding the construction of a didactics. Research ought first to provide a minimum of information concerning the formation and transformation of knowledge. Certain constants may be predicted on the basis of common teaching experience and a ''modest, everyday'' epistemology. This situation can be illustrated by two ways in which a form of knowledge can evolve. Closed, definitive forms of knowledge develop through an additive process and can result in a new form of knowledge which is adapted in advance of a specific situation; on the other hand, knowledge of the generative type develops through a growth process, that is, via the incorporation of new experiences and differentiation. A metaphor which became somewhat overused some time ago serves to illustrate this scheme of analysis. Some potentialities for action take shape like a bicycle: a set of prefabricated parts are put together according to a rigid order; once they have been assembled, they form an effective instrument. Other potentialities take shape in the manner of an apple tree: the sapling of an apple tree is planted; it is provided a series of conditions which are favorable to its growth; and it is left on its own to grow into an apple tree. Schools, it may be observed, attempt all too often to obtain apple trees by assembling a trunk, branches, and leaves . . .

In the first case, the product is predictable; however, if one component is removed, it becomes nonfunctional. It offers an image of an automatized approach of the kind obtained by assembling habits. In the case of the apple tree, development is uncertain; it is an approach which for the most part eludes the control of the producer. However, if one branch is removed from the apple tree, it compensates for this loss and continues to grow. That is the image of knowledge according to the constructivist ideal.

In the day-to-day reality of teaching, the two procedures are often disturbingly confused, for the simple reason that our didactic interventions are themselves pieced together in an almost haphazard fashion out of incompatible elements.

If we were to apply our (future) analytical framework to a given field (for example, medicine, plumbing, or accounting), we would be sure to discover a more or less correctly organized composite of potentialities for action occurring at varying levels, some of which would be fluid and capable of generating knowledge, with others being closed and immutable, while still others would be of general scope, as opposed to those of a topical nature, and so on. A ''modest, everyday'' epistemology in good working order might make it possible to determine what, within this whole, has a functional reason for existing and what ought to be considered as an accident or a cultural malformation. When applied to teaching options, this reflection calls forth a most daunting question: for any citizen who has gone to school, what categories should his or her universe of knowledge consist of?

If it is allowed that different categories of knowledge function according to different modes and that different types of human activity require different types of potential for action, it is certainly possible to elaborate a basis for theorizing teaching objectives. Two lines of research are available for constructing a theory capable of operating these choices.

It is necessary to grasp the modes by which different categories of knowledge are transformed (genesis, development, adaptation). Once these modes of transformation have been established, didactic intervention should be developed to the greatest degree in accordance with modes which are spontaneous, and with a view to producing optimal synergy between the action of the teacher and the modes under which potentialities for action function.

Within this nascent theory, research should integrate a principle of economy and the means by which to incorporate it. It is obvious that a limited, closed habit is easier to develop – is less costly, in other words – than a type of knowledge which leaves room for invention rather than limiting itself to automatism, and that it is more economical in the short term to inform than to explain. It is conceivable that with an adequate type of epistemology, it would be possible to evaluate the cognitive cost of a particular category of knowledge. How is this cost to be measured, in terms of experience, time, and effort? We must, for the time being, make do with merely formulating this question, in the hopes of some future response.

It is nevertheless possible to outline a number of lines of inquiry worth pursuing. It would certainly be possible to bring out how certain assemblages of closed-type knowledge (sets of procedures or algorithms, or types of discourse which simulate scientific knowledge) are economic in the short term (i.e., offer a payoff in a school setting) but costly in the long term, because they are unable to withstand changes in conditions and resist modification. An adequate description of the conditions of internal economy could, to a certain extent, explain the illusions under which teaching has labored. The expansion of ''generative''-type potentialities appears costly because it is slow during its preparatory stages, whereas the assembling of closed-type knowledge provides proof of performance from the very start.

Observations of this nature have been made by exceptional teachers at all times; lacking any "scientific demonstration," however, they have been subordinated to the fiats of experts. In a word, in didactical constructivism, epistemological constructivism might well find the tools with which to substantiate the strong intuitions which can result from classroom experience.

Conclusion

Speculation is not always a serious affair; indeed, it is enjoyable only to those who engage in it. However, it becomes a necessity at certain moments in the history of a profession.

It has become apparent to me that didactics suffers from a number of concealed difficulties which have kept it from becoming scientific. Whereas the epistemology of science has admitted constructivism into its own structures, didactics appears to have imported it as a very general ideology, without successfully incorporating it into its paradigms. This resistance may be related to the fact that teaching is concerned with humans and is hence dependent on various types of psychology, as much scientific as intuitive in nature, and which bear on the activity of the teacher and the student both.

Didactics would appear to lack an intrinsic epistemology. Theoretically speaking, it is capable of accepting constructivism, which frees science from an external object. Owing to just this lack of a specific epistemology, the object of didactics is poorly defined. It is in fact dual: it is comprised, on the one hand, of the object seen as external to knowledge (which it has been constructivism's aim to release it from), and, on the other, of the subject seen as external to knowledge (which has been imposed on it by psychology).

If, in the preceding speculations, it is admitted that didactics might work out its own modest epistemology, which eliminates both the external object of science to which reference is made and the external subject of psychology, then it becomes possible to accept the notion that didactics should be provided with models of knowledge which relate both to unspecified objects and unspecified subjects. The principles of didactic action might then be constructed on the basis of a gradual, ongoing development of a didactical epistemology which is tailored to such action.

As for epistemological constructivism, it could gain new access to didactics by defining specific paths by which the transformation of selected types of knowledge could be pursued and, accordingly, the strategies which are most appropriate for the interventions required in a given situation.

What then is to be made of the respective roles of the knowledge to be taught and psychology? In principle, the first serves to define the objects of knowledge to be taken over by teaching. To a certain extent, it can even determine the type of potential for action which is best suited for certain teaching objectives. Psychology, on the other hand, will provide the tools necessary for describing and analyzing cognitive actions whose potentialities it is the aim of didactics to provide.

Finally, research may be undertaken in view of a process of construction which deals jointly with its own epistemology and didactic action. The models that constructivism has to offer promise to make this undertaking fertile from the moment that such projects get underway.

Chapter 4
Toward a pragmatic social constructivism

JIM GARRISON

Constructivism must be careful not to confine itself to the purely cognitive domain of human experience. Educators must strive to include the body, its actions, and its passions more prominently in the curriculum. The pragmatic social constructivism of George Herbert Mead and John Dewey allows us to do so. Mead and Dewey maintained a lifelong friendship and were colleagues for many years during which they visited each other nearly every day. So intermeshed was their influence on each other that it is often impossible to determine who originated what. Such entwinement is typical of socially constructive contexts and illustrates a central thesis of pragmatic social constructivism – it decenters the locus of mind and self.[1]

The philosophy of consciousness

To grasp pragmatic social constructivism it is easiest to begin with what it is not. Pragmatic social constructivism rejects the philosophy of consciousness that dominates modern thinking about the mind and the self. In the philosophy of consciousness, mental phenomena are assumed to always be conscious. It is also usually assumed that consciousness includes immediate introspective apprehension of one's own mental states. Descartes' "I think, therefore I am" is the classic statement of the philosophy of consciousness. Subjective thought (the Cartesian *cogito*) provides personal identity in this philosophy.

The philosophy of consciousness reinforces Western folk psychology, a psychology that is ensconced in the philosophy of Immanuel Kant and that has exercised tremendous influence on Western psychology, sociology, and moral thought. It assumes we are all born with the same universal, essential, and unchanging personal identity, or self. Usually this essence is called "Rationality," and it is presumed adequate to grasping the universal moral laws that apply to all persons, in all cultures, in all places, at all times. Persons are seen as social atoms; their identity is assumed independently of personal relationship or cultural context. Moral agents also are assumed to have innate free will, existing in the mind apart from the body and the forces of nature. This "will" commands the body, its acts, and its passions; in turn the will should obey the dictates of timeless Reason.

Western folk psychology assumes sharp mind versus body, passion versus reason, and self versus society dualisms; these give rise to the subject versus object and knower versus known dualisms. The whole task of epistemology is to determine how a disembodied subject can come to know an embodied physical object with certainty. The Kantian answer is that transcendental Reason, along with other functions such as "schematism," acts to construct forms that structure the flux of experience into objects. Pragmatic social constructivism completely rejects what Dewey (1922) calls the "false psychology of original individual consciousness" (p. 62).

The primacy of action

Embodied action rather than abstract Reason lies at the core of pragmatic social constructivism. For the pragmatist, the "I can do" rather than the "I think" constitutes the (relatively) stable core of personal identity. At the most basic level, the biological organism must act effectively to coordinate itself with the environment that sustains it. All living beings must act by virtue of being alive; it is not action but the redirection of action that requires explanation.

For Dewey and Mead, emotional and intellectual clarity emerge together in the larger unity of an agent's embodied effort to coordinate action in an indeterminate situation. Dewey established the primacy and unity of activity at least as early as his 1895 reconstruction of William James's theory of emotion:

> In Mr. James's statement the experience is . . . split up into three separate parts: First comes the object or idea that operates only as stimulus; second, the mode of behavior [activity] taken as discharged of this stimulus; third, the *Affect*, or emotional excitation, as the repercussion of this discharge. No such seriality or separation attaches to the emotion as an experience. . . . We are easily brought to the conclusion that *the mode of behavior* [*activity*] *is the primary thing, and that the idea and the emotional excitation are constituted at one and the same time; that, indeed, they represent the tension of stimulus and response within the co-ordination which makes up the mode of behavior.* (p. 174)

In the unity of the act, the agent is attempting to harmoniously coordinate her behavior within the world. When the initially unified activity is subsequently reflected upon, it becomes possible to distinguish between activity, the feeling, and the idea (interpretation, object, hypothesis, etc.). Yet this is only a functional distinction useful for practical purposes. Dewey warned against allowing such useful practical distinctions to harden into untenable dualisms between mind (ideas, etc.), bodily activity (behavior, etc.), or affect (desire, etc.).

The relation between affect and ideas is circular. Each contributes alternatively to the successful coordination of the act and to the clarification of one other. We feel differently about a student's disruptive behavior if we know she is abused at home. We think differently about a child for whom we feel affection. The notion of the unity of action as a circular coordination was clarified in Dewey's article "The Reflex Arc Concept in Psychology."

Psychology in Dewey's day, as in ours, saw its task as determining causal, lawlike relations between stimuli and response. External stimuli were seen as independent variables that cause internal mental processing resulting in an external response (the dependent variable). Dewey (1896) observes: "The older dualism between sensation and idea is repeated in the current dualism of peripheral and central structures and functions: the older dualism of body and soul finds a distinct echo in the current dualism of stimulus and response" (p. 96).

The "older dualism" of sensation and idea find a distinct echo in the current dualisms of contemporary cognitive psychology with its notion of input information (stimuli), information processing hardware (central structures), and information output (response). On the computer model, neo-Kantian cognitive schemas serve as the program software. Dewey rejects any idea of a priori forms of thought or Rationality (hardware) that structure experience (information input/output). He sees all of these as descendants of Western folk psychology.

Dewey argues that the unity of the whole act precedes the discrimination of stimuli and response, that is, what is stimuli and what is response emerge as the act unfolds. According to Dewey: "What we have is a circuit, not an arc. . . . This circuit is more truly termed organic than reflex, because the motor response determines the stimulus, just as truly as sensory stimulus determines movement. Indeed, the movement is only for the sake of determining the stimulus, of fixing what kind of a stimulus it is, of interpreting it" (p. 102).

We do not know which is which until the completion of the act. This is because the actions of the agent construct the stimulus object as much as the stimulus object constructs the agent's response. The organism is as active in constructing its environment as the environment is active in constructing the organism. Dewey was a transactional realist (see Garrison, 1994). When two events interact in an evolving universe, what is already fully actualized in the first event actualizes the potential of the second event, and conversely. Good teachers know this from their relationships with their students.

To better explicate the agent's active construction of her environment, Dewey borrows the notion of selective attention from James. Selective attention is driven by embodied emotions; agents attend to what interests them. Dewey generalizes James's insight into what might be called selective operation. What emerges as the stimulus-object in a constructivist transaction depends, in part, on what operations agents perform. Selective operation *constructs* what it is that the agent will think about and respond to. This is not creation from nothing; the material situation provides real constraint on construction. Instead of a reflex arc with three disconnected mechanical parts, what actually occurs "is a whole act, a sensori-motor co-ordination" (Dewey, 1896, p. 100). What the organism is striving to do is coordinate (unify) its conduct in some specific context. The result is a "circuit, a continual reconstitution" or re*construction* of the situation (p. 99). Since the whole situation includes the organism, it is as likely to be reconstructed as its environment. When the organism is reconstructed, learning occurs. Learning for Dewey was not the simple substitution of new experience for old; it was developmental. New experiences, new learning, must be incorporated into previously existing habits of conduct. Dewey was a social constructivist (see Garrison, 1994).

Instead of beginning with stimulus and response as distinct events, Dewey urges us to recognize them as unified within the total act of an organism striving to coordinate its behavior within its environment. According to Dewey (1896, 1972), "Stimulus and response are not distinctions of existence, but teleological distinctions, that is distinctions of function. . . . With regard to this teleological process, two stages should be discriminated" (p. 104).[2] In the first stage everything is functioning smoothly without disruption:

> The relation represents an organization of means with reference to a comprehensive end. It represents an accomplished adaptation. . . . The end has got thoroughly organized into the means. . . . Regarding such cases of organization viewed as already attained . . . it is only the assumed common reference to an inclusive end which marks each member off as stimulus [or

stimulus-object] and response, that apart from such reference we have only antecedent and consequent . . . the distinction is one of interpretation. (pp. 104–5)

For Dewey, the means always constitute the end, nor is the relation linear; it is a coordination. Once coordinated it is possible to say that, given the agent's purposes, or the researcher's interpretation, something in a situation *was* stimulus (or means) and something else response (or ends). Objects (and their identity and essence) *emerge* for Dewey as a consequent of inquiry intended to transform (coordinate) some indeterminate, doubtful situation into a determinate, safe, and secure end. It is not possible to determine what is what prior to the act; determination is possible only as a consequence of successfully constructing an end that satisfies the needs and desires of the agent. Since the agent is herself among those things included in a situation, the agent's mind and self are among those new "objects" that emerge at the end of the process of reconstructing a situation. This is how learning occurs.

Disruption of unified action is the second stage of teleological functioning; it occurs when the agent's action is disrupted and it does not know how to continue. The emotional experience ranges from discomfort to panic; cognitively the experience is experienced as doubt. In such circumstances, "the response is not only uncertain, but the stimulus is equally uncertain; one is uncertain only in so far as the other is" (p. 106). This is the *context* of all inquiry, including scientific inquiry. Note that there is no problem, merely doubt and discomfort, until the stimulus-objects that condition inquiry are constructed through emotionally driven selective attention, cognition, and experimental action. This is the hidden meaning of the saying that a problem stated is half solved.

One final point; it is important to make functional distinctions, but we must not hypostatize them. One of the most common ways this occurs is by assuming that the consequent of a unified act was there at the beginning. At best, it was only there potentially, not actually. Perhaps an external observer of the action, or the actor *after* the action is complete, can interpret the action and make the functional distinctions. Dewey used the term "psychological fallacy" to describe the following mistake:

A set of considerations which hold good only because of a completed process is read into the content of the process which conditions this completed result. A state of things characterizing an outcome is regarded as a true description

> of the events which led up to this outcome; when, as a matter of fact, if this outcome had already been in existence, there would have been no necessity for the process. (pp. 105–6)

The basic error is mistaking the consequences of a constructive process for antecedently existing, or transcendental, structures of knowledge and interpretation. Mind, self, and meaning are all *emergent* for Mead and Dewey; they do not exist innately at birth.

Mead's theory of the emergent self

Mead's 1903 paper "The Definition of the Psychical" marks a decisive turn in his thought. It is a difficult paper to follow and it contains a number of flaws which were later corrected. Nonetheless, it introduces many themes important to pragmatic social constructivism.

Mead explicitly takes his departure from Dewey's "Reflex Arc" paper. He begins by further refining the two teleological stages described by Dewey: "Insofar as the coordination is unbroken, the end is for the time being adequately expressed in terms of the means, i.e., the object and its background [context] which provide an adequate stimulus for continuance of the activity, and thus the distinction between the act and the conditions of the act does not appear"(Mead, 1903, p. 50).

Note that Mead is describing the first stage of teleological functioning. Here the stimulus-objects and the habitual responses are unified indistinguishably within the act. It is what Mead does with the second teleological case that is most interesting:

> When the coordination is broken up – or, in other words, when an adequate stimulus for the expression of the impulse is not given, but the conflicting tendencies to act deprive the object of its power as a stimulus – then consciousness is divided into two fields: that within which the new stimulus or objects must be *constructed*, and the rest of experience with which reference to the new possible object can have no other content than that of conditions of its formation. (p. 50; emphasis added)

When certain stimulus-objects no longer control an agent's responses, the agent does not know how to act. Still, she feels the impetus to act in multiple ways, and so she finds herself in cognitive doubt and emotional conflict. Diverse habits of action struggle to be heard, the situation demands immediate action. This is the field of constructive action where the agent must construct new stimulus-objects by means of creative response.

Mead regards "the psychical, not as a permanent phase . . . but as a 'moment' of consciousness" (p. 29). He received the insight from Dewey: "The position taken by Dewey is that in this psychical situation the object is gone, and the psychical character of the situation consists in the disintegration and reconstruction" (p. 42). The "psychical situation" is the transitory phase of existence, the disruptive field of the second teleological case. The agent's previous constructions have been deconstructed and the agent must reconstruct the situation (including herself) to continue functioning effectively. It is appropriately called psychical because the stimulus-objects that normally control the agent's behavior have disintegrated; the agent must call on her own creative resources to imaginatively create hypothetical interpretations (ideas) for reconstructing the situation.

Mead does not want to be caught in a dualism where the subjective "psychical" situation is either reduced to physiological processes or dismissed as mere mental epiphenomena. It is a situation in which an embodied being is internally involved in reconstructing itself and its world simultaneously. The psychical cannot be found within the dominion of the dualistic: "The disintegration of the object means a return, with reference to a certain *field*, to the original phase of protoplasmic consciousness, and within these limits there is neither mind nor body, only subjectivity. The reconstruction is the immediate process of attention and apperception, of choice, of consciously directed conduct" (p. 49). The pragmatist locates the construction zone in a field of action outside the atomistic dualisms of modernity.

In defining the psychical, Mead has at least three goals. First, he wants an antidualistic definition of the psychical that emphasizes the drive to unify our action (or conduct). I believe he should have chosen a word less closely associated with mental substance than psychical, but he nevertheless achieves his goal. Second, he wants to answer questions of cognitive validity in terms of concrete construction, deconstruction, and reconstruction. Third, he wants to give the individual a unique and creative role in the course of natural events.

Mead's definition of the psychical delineates a functional understanding of the individual as necessarily unique and creative: "And it is in this phase of [psychical] subjectivity, with its activities of attention in the solution of the problem, i.e., in the construction of the hypothesis [interpretation] of the new world, that the individual qua individual has his functional expression or rather is that function" (p. 52).

The center of our being is the functional "I can do." Human nature is a part of nature that can function to continue the creation. Individuality functions freely to re-create the world:

> But it is evident that, as the function of the world is to provide data for the solution, so it is the function of the individual to provide the hypothesis [idea] for that solution. . . . This is the self in the disintegration and reconstruction of its universe, the self functioning, the [psychical] point of immediacy that must exist within a mediate process. . . . It is the self of unnecessitated choice, of undreamt hypotheses, of inventions that change the whole face of nature. (pp. 53–4)

In the transaction between self and world both are transformed. Mead remarks "one of the results of the reconstruction will be a new individual as well as a new social environment" (p. 53). In the pragmatic construction zone *all* objects are open to creative reconstruction. Constructivist educators must realize they are altering their students' identity in ways that cannot be predicted in advance.

Mead provides an easily accessible example of the "psychical situation" from everyday social experience. Think about some occasion when you were forced to reconstruct your idea (interpretation) of someone close to you. As long as they behaved as you expected your transactions continued without disruption; but when they did something seriously "out of character" (perhaps they lied) you did not know how to respond. Your understanding of them disintegrated, you were unable to coordinate your actions with theirs. Your task then was to find means to the end of restoring coordination to your conduct. Because mutual relationship helps construct our personal identity, reconstruction includes ourselves. Because social relationships are transactions, "The contradictory attitudes of approval and abhorrence include in their sweep" not only the person in question, "but also ourselves insofar as mutual interrelationship has helped to form our selves" (p. 51). Relationships will become very important later when we discuss symbolically mediated interaction.

There is another move Mead makes in this essay that will become especially interesting. Mead develops a distinction between the "I" and the "me" in which the "me" is the individual self as a stimulus-object of consciousness. The individual as a "me" is "an empirical self" that "belongs to the world which it is the function of this phase of consciousness to reconstruct" (p. 53). There are many instances of the "me." For example, the same self can be a teacher, a student, a parent, and a child simultaneously. The "I" is the creative psychic self, the self in disintegration that reconstructs its universe; it is the self functioning. The multiple instances of the empirical "me" can serve as a stimulus-object to the reconstructive "I." The "I," however, "cannot be an object" (p. 46). It is the function that appears "in the shifting of attention in the adaptation of habitual tendencies to each other, when they have come into conflict within the coordination" (p. 45). The "I" is the creative aspect of self capable of reconstructing the multiple instances of "me."

Before moving on, let us note some shortcomings of Mead's definition of the psychical. At this stage, Mead still thinks that the "I" can somehow be immediately and directly experienced through reflection, although he had effectively demolished any such possibility. What is missing is: (1) the social origin of the self, (2) a concept of the intersubjective constitution of meaning, and (3) a way of bringing these two together. Mead is still constrained by a monologic framework. What is needed is a more dialogical, less narrowly individualistic, understanding of the mind, self, and meaning or, rather, a social constructivism that emphasizes symbolic interaction.

Mead's theory of symbolically mediated social interaction

Mead built his theory of the socially constructed origin of mind, self, and meaning out of elements borrowed from a number of psychological and sociological theories prominent in his day. Reviewing the borrowed elements readily reveals the nomenclature of Mead's theory.

From Darwin, Mead borrowed a biological and embodied orientation toward mind and meaning; he then extended evolutionary thinking to include the idea that minds, selves, and meanings emerge and evolve as species do. From Wilhelm Wundt, he borrowed the insight that language emerges from gestures, especially the vocal gesture. Mead, though, rejected the notion that gestures express antecedently existing ideas or emotions.

From James Baldwin, Mead derived the idea of the social origin of the self, but he rejected Baldwin's dualism. Mead is also indebted to William McDougall for the doctrine of social instincts, but he denied McDougall's commitment to a self and mind that exists from birth. Finally, Mead adopted Josiah Royce's insight into the essentially social character of linguistic meaning and the necessity of using symbols in communication. What Mead (1909) rejected was Royce's emphasis on imitation as "the means of getting the meaning of what others and we ourselves are doing" (p. 101). In Mead's opinion, the origin of meaning, along with the consciousness of meaning, lies elsewhere: "The probable beginning of human communication was in cooperation [social coordination], not in imitation, where conduct differed and yet where the act of the one answered to and called out the act of the other" (p. 101). For Mead, the emergence of meanings in social action is merely a special case of the emergence of stimulus-objects in the overall effort to coordinate our actions.

The one mistake common to all of Mead's mentors is that none of them move completely beyond the philosophy of consciousness; a ghost of an innate a priori mind, self, or meaning haunts their work. Mead states the tension straightforwardly: "We cannot assume that the self is both a product and a presupposition of human consciousness, that reflection has arisen through social consciousness and that social intercourse has arisen because human individuals had ideas and meanings to express" (p. 97). Minds, selves, meanings, and the consciousness of them are, for the pragmatic social constructivist, emergent social constructions that evolve much as species evolve.

I begin with the emergence of mind through the social construction of significant symbols. Mead's explication of meaning is often confused; what follows is my attempt to clarify his work. I begin with Mead's basic definition: "Meaning is a statement of the relation between the characteristics in the sensuous stimulation and the responses which they call out" (Mead, 1910, p. 129). Response to sensuous stimulation alone will not yield the sort of symbolic meanings associated with having a mind, although it does provide the basis for the use of the significant symbols associated with the emergence of mental functioning. Dewey (1925) distinguishes two kinds of meaning, sense and signification:

> The qualities of situations in which organisms and surrounding conditions interact, when discriminated, make sense. Sense is distinct from [subjective] feeling, for it has a recognized reference. . . . Sense [denotation] is also different from signification [connotation]. The latter involves use of a quality as a sign or index of something else, as when the red of a light signifies danger. . . . Whenever a situation has this double function of meaning, namely signification and sense, mind, intellect is definitely present. (p. 200)

An agent may sense the meaning "red" without interpreting it as meaning "stop." Minds emerge when organisms make significant interpretive *use* of their sense of things, but how does this happen? Mead and Dewey's answer is by the social use of behavioral gestures.

The social use of gestures already exists below the level of human interaction: "Thus there is a conversation of gesture, a field of palaver within the social conduct of animals. . . . The first function of the gesture is the mutual adjustment of changing social response to changing social stimulation" (Mead, 1910, p. 124). Note the introduction of a dialogical (conversational) framework to explain the coordination of social behavior. Animals in social situations may construct discriminations and responses that make sense of the gestures of other animals with which they are interacting. Mead provides an explanation for why social animals often perform highly intricate functions; they are able to coordinate their behavior in ways that display a primitive capacity to socially construct meaning. They have a sense of reciprocally coordinated action, but they impart no significance to the gestures, no symbolic meaning.

Social transactions resemble transactions with other stimulus-objects, though there is an immensely important distinction: "The difference is found, however, in the fact that we are conscious of interpreting the gestures of others by our own responses or tendencies to respond" (p. 130). An agent's responses to exclusively physical objects does not influence how the object responds, but things are very different regarding the responses of social objects. In social interaction, gestures – our own as well as others' – must be recognized, interpreted, and responded to. The symbolic mediation of social transactions emerges in the give and take of communication among creatures like ourselves capable of using sensible meanings as significant symbols: "It [social interaction] does not become communication in the full sense, i.e., the stimulus does not become a significant symbol, until the gesture tends to arouse the same response in the individual who makes it that it arouses in the others" (Mead, 1927, p. 312). The agent who is able to interpret and use the sense of a gesture to determine her own response must grasp the significance of both the gestures of others and her own; such an agent has a mind.

The gesture as a significant (linguistic) symbol helps agents coordinate their behavior with respect to other stimulus-objects in the social environment. Significant (linguistic) meaning for Mead involves interpreting the significant symbol as a triadic relation between the organism that is the agent of the gesture, the organism to whom the gesture is directed, and the emerging stimulus-object that will be co-designated by the end of the social act. Mead and Dewey agree that language, the use of significant symbols originating in symbolically mediated action, marks the emergence of the mind.

Mead (1910) offers an example of a symbolically mediated social transaction that prompts the emergence of a conscious awareness of the meanings that agents already use; think of a boxer or fencer:

> His own gesture thus interprets his opponent's attitude and must be held in consciousness as changing the situation to which he must respond. . . . Within social conduct the feels of one's own responses become the natural objects of attention, since they interpret first of all attitudes of others which have called them out, in the second place, because they give the material in which one can state his own value as a stimulus to the conduct of others. Thus we find here the opportunity and the means for analyzing and bringing to consciousness our responses, our habits of conduct, as distinguished from the stimulations that call them out. . . . Language . . . is but a form – a highly specialized form – of gesture. (p. 132)

The interpretation and use of sensible meaning constructs signification. A being capable of symbolically mediated interaction (a being with language) has a mind and is capable of becoming consciously aware of the meanings it possesses; it can come to interpret its own symbolic acts as others do. We know this, for instance, when the agent can lie (e.g., a fencer feigning a lunge). Such a being is on the verge of becoming a self; self-identity, though, requires not merely consciousness but *self*-consciousness.

The question remains, exactly how do agents become self-consciously aware of the meanings they possess, the significant symbols they use, or, simply, their minds. Mead's (1922) answer is through vocal gestures:

> If an individual uses such a [significant] gesture and he is affected by it as another individual is affected by it, he responds or tends to respond to his own social stimulus, as another individual would respond. . . . The vocal gesture is of peculiar importance because it reacts upon the individual who makes it in the same fashion that it reacts upon an other. . . . The self arises in conduct, when the individual becomes a social object in experience to himself. This takes place when the individual assumes the attitude or uses the gesture which another individual would use and responds to it himself, or tends so to respond. . . . He acts toward himself in a manner analogous to that in which he acts toward others. Especially he talks to himself as he talks to others and in keeping up this conversation in the inner forum constitutes the field which is called that of mind. (p. 243)

This is a dialogical theory of the self emerging by becoming reflexively conscious of one's own mind and the meanings it possesses. An agent's vocal gesture acts on the agent much as it acts on others toward whom it is directed. It may call out the same response on the part of the initiating agent (i.e., the same meaning) as it would in the other toward whom it is directed.

Mead carefully distinguishes between having a meaning and being conscious of it: "The association of one content with another content is not the symbolism of meaning. In the consciousness of meaning the [sensed] symbol and that which is [significantly] symbolized . . . must be presented separately. Association of contents of stimulation tends to become a complete merging and loss of distinction" (p. 128).

This separation only holds for the consciousness of meaning, not for the existence of the meanings themselves. We may have and use meanings without being conscious of them; as already noted, we use a red light as a symbol for the response "stop" and sometimes know it consciously [illegible] drive across town quite successfully, although complexly directed, without ever consciously thinking about [illegible] traffic signals. We have and use the meaning, we just are not consciously aware of it at the time. Mead remarks: "In fact it is essential to the economy of our conduct that the connection between stimulation and response should become habitual and should sink below the threshold of consciousness" (p. 127). Like Pavlov's dogs, the bell rings and without conscious thought we answer. Unlike dogs, we can become conscious of the meanings we possess, our habits, and reconstruct them if we so desire. Dewey (1925) expresses the situation well: "Mind denotes the whole system of meanings as they are embodied in the workings of organic life; consciousness in a being with language denotes awareness or perception of meanings . . . the field of mind – of operative meanings – is enormously wider than that of consciousness" (p. 230).

Embodied meanings for Dewey, as for Mead, are habits. Animals embody meanings insofar as they have sensible habits of response, but they do not have minds as such. Mental functioning assumes sociolinguistic coordination mediated by symbols. Insofar as some animals (e.g., primates) can, perhaps, coordinate their conduct by symbolic mediation, they have minds. They have them, but they do not know they have them, or rather, they are not conscious of them. To have a self an organism must have self-consciousness of the meanings it possesses.

Beliefs for Dewey and Mead are habits, and habits are embodied dispositions to act which evince emotion. For Dewey (1922) habits of sensible response, and especially significant symbols, compose the mind: "Concrete habits do all the perceiving, recognizing, imagining, recalling, judging, conceiving and reasoning that is done. . . . Yet habit does not, of itself, know, for it does not of itself stop to think, observe or remember'' (p. 124). Habits are never entirely separate from a specific context of action, including the community in which the agent resides. Habits are in the body, but they mediate a dispersed field of action; cognitive habits use symbols to mediate such a field. In a world without automobiles, cognitive dispositions to act, such as monitoring traffic signals (symbols), are meaningless. All habits are intelligent, but they are not inquisitive or reflective; so what sparks conscious reflection and self-awareness of the meanings that we possess?

We have meanings, that is, embodied and impassioned habits, but we do not know we have them until our unconscious, habitual functioning is disrupted. Mead (1913) expressed it this way:

> As a mere organization of habit the [conscious] self is not self-conscious. It is this self which we refer to as character. When, however, an essential problem appears, there is some disintegration in this organization, and different tendencies appear in reflective thought as different voices in conflict with each other. In a sense the old self has disintegrated, and out of the moral process a new self arises. (p. 147)

The self that merely possesses consciousness and a mind is a self only potentially. Actual selfhood emerges when we become conscious of our minds and their meanings. When stimulus-objects, including other people, lose their control of us (when habitual modes of functioning fail), the ''I'' must function creatively to reconstruct the situation. The agent does not become self-conscious of the meanings she possesses until her interpretations of her own gestures, gathered from the attitude of the other, are disrupted. On such occasions agents must inquire into the meanings they possess and, therefore, themselves. Fully understanding such a self-conscious reflexive relation requires returning to a discussion of the relation of the ''I'' to the ''me'' and eventually, to the concept of role-taking.

When the agents act toward themselves as they would toward others, they become their own stimulus-objects. Such an object is a ''me.'' It is the vocal gesture that gives rise to the ''me,'' that is, the empirical self as a social-object among others. The vocal gesture is not strictly necessary; any source of self-stimulation could, in principle, do:

> The vocal gesture is not the only form which can serve for the building-up of a ''me,'' as is abundantly evident from the building-up gestures of the deaf mutes. Any gesture by which the individual can himself be affected as

others are affected, and which therefore tends to call out in him a response as it would call it out in another, will serve as a mechanism for the construction of a self. (Mead, 1912, p. 140)

Minds emerge when agents can manipulate sociolinguistic meanings; selves emerge when the agent can take the perspective of others in interpreting their own symbolic acts, thereby becoming self-consciously aware of their minds (as a system of meanings). Self-awareness involves the "I."

A self comprises an "I" as well as a "me." It is the "I" that provides reflective self-awareness of the empirical "me." Recall that the "I" is operative only when the habitual functioning of the "me" is disrupted. The "I," however, never appears because it is, as we saw earlier, the expressive functional "I can do" at the center of reconstructive action:

It is only the "me" – the empirical self – that can be brought into the focus of attention, that can be perceived. "I" lies beyond the range of immediate experience. . . . The "I" therefore never can exist as an object in consciousness, but the very conversational inner experience, the very process of replying to one's own talk, implies an "I" behind the scenes who answers to the gestures, the symbols, that arise in consciousness. (pp. 140–1)

Thinking here is represented as an internalization of social dialogue. The "I" is the individual agent's basis of functioning from birth as a biological inheritance and evolves through the unique personal experience of the individual's life history. This is the basis of unique creativity in individuals. This uniqueness interprets and resists the social roles that comprise the varied constructions of the "me." This brings us to the idea of role play in Mead.

There are as many instances of the empirical "me" as social roles that the agent plays:

It is also to be noted that this response to the social conduct of the self may be in the role of another – we present his arguments in imagination. . . . In this way we play the roles of all our group; indeed, it is only insofar as we do this that they become part of our social environment – to be aware of another self as a self implies that we have played his role or that of another with whose type we identify him for purposes of intercourse. (p. 146)

For Mead, individuals are an internal plurality, a community. Initially, the role play is very literal; later it is possible to abstract from the specific roles: "The features and intonations of the *dramatis personae* fade out and the emphasis falls upon the meaning of the inner speech'' (p. 147). Pragmatic social construction is dramatalogical; the construction and reconstruction of dramatic narratives are crucial to the emergent construction and subsequent reconstruction of the self. The community at large provides narrative scripts for playing the various roles that constitute the different senses of ''me'' that make up the empirical self. For the most part, most of the time, all of us live socially prescripted lives.

Mead (1922) distinguishes between role-taking in play and games. He begins with play:

> The self arises in conduct when the individual becomes a social object in experience to himself. This takes place when the individual assumes the attitude or uses the gesture which another individual would use and responds to it himself, or tends so to respond. . . . It arises in the life of the infant . . . and finds its expression in the normal play life of young children. . . . He acts toward himself in a manner analogous to that in which he acts toward others. Especially he talks to himself as he talks to others and in keeping up this conversation in the inner forum constitutes the field which is called that of mind. (p. 243)

Playing with dolls is the classic example of children's role-play; the child responds in tone of voice and attitude toward the doll as his parents respond to his own cries and chortles. Mead (1924–5) explicitly refers to the work of Froebel and kindergarten play (p. 285). Social construction is not a new educational idea.

Play readily evolves into games: ''For in a game there is a regulated procedure, and rules. The child must not only take the role of the other . . . but he must assume the various roles of all the participants in the game and govern his action accordingly'' (p. 285).

Mead's example is that of a baseball player who must understand the function of every other player and their organized responses to her, in order to understand how she herself is to play. The rules, values, and norms of games are abstracted from play much as the agent abstracts the concepts and categories of thought from the dramatis personae. The abstraction of roles and norms leads to the notion of the ''generalized other.''

It is the generalized other that provides the most socialized sense of self. In an organized community (a team or a nation) each individual must functionally coordinate her conduct with every other individual in order to secure the common goals of the community. Each participant must refer her conduct to that of every other member. The generalized other exercises social control over every member of a community:

> We assume the generalized attitude of the group, in the censor that stands at the door of our imagery and inner conversations, and in the affirmation of the laws and axioms of the universe of discourse. . . . Our thinking is an inner conversation in which we may be taking the roles of specific acquaintances over against ourselves, but usually it is with what I have termed the "generalized other" that we converse, and so attain to the levels of abstract thinking, and that impersonality, that so-called objectivity that we cherish. In this fashion, I conceive, have selves arisen in human behavior and with selves their minds. (p. 288)

This passage pulls together many things. I showed earlier how Mead distinguishes the mind from self-consciousness. Here also is the dialogical notion of the self as an internalization of the conversation of the community. The conduct of the various roles played by the multiple instances of "me" is socially controlled by the approving or disapproving responses of others (e.g., parents and teachers).

It is the notion of a generalized other that radically decenters the pragmatist social constructivist comprehension of the self: "Mind is then a field that is not confined to the individual, much less is it located in a brain. Significance (meaning) belongs to things in their relations to individuals. It does not lie in mental processes which are enclosed within individuals"(Mead, 1922, p. 247). Mind, and self-consciousness of the meanings that make up the mind, must be understood as a property of fields of action; it cannot be adequately comprehended in terms of individual psychological atoms colliding into each other.

The educational consequences of pragmatic social constructivism

Living creatures must act; recognizing the "I can do" is the most important lesson of pragmatic social construction. If we understand beliefs as embodied dispositions to act which evince emotion, it becomes necessary to rethink education so as to overcome the classical dualisms of mind–body, self–society, and so on. We must reconstruct the curriculum so as to "reconnect" the extremes of these fundamentally circular processes.

The teachable moment occurs when students' habits of functioning are disrupted and it is necessary for them to reconstruct some situation. These are artistic contexts of creative action. For the pragmatic social constructivist, teaching in the construction zone is a transactional, artistically transformative, and creative activity. Meaning is made, it is not a matter of downloading information into our students' central processors. Minds and selves are too decentered for that.

Teachers teach subject matter to students in some context. The minds and selves of teacher and student are distributed in a field of action only partially delineated by the subject matter. Pragmatic social constructivism urges educators to consider the entire context, the environmental ethos of schools and community within which the student as a creative individual must function in organic interconnection. Decentering minds and selves within fields of action has important implications for democratic education.

Freedom for pragmatic social constructivists is an achievement, not an innate natural endowment. It is the product of creatively reflecting on self and society. Knowledge is not enough for freedom, we must create possibilities. If we become imaginatively aware of a possible alternative to oppressive conditions we might learn to desire it. Aesthetic education is part of moral education, and educating eros is a part of moral education. If we can become reflectively aware of environmental contingencies, especially social contingencies, we may seek to reconstruct ourselves by reconstructing the contingencies of our world.

We all play roles (various versions of "me") on the stage of life that are prescripted for us by culture; it has us before we have it. The task of democratic education is to disrupt these habitual scripts so that each individual is free to become the author of her own life. The most direct way to acquire new scripts is through dialogue with those who tell different stories in a different vocabulary from ourselves. That is why pluralistic democratic education is our best hope; it is also why an international collection of readings, such as may be found in the present volume, is so needed.

Part III
Teaching within the constructivist mode: practices and promises

Chapter 5
Individual construction, mathematical acculturation, and the classroom community

PAUL COBB, MARCELA PERLWITZ, AND DIANA UNDERWOOD-GREGG

For the past six years we, together with Erna Yackel and Terry Wood, have conducted a classroom-based research and development project in elementary school mathematics.[1] In this paper, we draw on our experiences of collaborating with teachers and of analyzing what might be happening in their classrooms to consider three interrelated issues. First, we argue that the teacher and students together create a classroom mathematics tradition or microculture and that this profoundly influences students' mathematical activity and learning. Sample episodes are used to clarify the distinction between the school mathematics tradition in which the teacher acts as the sole mathematical authority and the inquiry mathematics tradition in which the teacher and students together constitute a community of validators. Second, we consider the theoretical and pragmatic tensions inherent in the view that mathematical learning is both a process of individual cognitive construction and a process of acculturation into the mathematical practices of wider society. In the course of the discussion, we contrast constructivist attempts to cope with this tension with approaches proposed by sociocultural theorists. Finally, we use the preceding issues as a backdrop against which to consider the development of instructional activities that might be appropriate for inquiry mathematics classrooms.

Classroom mathematics traditions

In the course of our work, we have conducted a series of second- and third-grade teaching experiments with seven- and eight-year-old students at both a rural/suburban site and an urban site that serves an almost exclusively African-American student population. Each of these experiments lasted for the entire school year and involved intense collaboration with classroom teachers who were responsible for all instruction. Our pragmatic goal in these experiments was to develop instructional strategies and complete sets of instructional activities that support students' personal construction of increasingly sophisticated conceptual operations and methods in mathematics. The data gathered during each experiment consist of video-recordings of all lessons for the school year, copies of all the children's written work, field notes, and video-recordings of clinical interviews conducted with all students at the beginning, middle, and end of the school year. Approximately fifty second- and third-grade teachers currently use the instructional activities developed in these experiments as the basis for all their mathematics instruction.

Our original intention before we began the first teaching experiment was to use detailed cognitive models of children's arithmetic concepts (Steffe, Cobb, and von Glasersfeld, 1988; Steffe, von Glasersfeld, Richards, and Cobb, 1983) to account for mathematical learning as it occurred in the social setting of the classroom. These models had been developed by analyzing clinical teaching sessions in which one researcher interacted with a single child. However, our initial experiences in the first experiment were enough to convince us that the cognitive models were, by themselves, insufficient to account for the children's mathematical learning. This experiment was conducted in a second-grade classroom at the rural/suburban site. The general instructional approach we and the collaborating teacher developed was problem-centered and reflected the constructivist tenet that students reorganize their ways of knowing to eliminate perturbations in the worlds of their personal experiences (von Glasersfeld, 1987a). The instructional activities were therefore designed to be personally problematic for children at a variety of different conceptual levels. Further, we viewed social interactions as a potential source of perturbations and attempted to ensure that the children explain and justify how they had interpreted and solved tasks. In addition, we placed a high priority on the development of intellectual and social autonomy and hoped that the teacher and children would together become a community of validators.

Contrary to our expectations, it soon became apparent that the teacher's pedagogical agenda conflicted with the beliefs that the children had developed during first grade about their own role, the teacher's role, and the general nature of mathematical activity in school. As a consequence, the teacher spontaneously began to guide the renegotiation of classroom social norms on her own initiative

(Cobb, Yackel, and Wood, 1989). For example, the following incident occurred during the first day of school when the teacher and children discussed solutions to the word problem, "How many runners altogether? There are six runners on each team. There are two teams in the race."

Teacher: Jack, what answer – solution did you come up with?
Jack: Fourteen.
Teacher: Fourteen. How did you get that answer?

In this brief exchange, the teacher expected Jack to explain how he had interpreted and solved the problem. However, Jack seemed to interpret the teacher's question as a request for an answer and presumably expected her to evaluate his reply. Instead, she accepted his answer without evaluation and restated her initial question. This conflict in expectations indicates that the teacher was not merely attempting to elicit an account of Jack's solution but was also negotiating with him how to engage in mathematical discourse in her classroom. The episode continued:

Jack: Because 6 plus 6 is 12. Two runners on two teams . . . (Jack stops talking, puts his hands to the sides of his face and looks down at the floor. Then he looks at the teacher and then at his partner, Ann. He turns and faces the front of the room with his back to the teacher and mumbles inaudibly.)
Teacher: Would you say that again. I didn't quite get the whole thing. You had – say it again please.
Jack: (Softly, still facing the front of the room.) It's six runners on each team.
Teacher: Right.
Jack: (Turns to look at the teacher.) I made a mistake. It's wrong. It should be twelve. (He turns and faces the front of the room.)

Once he realized that his answer was incorrect, Jack interpreted the situation as one that warranted acute embarrassment. In effect, he acted as though the teacher had publicly evaluated his answer. This further conflict in expectations confounded the teacher's intention that the children should publicly express their thinking and, more generally, engage in mathematical practices characterized by conjecture, argumentation, and justification.

Thus far, Jack and the teacher had been talking about mathematics – the themes were Jack's answer and his solution. At this point in the episode, the teacher initiated a new conversation in which she and the children talked about talking about mathematics. The issue of how to interpret situations in which a mistake has been made then became an explicit topic of conversation.

Teacher: (Softly.) Oh, okay. Is it okay to make a mistake?
Andrew: Yes.
Teacher: Is it okay to make a mistake, Jack?
Jack: Yes.
Teacher: You bet it is. As long as you're in my class it is okay to make a mistake. Because I make them all the time, and we learn from our mistakes, a lot. Jack already figured out, "Oops, I didn't have the right answer the first time," (Jack turns and looks at the teacher and smiles) but he kept working at it and he got it.

In contrast to exchanges in which the teacher and children talked about mathematics, this interaction fits the elicitation-reply-evaluation pattern of traditional classroom discourse (Mehan, 1979), the evaluative statement being, "You bet it is." Both here and on other occasions when she initiated the explicit renegotiation of classroom social norms, the teacher attempted to tell the children how they ought to interpret particular situations. In this case, she emphasized that Jack's attempts to solve the problem were appropriate in every way, while simultaneously expressing her belief that it was more important in her classroom to contribute to the discussion by explaining a solution than it was to produce correct answers. Observations made in this classroom later in the school year indicated that the interventions the teacher made to initiate and guide the renegotiation of classroom norms were generally successful.

As the sample episode illustrates, the classroom can be seen to be composed of two mutually supporting levels of conversation: (1) talking about mathematics, where the teacher and children negotiate mathematical meanings; and (2) talking about talking about mathematics, where the teacher and students negotiate their obligations and expectations for doing and talking about mathematics.

In cognitive terms, the distinction is analogous to that which Lampert (1990) has made between beliefs *of* mathematics and beliefs *about* mathematics. Further, with reference to the philosophy and sociology of science (Barnes, 1982; Latour, 1987), the distinction is analogous to that between: (1) the evolution of a scientific research program or research tradition; and (2) the development of scientific theories and constructs within the evolving tradition.

This last analogy suggests that it is reasonable to talk of the teacher initiating and guiding what might be called a Kuhnian revolution in the classroom mathematics tradition (Cobb, Wood, and Yackel, 1991). It should be noted that our notion of a classroom mathematics tradition is closely related to a variety of other theoretical constructs including the classroom discursive practice (Walkerdine, 1988), the tradition of classroom practice (Solomon, 1989), the classroom didactical contract (Brousseau, 1984), and the classroom subculture or microculture (Bauersfeld, Krummheuer, and Voigt, 1988).

In the years following the completion of the first classroom teaching experiment, we have continued to analyze the mathematics traditions established in project classrooms and in conventional, textbook-based classrooms, and we have followed Richards's example (1991) in calling them the inquiry mathematics tradition and the school mathematics tradition respectively. Our analysis indicates that the taken-as-shared mathematical practices established in traditional classrooms generally have the quality of what we call *procedural instructions* (Cobb, Wood, Yackel, and McNeal, 1992). They are instructions in the sense that the consequence of transgressing them is ineffectiveness, rather than merely error per se (see Much and Shweder, 1979). They are procedural in the sense that the symbols manipulated when engaging in classroom mathematical practices do not necessarily refer to anything beyond themselves.

As an illustration, consider the following episode which occurred in a traditional third-grade classroom in the same school at the rural/suburban site with eight-year-old children. The teacher and children were working through four textbook tasks that each involved a pictured collection of base-ten longs and individual cubes. One task showed three longs and six cubes.

Teacher: How many tens do you see? Monica?
Monica: . . . [No response].
Teacher: [Problem] number three.
Monica: Three.
Teacher: How many ones do you see? James?
James: Four.
Teacher: Not in number three, James.
James: . . . [Inaudible].
Teacher: Six. And what number is that, James?
James: Sixty.

At this point, James's and the teacher's interpretations of the task were clearly in conflict. We can imagine a variety of possible ways in which the episode might have continued. For example, the teacher could have asked James to explain his response, or she could have asked the other children whether they agreed with his answer. Instead, their subsequent actions indicated that doing mathematics was, for them, a matter of following procedural instructions.

Teacher: Look at number three, James. How many tens do we see? (Moves toward him.)
James: Three.
Teacher: And how many ones?
James: Six.
Teacher: And what number is that?
James: Sixty-three.
Teacher: Okay, let's look, James. Look, James, look. How many tens do we see? Three tens. How many ones? Six ones.
James: Thirty-six.
Teacher: Thirty-six. Good.

When we consider what James learned in the course of this exchange, it seems unlikely that he constructed conceptual units of ten that were themselves composed of ones. In all likelihood, he found a way of producing an answer that was acceptable to the teacher by focusing on the number words "three" and "six." Thus, it appears that the teacher was unknowingly guiding his construction of a procedural instruction that did not refer to anything beyond itself. We also note that the teacher had to pose increasingly specific questions before James gave a response that she could evaluate positively and thus conclude the exchange. The consequence of James's error therefore seemed to be ineffectiveness in that he was unable to participate in the constitution of an elicitation-response-evaluation pattern that characterized smooth interactions in this classroom.

More generally, an analysis of public discourse in this and other conventional textbook-based classrooms gives no indication that symbol-manipulation acts developed within the school mathematics tradition carry the significance of mentally acting on abstract yet personally real mathematical objects. Further, because there was nothing beyond the symbols to which the teacher and the children can publicly refer, an explanation in these classrooms involves stating a sequence of instructions for manipulating symbols. As a consequence, mathematics as it is interactively constituted in these classrooms is a ritualistic, self-contained activity divorced from other aspects of children's lives, including their out-of-school pragmatic problem solving.

In contrast, in project classrooms, the manipulation of conventional symbols typically seemed to signify acting on taken-as-shared mathematical objects for the children. For example, in the second-grade classroom in which we conducted the first teaching experiment, children proposed 52, 42, and 48 as answers to a task that involved finding how many would have to be added to 38 to make a pictured collection of eight strips of ten squares and six individual squares (i.e., 86). The teacher framed this conflict in the children's answers as a problem that needed to be resolved: "So how are we going to figure this out? We've got three different answers." One group who gave 48 as their answer explained their solution as follows:

Jason: We took away 50 [from the eight strips of ten], and we have 30 left, and then there is 6 [individual squares] here so we knew that wouldn't work so . . .

Teacher: Right.

Jason: . . . we have to take 2 off one of the ten bars [that we took away] and then add it to the 30, and that makes, and that, and that would make all up . . . and that would make 48 [that we have taken away].

Teacher: Forty-eight. Okay. Who did it a different way?

The metaphor of acting in physical reality was implicit in Jason's explanation, suggesting that he experienced numbers as arithmetical objects that were abstract and yet had a manipulable quality. More generally, this metaphor of acting in physical reality permeated classroom discourse whether or not task statements involved pictures and diagrams.

As the episode continued, one child said that he agreed with 48, and the teacher asked his small group partner, Chuck, for his opinion.

Chuck: I agree with 48.

Teacher: Why do you agree with that? I want you to explain it to me.

Chuck: Well, like . . . (shrugs his shoulders).

Teacher: That's not a good enough answer, Chuck. Did you hear Chuck's answer? Look at me [to the class], this was Chuck's answer (shrugs her shoulders). That's not good enough.

Here, Chuck was ineffective even though he agreed with the correct answer. In contrast, children who could explain how they had arrived at what later proved to be an incorrect answer continued to be effective in this classroom. The teacher explicitly addressed this issue at the conclusion of the episode: "It doesn't matter if you have 48, 47, 49 or whatever. . . . It isn't the idea that your answer is right as much as how in the world are you gonna try to get an answer." Thus, the consequence of transgressing a mathematical norm in this classroom was error per se rather than ineffectiveness.

More generally, the sample episode illustrates that to be effective in an inquiry mathematics classroom is to engage in mathematical argumentation. As part of this process, students are obliged to give explanations and justifications that others might be able to interpret in terms of actions on mathematical objects. It also appears that the teacher and children in an inquiry mathematics classroom are acting in a taken-as-shared mathematical reality and that they elaborate this reality in the course of their ongoing negotiations of mathematical meanings. And, to say that their negotiations are about the nature of such a reality is to say that generally accepted arguments establish *mathematical truths* rather than specify procedural instructions. We should stress that this use of the term *truth* does not imply that particular mathematical meanings and practices are immutable and ahistorical or that mathematical objects have a Platonic existence independent of human activity. In this regard, we find von Glasersfeld's (1990) critique of correspondence theories of truth compelling. Instead, we subscribe to the view proposed by Peirce (1935), Rorty (1978), Bernstein (1983), and numerous others that truths are established by members of communities and that they serve a regulative function within those communities. It is for this reason that members of a community who transgress a currently established truth are expected to explain and justify their actions in ways that satisfy the standards of argumentation of the community. In the process, the truth and, indeed, the community's standards of argumentation may be modified.

The contrast we have made between school mathematics and inquiry mathematics, and between procedural instructions and mathematical truths, are captured succinctly by Davis and Hersh's (1981) observation that "mathematicians know they are studying an objective reality. To an outsider, they seem to be engaged in an esoteric communication with themselves and a small group of friends" (pp. 43–4). In a school mathematics classroom, the focus seems to be on a self-contained, esoteric form of communication that involves the concatenation of conventional written and oral symbols. In an inquiry mathematics classroom, the teacher and students elaborate a taken-as-shared mathematical reality in the course of their interactions – their personal experience is that of coming to know an objective mathematical reality.

Individual construction and mathematical acculturation

An issue that continues to preoccupy us is that of reconciling the cognitive and social aspects of children's mathematical learning. On the one hand, we can take a cognitive perspective that emphasizes the sovereignty of children's mathematical experiences and focuses on their personal ways of knowing (von Glasersfeld, 1991). From this point of view, it is reasonable to characterize learning as a problem-solving process in which children reorganize their mathematical activity in an attempt to resolve what they find problematic within the worlds of their experiences. On the other hand, we can also view mathematical learning as a process of acculturation into the mathematical ways of knowing institutionalized by wider society. From this perspective, one way in which a child might resolve what he or she finds personally problematic is not necessarily as good as any other. Thus, for example, when we conduct classroom teaching experiments, we tentatively outline potential conceptual constructions and attempt to guide the children's mathematical development in certain directions but not others.

This tension between mathematical learning as individual construction and as a process of acculturation is not merely a theoretical diversion. Instead, it finds expression in the activity of teachers as they attempt to teach through inquiry and to develop forms of pedagogical practice compatible with constructivism. Lampert (1985) made this point succinctly when she said that her job as a mathematics teacher involves "an argument between opposing tendencies within oneself in which neither side can come out the winner. From this perspective, my job would involve the tension between pushing students to achieve and providing a comfortable learning environment, between covering the curriculum and attending to individual understanding" (p. 183).

As Lampert's comments about "pushing students to achieve" and "covering the curriculum" indicate, the characterization of learning as a process of acculturation finds expression in sanctions and controls designed to ensure that teachers fulfill certain obligations to the school as a social institution and to wider society. The tension with which teachers have to cope became very real to us when we conducted classroom teaching experiments and helped a reasonably large number of teachers establish inquiry mathematics traditions in their classrooms. For example, in order to gain permission to conduct the teaching experiments, we agreed to address all of the participating school district's objectives for second- and third-grade mathematics regardless of whether we could justify them either in terms of our own beliefs about what is worth knowing and doing mathematically, or in terms of current analyses of children's mathematical learning. Further, State-mandated accountability tests of so-called basic skills were administered two-thirds of the way through the school year in both second and third grade. Children who were deemed to have failed these tests had to attend summer school and, if necessary, repeat the grade level the following year. Thus, from our point of view, it was imperative that the third-graders be able to add and subtract three-digit numbers by March of the school year. As a consequence, we experienced the tension as we supported their construction of increasingly sophisticated yet personally meaningful computational algorithms that reflected their developing conceptions of place-value numeration.

Stepping back to consider this tension in theoretical terms, we first note that Piaget's writings have been repeatedly critiqued, often unfairly in our view, for downplaying the social and cultural aspects of knowing. Further, there has been an increasingly vociferous reaction against the individualist focus of mainstream American psychology in recent years. In this intellectual climate, a gamut of sociocultural theories that build on the work of Vygotsky and Russian activity theorists has become increasingly influential in the United States. Theories of this type typically capitalize on the observation that, historically, the evolution of currently accepted mathematical ideas and theories involved more than the insights of the prototypical mathematical genius. In this regard, constructivist and sociocultural theorists agree that the construction and validation of mathematical concepts are collective as well as individual activities and that they occur via a process of argumentation within a community. Further, both groups of theorists speak of a mathematical worldview or culture that involves taken-as-shared concepts, conventions, and models together with a background of largely unarticulated suppositions and assumptions. As a consequence, both contend that teachers should help students learn to use models and symbolisms and should support their construction of normative mathematical concepts.

The issue that separates constructivist and sociocultural theorists concerns the role that so-called cultural tools such as models and symbolisms play in conceptual development. From the sociocultural perspective, a teacher who teaches students to engage in the practices of the mathematics community and to use mathematical conventions, models, and symbolisms appropriately is simultaneously introducing them to the theoretical ideas and concepts of the discipline (Davydov, 1988). In this view, students who engage in mathematical practices involving conventions, models, and symbolisms must necessarily be constructing the taken-as-shared concepts of the mathematics community. As a consequence, sociocultural theorists sometimes describe mathematical conventions, models, and symbolisms as objective mediators that carry meaning from one generation to the next.

This general line of argument is untenable from the constructivist perspective even if only the social and cultural aspects of mathematical activity are considered because it assumes that the use of models and symbolisms can be cut away from a complex network of consensual suppositions, assumptions, and construals that give them meaning and significance within the culture of an established mathematics community. In other words, the rationale for teaching students to use cultural tools appropriately is plausible only if it can be shown that the introduction of those tools somehow transports a complex of interrelated concepts and background assumptions intact from the mathematics community to the classroom community. From the constructivist perspective, it appears that in their attempt to transcend the limitations of a purely cognitive focus, sociocultural theorists go to the opposite extreme and characterize learning almost exclusively as a process of acculturation.

Sociocultural approaches that subordinate the individual to social and cultural processes can be contrasted with the view that neither the individual nor the social and cultural aspects of mathematical activity should be given priority over the other. The overriding educational task is then not to introduce aspects of a pregiven mathematical culture into the classroom. Instead, it is to guide the development of individual children's thinking and the evolution of the mathematical practices established by the classroom community so that they become increasingly compatible with those of wider society. In this scheme, the mathematical practices established in the classroom are not treated as entities that can be brought in from the outside. Instead, they are viewed as co-constructions created by the teacher and students together in the course of their classroom interactions. From this perspective, one of our goals when analyzing classroom video recordings is to explain how the teacher and students negotiate increasingly sophisticated ways of interpreting and acting with conventional arithmetical symbols such as multidigit numerals.

In general, the central issue for the sociocultural theorist is to explain how students learn to engage in the mathematical practices of wider society and thus acquire their cultural inheritance – mathematics as objective cultural knowledge. In contrast, our primary concern is to explain the evolution of both individual students' thinking and the mathematical practices of the classroom community. Such an approach reflects the view that students' individual mathematical activities and the mathematical practices established by the classroom community are reflexively related. In proposing this relationship, we do not merely contend that individual and collective mathematical actions are interdependent, but instead claim that one literally does not exist without the other. On the one hand, the teacher and students together regenerate the taken-as-shared mathematical practices of the classroom community as they coordinate their individual mathematical activities. On the other hand, students' participation in the establishment of these practices both enables and constrains their individual mathematical activity.

This account of the relationship between the individual and social aspects of mathematical activity focuses on emerging systems of meaning in the classroom. A sociocultural theorist might therefore object that we have ignored the mathematical meanings and practices institutionalized by wider society. We can best address this issue by considering the development of instructional activities that might be appropriate for inquiry mathematics classrooms. In doing so, we will also clarify the teacher's role in guiding both individual students' cognitive development and the classroom community's establishment of mathematical practices.

Instructional development

From the constructivist perspective, the challenge when developing instructional activities for inquiry mathematics classrooms is to make it possible for *mathematically significant issues* to arise out of *children's own constructive efforts* in the course of *classroom social interactions*. In talking of mathematically significant issues, we of course mean that the issues are significant with respect to the mathematical practices of wider society. Thus, mathematical learning is a process of acculturation. In stressing that children's constructive activity is the source of these mathematical issues, we are simultaneously emphasizing that learning is a process of active individual construction. Further, the reference to social interaction indicates that children make these constructions as they participate in the mathematical practices of the classroom community. Thus, individual learning and the evolution of these practices are inextricably related.

As an illustration, we will present a sequence of brief episodes taken from a third-grade classroom teaching experiment conducted at the rural/suburban site. Here, we made only minor modifications to a sequence of instructional activities developed by Streefland (1991). The activities were designed to support the emergence of the issue of the equivalence of fractional partitionings both as a focus of individual children's activity and as a topic of conversation. The initial tasks in the sequence involved dividing pizzas fairly. In one of the first tasks, the children worked in pairs to share two pizzas between four people. The task statement showed a picture of two circles.

The children's explanations during the subsequent whole class discussion indicated that some groups had divided each pizza in half whereas others had divided each into quarters. The teacher recorded these solutions by writing "1/2" and "1/4 + 1/4" to symbolize the portion that each person would receive. One child then commented on the second solution as follows:

Richard: Yeah, but instead, in this one [the drawing of two pizzas divided into fourths], you'd get two pieces, or you'd get a big half.
Teacher: Well, do they still get the same amount?
Richard and Dawn: Yeah.
Richard: Yeah, they still get the same amount. Both of those equal a half.
Teacher: What could you find out here? Do you know?
Richard: They're both the same, but just done differently.
Teacher: So two-fourths is the same, or equal to, one-half, right? (writes "1/4 + 1/4 = 1/2").

Here, the issue of the equivalence of the different partitionings emerged naturally in the sense that the question of whether a person would receive the same amount of pizza to eat in the two cases was both *personally meaningful* and *relevant* to the children. More generally, when we speak of some event in the classroom as being natural, we mean that it was experienced as a natural development by the children in that it grew out of their activity in a personally meaningful and relevant way. We can also note in passing that the teacher redescribed Richard's response by talking of two-fourths as being equal to one-half, and by using conventional written symbols to record the solutions. We will return to this point once we have presented the remaining episodes.

In a subsequent task, the children shared four pizzas between eight people. Their various solutions involved dividing pizzas into halves, quarters, and eighths. Referring to these solutions, the teacher asked, "Do you get more pizza one way than another?"

Jenna: It wouldn't make a difference.
John: Well, in a way they're the same, and in a way they're different.
Teacher: How are they the same?
John: They're the same because if you put 4 eighths together, it equals a half.

He subsequently elaborated:

John: I know a way you can tell. Four plus 4 equals 8, and 1 plus 1 equals 2.
Teacher: Four plus 4 equals 8. Now how does that help us?
John: It tells us that it's just half.
Teacher: So, in other words, you're saying that if we add 4 eighths and 4 eighths (writes "4/8 + 4/8 = 8/8"), that would equal 8 eighths, would be the whole thing.
Jenna: What could we do with the [solution that involved dividing pizzas into] fourths?

Jenna's final question indicates that the task for her was now not simply to partition pizzas fairly but also involved demonstrating the equivalence of different partitionings. This goal, which became increasingly taken-as-shared, was not given to the children by either the instructional developers or by the teacher. Instead, it grew out of the children's mathematical activity with the teacher's guidance.

It is also apparent that this shift in taken-as-shared goals was accompanied by a change in classroom mathematical practices. Initially, these practices had involved partitioning and comparing amounts of pizza per se. The above exchange indicates that drawings of pizzas now seemed to signify fractional parts of a numerical whole. Thus, neither John nor Jenna referred to amounts of pizza but instead spoke of fourths and eighths. What these terms might have meant for the children is, of course, an open question. We can, however, note that there were significant qualitative differences in the ways that individual children reorganized their partitioning activity. For example, during a subsequent discussion, one child explained that three-sixths was equal to one-half by dividing a circle in half and then partitioning one of the halves into three equal pieces called "sixths." However, another child explained, "I do it backwards. . . . Six-sixths . . . Half of six-sixths is three-sixths and so that would be . . . Since six-sixths is a whole, then three-sixths is one-half."

It would seem that this child had internalized partitioning activity to a considerable degree and could conceptually compose and decompose fractional units of some type. These qualitative differences in the children's mathematical interpretations subsequently made it possible for the process of establishing the equivalence of partitionings to itself become a natural topic of conversation.

We should stress that the instructional activities we have discussed are the first in an elaborate sequence developed by Streefland. Nonetheless, they are sufficient to allow us to make three points about instructional development. First, the initial instructional activities in a sequence should give rise to situations that are real in the worlds of children's personal experiences, thus making it possible for them to immediately engage in informal mathematical activity (Treffers, 1987). In the case of the sample sequence, for example, the activity of dividing pizzas was experientially real for the children. Second, in keeping with the view that mathematical learning is a process of acculturation as well as a process of individual construction, the instructional activities should be justifiable with respect to the potential endpoints of the learning sequence. Consequently, it is essential that children's initial, informal activity constitute a basis from which they can reflectively abstract and thus make the transition to more formal yet personally meaningful mathematical activity. We should stress that, in this view, children progressively mathematize their activity in the situation rather than the situation per se, and that this involves the internalization and interiorization of activity (Piaget, 1980). With regard to the sample activity sequence, for example, the children who could conceptually compose and decompose fractional units of some type had internalized their activity of partitioning. Third, the teacher must be able to capitalize on children's interpretations, solutions, and explanations when guiding the development of classroom mathematical practices. Only then can the teacher fulfill his or her obligations to the school and to wider society without steering or funneling children to predetermined responses that he or she has in mind all along (Bauersfeld, 1980; Voigt, 1985). Mathematics, as it is realized in the classroom, is then a genuine process of argumentation rather than a sterile social guessing game.

The last of these three points is particularly significant in that it brings together issues concerning individual construction, mathematical acculturation, classroom social interaction, and the nature of instructional activities. The sample episodes illustrate two ways in which the teacher capitalized on the children's activity. First, she was able to raise the issue of the equivalence of different partitionings simply by asking, "Do you get more pizza one way than another?" It was not merely a matter of luck that the teacher was able to use the children's solutions as a resource in this way. The classroom-based approach that Streefland used to develop the instructional activities involved analyzing the various ways in which individual children solve specific tasks. This enabled him to anticipate the range of solutions that might arise in any classroom including the one in which we conducted the teaching experiment. We can note in passing that this interest in the quality of different children's mathematical activity contrasts with sociocultural theorists' focus on pregiven social practices that, it is claimed, drive individual thought.

The second way in which the teacher capitalized on children's mathematical activity was to repeatedly redescribe the children's explanations in terms that they would not have used, but which nonetheless made sense to them. It was critical that the teacher initiate the negotiation of mathematical meanings in this way in that she was the only member of the classroom community who could judge which aspects of the children's activity might be significant with respect to their acculturation into the mathematical practices of wider society. As these redescriptions often involved the use of written symbols, a sociocultural theorist might argue that the cultural tools were carriers of meaning. However, detailed analyses of classroom interactions indicate that the children gave meaning to the teacher's use of conventional symbols within the context of their ongoing mathematical activity. Further, the analyses indicate that the children actively contributed to the classroom community's development of taken-as-shared meanings for the symbols. Consequently, the claim that conventional ways of symbolizing carry the mathematical meanings institutionalized by wider society into the classroom does not hold up under close scrutiny. It seems more reasonable to say instead that the use of conventional symbols to redescribe the children's mathematical activity was one way in which the teacher guided both their mathematization of their initially informal activity and the classroom community's establishment of increasingly sophisticated mathematical practices. Thus, whereas sociocultural theory is concerned with the transmission of meaning from one generation to the next, constructivism is concerned with the process of guiding the emergence of individual and collective systems of meaning in the classroom.

An issue for the future

In the course of the discussion, we have attempted to clarify what we mean by an inquiry mathematics classroom tradition. We have also stressed the importance of developing instructional activities that make it possible for the teacher to guide the emergence of significant mathematical issues by capitalizing on children's mathematical activity. The astute reader will, however, have noted that although we have considered the starting points and potential endpoints of a learning sequence, little has been said about instructional activities that might support children's transition from informal, pragmatic problem solving to more formal mathematical activity. Observations made during a recent classroom teaching experiment indicate that instructional activities in which students are encouraged to create models of their informal mathematical activity can be helpful in this regard. We are currently collaborating with researchers at the Freudenthal Institute in the Netherlands to investigate the hypothesis that these models of informal activity will evolve into models for more formal mathematical activity (Gravemeijer, 1991; Treffers, 1991). These models are not restricted to conventional symbols, but can involve pictures, diagrams, and nonstandard notational schemes. Cognitively, it appears that students' use of models to record prior activity facilitates their reflection on and progressive mathematization of that activity. Socially, the development of models appears to provide opportunities for crucial conceptual acts to become explicit topics of conversation. To the extent that this approach proves viable, students' formal mathematical activity will involve the conceptual manipulation of experientially real mathematical objects and yet be anchored via the models in the rich imagery of the starting points. Further, instructional sequences of this type would make it possible for teachers to achieve their pedagogical agendas while simultaneously building on students' mathematical thinking during genuine discussions.

Significantly, despite its pragmatic promise, the proposed approach to instructional development poses a challenge to the way in which constructivists (including ourselves) have tended to characterize the relationship between languaging and thinking. As Walkerdine (1988) observed, languaging and symbolizing play little if any role in such key processes as reflective abstraction, internalization, and interiorization that constructivists typically use to account for conceptual development in mathematics. It would seem that we and other constructivists have sometimes equated positivist characterizations of language with the very activity of languaging. As a consequence, in dismissing the first, we have often assumed that the second plays no role in students' construction of increasingly sophisticated mathematical concepts. Thus, whereas sociocultural theorists frequently treat symbols and other cultural tools as preexisting carriers of meanings, we have tended to assume that conceptual construction precedes symbolization. The challenge is to transcend these dichotomous views of the relationship between languaging and conceptualizing. As part of this process, it might be productive to view ways of symbolizing as both individual constructive activities and as mathematical practices established by the classroom community. One of our current interests is in fact to explore the reflexive relationship between these individual and collective activities, and thus between learning and communicating in the classroom.

Chapter 6
The construction of answers to insoluble problems

MARIA-LUISA SCHUBAUER-LEONI AND LADISLAS NTAMAKILIRO

The cognitive answer as a construction

In order to show the relevance of using ''insoluble problems'' as a means of approaching the educational problematic of problem solving, we must first frame the constructivist approach which characterizes this research work.[1] This theoretical contribution is to be located in the socioconstructivist current which advocates a ternary model according to which the relationship of an ego to the world and its objects is always mediated by a real or potential alter (Gilly, 1991). It is within this psychosocial current, which challenges the validity of a constructivist perspective conceived of within an ''individualistic'' framework, that we join with other authors (Perret-Clermont and Nicolet, 1988) in: (1) refusing to limit the debate to the classic oppositions between ''innate/acquired, imitation/construction, the working out of answers *hic et nunc*/actualization of preexisting potentialities''; and (2) advocating ''that cognitive answers acquire the status of construction'' (Iannaccone and Perret-Clermont, 1990). By no means the easy way out, such a choice indeed entails approaching the problem of knowledge via the observable, ad hoc situations in which the answers of individuals manifest. The status of answers is at that point analyzed in accordance with the postulate that ''while an answer is never totally new, it is articulated in the *hic et nunc* of the social situation with which the individual is confronted and is based both on the experience which he or she has acquired and the 'cultural heredity' which he or she has available to him or her'' (ibid.). Hence, as a form of behavior, the observed answer is referred to the problem of its meaning, which, in this case is threefold – that is, meaning must be conceived of from the point of view of: the person whose actions took the form of an answer; the person who formulated the question; and, finally, the researcher who studies the phenomenon and interprets this series of actions in order to describe and explain them.

Like the historical and sociocultural current originating in the work of Vygotsky (1985), this psychosocial current holds to the principle of indissociability governing the individual and the environment, whereby cognitive activity is inscribed in an interindividual, cultural, and institutional context. By considering cognitive activity as essentially social and intersubjective in nature, these theoretical perspectives entail conceptual and methodological changes which themselves involve a shift in terms of what is held to be the minimum unit of analysis: Once the individual is no longer studied for his or her own sake but is viewed in terms of his or her interactions with others, it is the interaction itself which becomes the analytical unit (Grossen, 1993).

A ternary relational system and its contracts

We propose exploring the system of relationships represented by the triad of questioner–questionee–object of inquiry; indeed, this system appears to us as an inescapable subject of research within the approach we have adopted. Such systems of relationships have already been analyzed on the basis of the interpretative framework made possible by the existence of a "contract of communication" which not only gave body to each member of the triad but also linked all parties to one another (Ghiglione, 1987). The principle of a "contract of communication" refers to the existence of systems of tacit norms, values, and rules which structure every social relationship and which form the hub of theoretical preoccupations deriving from various fields such as ethnomethodology, social psychology, sociolinguistics, and linguistic pragmatics. The notion of a contract of communication has, moreover, been fine-tuned according to the specific nature of the contract in question as this in turn brings particular, ad hoc institutional cultures into play. Thus, for example, an experimental contract brings together the experimenter, the experiment participant, and the subject of the experiment under the governance of the culture prevailing in this particular area or space. The didactic contract, on the other hand, governs the interaction occurring between teacher, student, and subject matter within the teaching space (Elbers, 1986; Grossen, 1988; Schubauer-Leoni, 1986, 1988; Schubauer-Leoni, Bell, Grossen, and Perret-Clermont, 1989). As for educational settings, the notion of didactic contract (Brousseau, 1988; Chevallard, 1988; Schubauer-

Leoni, 1986, 1988) enables us to specify the nature of this contract. The rights and obligations which link the partners of a didactic relationship are determined, notably, by the social, institutionally inscribed project whose aim is to have children acquire a duly transposed kind of knowledge (Chevallard, 1991).

In a context of questioning of the type occurring in the face-to-face encounter between an experimenter and a child in connection with problem solving, the communication which develops between these two figures does so either in respect or in defiance of certain tacit rules whose main, time-honored features bring into play (following Ghiglione, 1987) principles of relevance, coherence, reciprocity, and influence.[2] Rules of such a general nature are at work in both a didactic contract and an experimental contract. The distinction which can be made between the two contracts depends, moreover, on the locus from which the situation is interpreted. One of us has, in fact, emphasized elsewhere (Schubauer-Leoni, 1988; Schubauer-Leoni et al., 1989) that differentiation of the didactic contract from the experimental contract is basically a matter of the tacit intentions and finalities which are ascribed to a situation by the actor enjoying greatest prominence (i.e., experimenter or teacher). As for children, they will tend to continue to refer meaning back to the didactic contract which they are party to on an everyday basis, even when the adult with whom they are confronted has constructed his or her questioning procedure beforehand to reflect an experimental contract (Grossen, 1988). Studying how the child functions in an experimental situation thus proves to be a particularly delicate operation, since it involves identifying the meanings which are ascribed by the child and experimenter according to the contracts which are tacitly referred to by each. Hence, certain cases may arise in which the actors interact at cross-purposes with one another because their realms of reference are not concommitant with one another. Studying what takes place in the context of an experimental situation must, then, take into account the articulation occurring between the rules of the experimental contract, as implemented by the experimenter, and the rules of the didactic contract conveyed by schooling practices, as imported into the experimental situation by the child.

Co-constructing a world which is taken as shared

Approaching an object of learning or evaluation within the didactic (or experimental) relationship amounts to co-constructing a suppos-

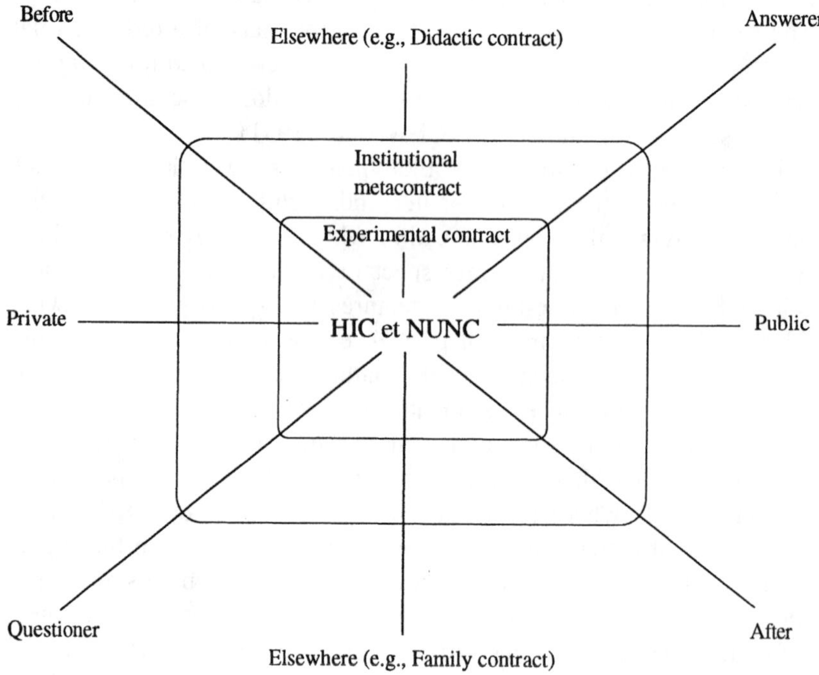

Figure 6.1. Coordinates of the construction of an answer within the framework of an experimental contract

edly common world *hic et nunc*. Such a construction indeed involves a variety of levels that interact closely with one another. Figure 6.1 offers a schema of the various levels of construction (represented in the form of coordinates) which are likely to be involved in the functioning of a child who is questioned within the framework of a tacit experimental contract.

The *hic et nunc* in which linkages occur between the actions of questioning and replying is represented as being governed in the first instance by an institutional metacontract, within Rommeiveit's meaning of the term (1974). We are dealing here with a contract with respect to the experimental contract governing an initial level of rights and obligations of interactors, hence, with an initial level of meanings with respect to what is supposed to occur in such a locus of verbal exchange. We locate the assumptions of Ghiglione (1987) at this metacontractual level. With reference to the model of Rommeiveit (1974) concerning the architecture of intersubjectivity which is necessary to all communication, the figure evokes the existence of an "elsewhere," which is equally assumed to be held in common by the actors who interact here and now. This "elsewhere" refers in particular to the existence of other contracts of which the actors may have had some experience: here, the didactic contract takes pride of place, but the family contract which presumably governs the interactions occurring within this institution is also mentioned. Another axis represents the temporal dimension which emerges in connection with all relationships involving questioning and which, as such, may well contribute to the meanings which actors develop respectively.

Figure 6.1 distinguishes between the respective roles of questioner and questionee along what may be called the human axis. In addition, borrowing from Chevallard (1988), this figure polarizes analysis along a new axis which is concerned with the split between a public element and a private element. The dichotomy between public and private refers, on the one hand, to what each partner elaborates for him- or herself privately, and which he or she does not deem necessary or useful to make apparent, and, on the other hand, to what subjects manifest to the interlocutor through a variety of channels and systems of signifiers within a given institution. However, this split is not an absolute one, as Chevallard (1992) has pointed out: "It is relative to institution 'I,' and what is concealed from a given institution could emerge in broad daylight with respect to some other institution" (p. 91). Moreover, it is indeed the room to maneuver represented by this split that provides the child with the possibility of playing with the institution and negotiating his or her place and freedom over the course of experiments involving questioning and answering.

We see this coordinate as being of major significance because it makes possible a distinction between two levels of rationality, which we have called level A (the child is focused both on processing the problem and producing an answer for him- or herself) and level B (the child focuses on the admissibility of this answer according to the presumed expectations of the questioner). Now these two levels of rationality are first subjected to private processing and then take on a "public" form via the externalization and formulation of answers for the experimenter. Obviously, this is a dialectical process, one that unfolds over time: a range of public manifestations, taken together with the reception which they meet, in turn stimulate new private productions, and so on.

We undertake the dissection of the events occurring in connection with acts of questioning and answering to satisfy the need for further analysis. However, we are in no way of the opinion that, as concerns the very functioning of the relationship, subjects indeed dissociate these different ingredients of their practical behavior as this is unfolding. In addition, it is not our intention to reduce cognition to linguistic phenomena. However, it is useful to rely on the verbalizations, explanations, and indeed justifications of questionees to bring out the processes of construction taking place on the various levels we have just outlined.

In the area of problem solving, other research in mathematics teaching (Brun and Conne, 1990) makes it quite clear that the functioning of a child who is confronted with a problem cannot be referred purely and simply to a "logic which is inherent to the behavior of the problem-solver, without (also) questioning the role played by the situation." In particular, it appears that the most widespread educational epistemologies require of teachers that they not only think up questions but that they also take charge of the answers if the children themselves fail to do so adequately. Brun and Conne (1990) have written, "The didactic contract essentially obliges the teacher to compensate for the foulups and the gaps which arise in the course of child/situation interactions, however well these interactions were thought out beforehand" (p. 271). Thus, through the repeated enactment of this didactic contract, the child becomes accustomed to dealing with legitimate problems, to which, necessarily, an answer can be provided and which also are subject to verification by a teacher who regularly confirms whether the answers provided are correct or incorrect.

By taking up the paradigm of the "insoluble" problem, the portion of research with which we are particularly concerned hereafter proceeds to introduce a break with the customary didactic contract. We are dealing here, in other words, with a tool for research or a methodological alternative as an experimental device by which to penetrate into the practical universe governed by the didactic contract and thus bring out the axes of rationality which were described above.

A contextual psychology of mathematical problem solving

Thus far, an individual's ways of thinking and answering have been described as being intimately bound up with the institutional, cultural, and interpersonal conditions of their manifestation. In order to understand the answering activity of a child confronted with an insoluble question, it is worth exploring a body of research which has brought out the effects of context on arithmetical problem solving.

In particular, we would like to mention the work of Säljö and Wyndhamn (1987), who showed how titling a page of problems for assignment purposes affected the public version of the child's work. Thus, depending on whether children were dealing with an activity designated as "math problems" or "math problems: multiplication," in which the information was highlighted (according to the typographical characters used) and then reinforced (or not) with a precise example of an appropriate answer, some children produced multiplication to solve a problem of capacity (volume).

Brossard (1994), who has pursued this avenue of research with a view to studying the cognitive functioning of students in a school setting, brings out a number of presumably interwoven levels of analysis: (1) a level involving the social representations which the child develops not only of the teacher but also of him- or herself as a pupil (at this level, actors are able to take stock of one another in various situations); (2) a didactic level which refers to class subject matters as well as to teachers' teaching strategies. With his sights set on honing analysis of children's cognitive functioning in the school setting at some future date, Brossard also proposes a distinction between the *exercise* (defined as the statement of the different problems and questions, by which the heading or title is fleshed out) and the *context* (defined as the "set of indicators related to the social environment," which children may or may not deem relevant). This research has served especially to show that children who otherwise are labeled in school as being "weak" turn out to be especially sensitive to the significance of the context which was subjected to experimental manipulation via the titling of the exercise.

Other major research, by Carraher, Carraher, and Schliemann (1985) and Lave (1988) in particular, has also emphasized the impact of contextual and cultural dimensions on the manifestation of cognitive strategies in approaches which may be adopted toward problems of arithmetic. A number of ethnographic studies by these researchers (Nunes, 1992) have shown how strategies vary according to the oral or written form adopted in dealing with arithmetic problems and according to the location (classroom or street) in which problems were presented.

In other research (Perret-Clermont, Schubauer-Leoni, and Grossen, 1996; Schubauer-Leoni, Perret-Clermont, and Grossen, 1992), one of us has observed that the answers produced by children who are questioned in the classroom are of a different kind than those provided outside the classroom in a one-on-one situation with the experimenter (that is, answers were formulated vis-à-vis the same experimenter by a group of children possessing comparable competency in terms of the mathematical problems used in testing). A similar but as yet unverified effect was obtained by manipulating the role given to the experimenter.[3] Taken together, this research focuses on the individual in context and seeks out the reasons for his or her behavior in individual/situational interaction. A similar principle underlies research in didactics, although in this case the primary object of inquiry consists in the situation itself, viewed in terms of a "milieu" (as defined by Brousseau, 1988) in which the learning subject develops and constructs knowledge.

Entitling problems the "right" way – and the other ways

A second type of research which we would like to examine deals with how problems are titled and the awareness children have of what a "good" title is, one that has been made the "right way." Following up on research conducted by De Corte and Verschaffel (1983), which concluded that primary school children were unaware of this question, Brissiaud (1988) made use of the paradigm of the "absurd" problem (which had already been experimented with in 1980 by the elementary-level research team of the Institut de recherche en enseignement des mathématiques [IREM] in Grenoble, France) to test out the same hypothesis. In this researcher's conclusion, all students perceive a certain anomaly in an insoluble problem; however, the decision to reject the problem is what some children prove "incapable" of achieving.

This type of research is far from representing an isolated case. In fact numerous other research projects have drawn on the paradigm of insoluble problems (e.g., the ship captain's age – from the title of a well-known work in mathematics education published in France [Baruk, 1985]; see also Alves Martin and Carvalho Neto, 1990).

Chevallard (1988) also drew on "absurd" problems to reveal the existence of a didactic contract and how it functions. It was in connection, particularly, with the article "Quel est l'âge du capitaine?" (How old is the captain?), published by the IREM in Grenoble (1980), that this author developed a conceptual framework with which to take up the didactic contract. In his discussion of how problems of this type are usually referred to as absurd, Chevallard (1988) points out that such problems are the object of research bearing on the contract rather than on the children. He introduces the notion of the relevance of titles or statements of problems by means of a distinction between relevance in mathematical terms from relevance in terms of the appraisals made in everyday life. And, in a distinction crucial for our analysis, he contrasts the presence of two different kinds of logic: one (sacred), which operates within the terms of the didactic contract and which (to take the case of this article) prompts children to state that the captain is twenty-six years old on the basis of the number of goats and sheep he has on board; the other (profane), which causes children, on occasion and at the request of the adult, to declare that they cannot really see what the relationship is between the sheep and the captain! Nevertheless, according to Chevallard (1988), these two types of logic coexist and fill different functions within the realm of teaching interaction. Only an answer to the problem is required by the didactic contract, whereas commentary on the problem comes within the scope of "epididactic" concerns. Thus, in terms of the usual didactic contract, the child need not concern him- or herself with the legitimacy of the question.

To continue in the vein developed by Chevallard (1988), we are not interested in making a simplistic use of a child's publicly formulated answer to provide indications of dysfunctioning in either the child, the teaching activity, or the school as institution. Rather, we are interested in approaching this answer as the manifestation of conflicts emerging between different types of rationality located along a public/private axis. An approach of this type may prove informative not only about the nature of the customary didactic contract and that of the experimental contract involved, but also about the child's functioning.

From the age of the schoolteacher to the area of the cabbage field

We conducted an experiment in four elementary classes of fifth- and sixth-grade children at the primary level (age ranges ten to eleven and eleven to twelve years accordingly) in the Canton of Geneva, Switzerland. Classes were mixed and were made up of children from three major social strata: upper, middle, and lower. Three classes were evaluated as a group, with each child providing a written answer in the classroom setting, whereas the fourth group (a group of fifth graders) underwent individual interviews outside the classroom.[4] The texts and verbal explanations provided by the children in the fourth group are analyzed in detail; these answers lent themselves particularly to research into the articulation of the public and private aspects of answering. In the remainder of our analysis and commentary, we will focus exclusively on the answering activity of this fourth group of children.

The experiment was conceived of as a series of four problems and was designed to lead gradually to a break with the usual didactic contract. Accordingly, the first task was prepared by the teacher himself and was perfectly suited to the ongoing development of the didactic contract in the classroom, whereas we prepared the remaining three tasks. The second problem was formulated in a way which, according to the teacher, was complex but nevertheless accessible. The third problem was formulated as follows: "A farmer has 87 rows of 150 cabbages. What is the area of the field?" The problem affords no solution and yet involves a notion which is complex for this level of schooling, namely, that of area. Further space will be devoted below to this aspect of the problem. The fourth and final task was a classic example of an absurd problem: "In a class, there are 12 boys and 15 girls. How old is the schoolteacher?"

Problems: how to manage them? how to manage their irrelevance?

The face-to-face encounter between the experimenter and each child took place in two phases which led from one into the other.

The first phase involved managing the four problems. The experimenter merely gave out the problems as had been formulated beforehand. Without providing any further commentary, she then collected the written answers of the children as soon as these were ready to be handed in: "We'll talk about this afterward," she announced.

The second phase consisted in the discussion that took place in connection with the work which had been performed. Children looked their answers over and, when the situation lent itself accordingly, dealt with the problems once more. It was during this phase that the questions planned by the experimenter were used to create conditions in which the children could come to terms with the relevance of the problem. Thus, once problem solving had been completed and written answers had been turned in, the children were involved in another type of exercise, one which was governed by another type of contract and which required that the children engage in discourse of a kind usually banished from the didactic contract – namely, the epididactic contract, within Chevallard's meaning of the term (1988). As staked out within this research project, it was the experimental framework itself which, delimited as it was by the questions put by the adult, also legitimized the habitually illegitimate – that is, the adoption of a position on the problem itself. In the context of the questioning process represented by phase two, not only did it become possible to talk about a problem, but indeed the newly inaugurated experimental contract implicitly compelled discussion of the problems by means of a shift in the register of the questions being put! By way of introduction to this phase, the children were asked to evaluate the work they had just performed in terms of success or failure: ''So how did it go? Do you think you got it or not?'' From the outset, this request for self-evaluation provided the children with an opportunity to make a statement concerning a certain relationship which they entertained toward the object of questioning. It also stimulated a number of questions in ourselves: Are they going to say that they did not really understand what it was they were supposed to do? That the answer looks good to them? That they usually come up with the right answer? That they could not have done otherwise?, and so forth. We have, then, a whole range of indicators which make it possible to bring out other facets of this relationship. Then, the children were asked if they had previously worked on similar problems in class, whether such exercises were ''good'' or ''bad,'' if they were useful in some way, and so on.

This discussion immediately followed upon the work done on the question of the age of the schoolteacher: hence, most of the time was spent talking about this particular problem. All the same, the area problem holds special interest because it serves, at a deeper level, to problematize the articulation of the emergent conflicts. Indeed, how is one to dissociate aspects related to the complexity of the problem (i.e., the notion of area) from those relating to maneuvering vis-à-vis the contract (i.e., actions and statements which are allowed versus the actions and statements which children are obliged to make in a situation such as this one)? The events that took place during the experiment do not permit of any definitive response, since we were unable to verify how children would react to a ''good'' problem in a way conducive to distinguishing notional difficulties from the conflicts triggered by the use of problems which are at odds with the usual didactic contract. Nevertheless, the experiment makes it possible to at least approach this problematic. Further research is projected so as to bring out this articulation with greater precision.

The notion of area and the didactic contract

Piagetian studies on genetic epistemology (Vinh-Bang and Lunzer, 1965) have been used in research in mathematics teaching to clearly establish the complexity of the conceptual field represented by the spatial measurements of length, area, and volume for classroom purposes (Rogalski, 1982; Vergnaud, 1983). According to Rogalski (1982), as concerns cognitive development, spatial measurements bring into play the "articulation of 'physical concepts', which touch on the properties of the transformations of material objects, and 'spatial' concepts, which are related to the organization of cognitive activities involving space." In addition, spatial measurements necessitate the coordination of aspects of number with aspects connected to the qualitative representation of space. An essential element of any problem of measurement centers on the concept of unit; in turn, constructing and using a unit of measurement presupposes the synthesis of two operations, namely, partition and displacement. In the school setting, children acquire the habit fairly early on of associating work on measurements to pregiven conventional units, which does not mean, however, that they have constructed the mathematical concept of unit of measurement. The conceptual field surrounding spatial measurements is thus a complex one; whereas constructions of notions of length and area permit of conservation from the age of about seven or eight, differentiation between perimeter and area does not appear to be acquired before twelve years of age (Vinh-Bang and Lunzer, 1965).

With respect to the measurement of areas, the official objectives for the school year figuring in our research project (grade five of the primary level with children ages ten to eleven years) are as follows: measurement of the area of a polygon by "tiling" (i.e., covering a given shape of unknown area with regular shapes of the child's choosing; the areas of these shapes have been previously determined); introduction of a standard unit (i.e., the cm^2); discovering the rule for calculating the area of a rectangle; finding the area of a polygon which may be broken down into rectangles over a grid.

Thus formulated, our problem is particularly misleading since it draws on notions contained in "tiling" to refer to a unit of measurement which is little used, to say the least – that is, a cabbage head. In addition, cabbages work quite well in covering a field, with the result that, semantically speaking, the problem appears to hold water! Furthermore, children who have learned that "you have to carry out a multiplication'' in order to find the area will easily be led to think that "150" and "87" are necessary. The various elements combine together surprisingly well and are in complete harmony with the most basic rules governing the didactic contract, which ward off any suspicion over the validity of how the problem is stated. The legitimacy of this problem appears all the more unquestionable in that it was positioned immediately after two other problems which were typical of both the school setting and the operative didactic contract. All the same, the teachers of the children who were questioned were all convinced that their students would see through the hoax at once, and say so!

Given all of the elements just referred to, and despite the opinion of the teachers concerned to the contrary, we expected a great many of the written answers of the children to contain a multiplication or some other arithmetical calculation (particularly addition) of the quantities figuring in the statement. Analysis of these answers should, then, bring out potential evidence of: (1) conflict between the requirements of the usual didactic contract; (2) the constraints which were removed by the proposed experimental contract; and (3) the information which was made available to the child in the form of the problem. On the other hand, we expected a significant proportion of children to reject the last problem (involving the age of the schoolteacher), given that the impossibility of handling such a problem appears more obvious, although the capacity to admit such a thing in the context of an experiment is and was by no means a foregone conclusion.

Answers to the insoluble problems

The first portion of this analysis deals with all the answers provided by the twenty-two fifth-grade children. Following this, we go into greater detail concerning the face-to-face encounters between the experimenter and the children, three of whom were selected to provide illustration of three different positions and relationships to the problems.[5]

Categories of written answers for the problem involving area

Division. Two children divided 150 by 87. One answered by using the remainder, or 63, and the other answered with the quotient, or 1.72. Neither of the two made mention of a unit.

Subtraction. Two children subtracted 87 from 150. One answered 63. The other made a computational error and answered 70. Here again, neither of the two referred to a unit.

Addition. Two children added 150 and 87. One gave 237 m as the answer, the other 250 m.

Multiplication. Sixteen children multiplied 150 by 87. Although these children's answers made use of multiplication, they nevertheless varied on account of computational errors and the different units which were selected. Eight of the sixteen made no mention of units. Of this number, five arrived at 13,050, whereas the other three showed signs of miscalculation. For example, one child answered 13,137. The other eight children "named" the unit they had used. Thus, three answered "13,050 m^2," one answered "13,050 m^3," another "12,050 m^2," one answered "13,050 cabbages" and another "13,150 cabbages."

Of the children in this class who were questioned by an experimenter in face-to-face encounters, not one discarded the problem during the phase given over to providing a written answer; in addition, all of the children made use of one of the four arithmetical operations acquired at school and used them to calculate the quantities referred to in the statement.

Aside from the difficulty represented by the notion of area, we noticed that of those students who made use of multiplication, a sizable number seemed to want to hedge in respect of the constraints posed by the problem, by means of solving the conflict in terms of "cabbages" or by transforming the unit of measurement in greater accordance more with their school-based notion of area (m^2 and m^3)!

Categories of written answers for the problem involving age of the schoolteacher

Addition. Sixteen children out of the twenty-two who were questioned added 12 and 15 to arrive at 27. Of this group, two tried other arithmetical operations (subtraction, multiplication, and division), but settled finally on the sum produced by addition. It is also worth noting that of these sixteen children, only five specified "27 years," whereas the others made do with writing "27" only.

No answer possible. Three children fall into this category. One child wrote, "Knowing the number of children won't tell you how old the schoolteacher is." The second child wrote, "There's no way you can know, because you don't know whether the schoolteacher is young or old." The third child simply wrote, "There's no way of telling."

Blank sheet. Three children fit into this category.

To be sure, a significant number of children used some computational operation in formulating their answers, even in response to the fourth question. All the same, we would point out that a number of those students who dealt with the question of area permitted themselves to reject the question of the schoolteacher's age. Transcriptions of the two interview phases and of the statement of the two problems will be subjected to further analysis hereafter so as to bring out specific features of these results.

Three children and their behavior toward insoluble problems

To begin with, we will situate these three children using a synthesis of their positions with respect to the two problems. Table 6.1 sets out their respective positions.

Each child is referred to by the first three letters of his or her given name. The child's quarterly grade in mathematics at the time they underwent questioning is also provided in parentheses.[6]

Sam (6 out of 6): interaction involving the area of the field

Phase 1

Sam: Do we have to say how many cabbages there are or how big the field is?

Experimenter: The question is, "What is the area of the field?"

Sam: So, how many cabbages are there altogether?

Experimenter: What do you think?

Sam: Well, I can't decide between the cabbages and how big the field is.

Sam is a student who has earned the highest mark in mathematics (6). Even from the outset of phase one, Sam voiced doubts and attempted to decode the expectations of the adult. The way he has framed the options is interesting in that it refers to the conflict between the knowl-

Table 6.1. Indicators of child's position toward problems

Children	The problem of the area of the field		The problem of the age of the schoolteachers	
	Phase 1	Phase 2	Phase 1	Phase 2
Sam	±	±	-	-
Lam	±	±	±	-
Vap	+	±	+	±

Key:
+ The child performs arithmetical operations (Phase 1) or justifies these (Phase 2) without conveying even the slightest doubt over the relevance of doing so.

± The child performs or justifies operations, but thanks to his or her statement, he or she reveals if not outright rejection of the problem at least a number of doubts over the relevance of these operations or indeed over some other aspect of the problem.

- The child explicitly rejects the problems.

edge of how many cabbages there are altogether, which is what can be established on the basis of the given quantities of the problem, and the content of the question, which involves the area of the field. By the same stroke, there appears to be no other solution to the conflict than to know "what you're supposed to say." In other words, the public term of this equation is presumed capable of removing the ambiguity of the statement and allowing the child to solve the conflict inhering to the problem as stated. When, at that point, Sam received no assistance from the adult, he appeared to resign himself to carrying out a multiplication. However, he did not give up on his own idea for all that, for he discussed the operation yet another time with the experimenter.

Sam: (Immediately after finishing the multiplication) Well, uh, I don't know . . . 13,050.

Experimenter: That's the area?

Sam: If it's cabbages, yes, I think. If it's meters, you can't do it because they don't even say whether it's a square or not and how long one side is. They don't say anything . . . you can't do it . . . it has to be the cabbages, it's got to be the area of the cabbages.

Sam was quite able to recognize the irrelevance of the unit of measurement that he had available to him for finding the area of the field, first declaring that the problem was impossible to solve on account of missing information that persons unknown had failed to provide him ("they don't even say"). He eventually submitted to the usual didactic contract, circumventing the conflict via an adapted version of the notion of area – that is, "the area of the heads of cabbage."

During phase two, the series of questions put by the experimenter did not help Sam reject the problem any more straightforwardly. Once more, he merely made do with a conditional rejection which allowed him to avoid making a break with the didactic contract. The question of whether he felt that he had managed to produce the right answer or not gave rise to the following discussion:

Sam: . . . If it's cabbages, then I got it, but if it's something else, then I didn't get it.
Experimenter: What else could it be?
Sam: If it's not cabbages, I don't know what it is.
Experimenter: So, it's the same thing when you find cabbages and you find the area?
Sam: You could say so.
Experimenter: You could say so. You don't look too terribly convinced. If you find the area, you mean it isn't the cabbages?
Sam: Oh no. It has to be the cabbages because otherwise there's nothing else you can do.
Experimenter: Uh huh.
Sam: If the cabbage heads all had the same length, then you could find the whole area . . . but they don't say what the cabbages measure.
Experimenter: Uh huh.
Sam: So, you have to count the cabbages. That gives you 13,050.

Sam makes himself increasingly explicit. He has understood quite well that the only possible approach depends on the total number of cabbages and that the problem and the contract which he believes he is confronted with require him to superimpose the number of cabbages onto area. "You could say it's the same thing," he says, transferring responsibility for this shift onto the situation. Now then, if only there were a way of knowing what a head of cabbage measured, and if it could be established that all the cabbages had the same dimensions, then it would be possible to find the area! The logic applying in a school setting and which makes use of "tiling" has been dug out; the problem may be preserved intact. We have here an excellent example of a problem being rectified when the way in which it has been stated makes it inadmissible within the prevailing contract.

Sam: interaction involving the age of the schoolteacher

From the outset of phase one, Sam rejected the problem outright, without even writing down any computational operation. It took this child no more than thirty seconds to categorically dismiss the problem: "It's impossible. I think it can't be done." He also did not waver in his decision despite being repeatedly questioned on the subject by the experimenter.

During phase two, the series of questions put by the experimenter did not elicit the slightest attempt at calculation from him. Thus, when asked if he thought he had gotten the right answer, Sam replied, "I got it because they didn't say anything. They only say that there are 12 boys and then they ask you what the age of the schoolteacher is. You can't do it. I have no way of knowing."

Lam (5 out of 6): interaction involving the area of the field

During phase one, this child, whom the institution has indicated as being rather good in mathematics (5 out of 6), made a quick interpretation of the problem and wrote out a multiplication.

Lam: Are there 150 cabbages in each row?
Experimenter: What do you think? What do you really think? What does the problem mean to you?
Lam: I took 87 times 150.
Experimenter: All right, then. But you're not sure?
Lam: No, I'm not.
Experimenter: No? Where's there a hitch for you?
Lam: Oh, I don't know (giggles). I don't know about the answer I got.
Experimenter: You're not sure of your answer, then. What do you think?
Lam: Not that it's kind of big, but . . .
Experimenter: Do you think it's kind of big?
Lam: Well, kind of (giggles).
Experimenter: Kind of.
Lam: I mean, it's almost . . . 87, almost 100. So that gives you almost 1,500.

During phase one, Lam acts in a way which shows that she was seeking to obtain additional indications as to what to do. When this attempt met with little success vis-à-vis the experimenter, she fell back (publicly, at least) on the answer she had come up with. Furthermore, in formulations that constantly voice her doubts, she sought to attain an apparently relevant register with her adult interlocutor. Her tactic was not only prudent, it also enabled her to save face. First Lam informed herself as to the given quantities of the problem and their possible interpretation (150 cabbages in each row?). Following this, she referred to the choice of performing multiplication ("I took 87 times 150"), gave evidence of a certain embarrassment (giggling), and spoke of the figure produced and how big this was. If analysis were limited to only these outer manifestations, one could hypothesize that either Lam is unsure of having calculated correctly or that she hesitates between an addition-derived solution (as entailed by estimation of a smaller figure?) and the multiplicative answer she indeed offered. Hence, only with phase two will it become apparent how her embarrassment is related to the contractual aspects of the problem.

During phase two, the experimenter put forward the question of area once again. Lam became embarrassed.

Experimenter: . . . Do you know what area is?
Lam: Area is . . . um . . . how big, how many square meters the field is?
Experimenter: Uh huh.
Lam: How many square meters the field is?
Experimenter: And that's what you were looking for?
Lam: Yes.
Experimenter: Yes. So what did you come up with?
Lam: I got 1,350. (13,050 was what was marked on her sheet.)
Experimenter: Thirteen hundred fifty. Tell me, you don't look too sure of this answer.
Lam: No (smiling).
Experimenter: No, tell me again what you think doesn't work.
Lam: I think, I did the multiplication right, but . . . I think that what I did isn't what you were supposed to do.
Experimenter: Well then, how could it have been done some other way?
Lam: . . . Uh, I don't know.

Thus, Lam did not harbor any doubts as to the accuracy of her computations. Unable, however, to make out the true nature of the problem, she attributed to herself the difficulty she had decoding the specific expectations with which she was confronted. But as she had to do something (with respect to the time-honored rules of the didactic contract), she preferred staking out the public position to the effect that she did not know.

Lam: interaction involving the age of the schoolteacher

During phase one, Lam finally wrote down "27" yet continued to state that "there's no way of knowing because you need more to go on." When questioned as to what she meant by additional indicators, she replied, "I don't know; say that her age is a multiple of 9." The sum which she wrote down was, in fact, extorted from her, within the meaning ascribed this term by Perret-Clermont, Schubauer-Leoni, and Trognon (1992); in effect, the experimenter required that Lam choose between "putting down nothing," "putting down 27," and "putting down that it was impossible."

During phase two, on the other hand, Lam publicly distanced herself from the problem, laughing outright, and declared that the problem was "impossible" and was a way of "saying happy birthday to the schoolteacher!"

Vap (3 out of 6): interaction involving the area of the field

During phase one, Vap, a "weak" student based on her middling marks in mathematics (3 out of 6), was one of the two children in her class who used addition to solve the problem of the area of the cabbage field. Upon reading the problem, she immediately proceeded to write down the operation: 150 + 87 = 237. Then she looked at the adult and wrote on her sheet: "250 m."

During phase two, when the experimenter asked how she felt she had done, Vap immediately replied that "it was hard!"

Experimenter: Why was it hard?
Vap: (Sighing) Because there was no way you could really tell how many meters long the field was.
Experimenter: There was no way of really telling. Why couldn't you tell?
Vap: You had to be there to measure it.
Experimenter: Have I got you right, you had to be there to measure it?
Vap: Yes.
Experimenter: And the way the problem is written, there's no way of telling?
Vap: You've got to be good in arithmetic.

Experimenter: You've got to be good in arithmetic . . . well, aren't you good in arithmetic?
Vap: No, not really.

Thus, Vap stated that there was no way you could "really" tell! You had to measure the field in person. Does this assertion imply that she had noticed that an adequate unit of measurement was missing? At all accounts, she searched for a measure of length ("how many meters long the field was") and not of area.

Experimenter: Did you get it, or didn't you?
Vap: I don't know.
Experimenter: You don't know?
Vap: I think so. Well, I think I didn't get it, I don't know.
Experimenter: You don't know how you did it. Tell me now how you went at it.
Vap: Well, I took 150 plus 87.
Experimenter: So why did you do it that way?
Vap: Because I thought it would give me the area.

Vap: interaction involving the age of the schoolteacher

During phase one, Vap was taken aback at first. She opened her eyes wide and asked the experimenter, "How many girls are there?" The experimenter confirmed what she had heard, "Twelve girls and 15 boys." Then, without further hesitation, and without carrying out any computation, Vap wrote down "27 years old."

During phase two, Vap didn't really believe the age she had first ascribed to the teacher. She held to her answer all the same because no other answer was possible or utterable. When asked whether or not she felt she had managed to find the right answer, she stuck to the facts, sighing as she declared, "Well, I added 12 plus, um, 15 . . . I did it that way because, if I didn't, I wouldn't have come up with something (laughs) . . . You can't do it any other way . . . because you couldn't tell, because there are a lot of schoolteachers who are old and they have 15 boys and 12 girls!"

Conclusion

The preceding excerpts, in which three children publicly produced answers, provide clear illustration in our opinion of the dynamics involved in the construction of answers to insoluble problems by grade-school children. The possibility of publicly pronouncing oneself on the irrelevance of a given question was particularly apparent in the case of the problem of the age of the schoolteacher, which all three children "privately" rejected, and which, in respect of the underlying contract, left them expecting a number of additional indications necessary to assuming their public version. In that connection, it is worth noting that only Vap, who was described by the institution as being weakest of the three in mathematics, did not dare to reject the problem in writing. On the other hand, these three children provided evidence of a different relationship to the problem of the area of the field. The complexity of the notion which this problem involved seemed to upset the relationship of public to private which is inherent to the act of answering. Indications of the different types of rationality which are brought into play by the split between public and private varied from one child to another, providing evidence of the inner conflict of each participant over conceptual aspects pertaining to the problem of area as opposed to aspects pertaining to the presumed receivability of the answer each gave. Delving into the interweavings of these constructions proved, in the case of this example, to be particularly instructive.

The phenomena involved in the interaction just described remain most complex, however, and the results of this study stand to benefit from further analysis not only in terms of what has been termed contextual psychology (qua science of the knowing subject in context) but in terms also of didactic theory (qua science of the conditions for the emergence of knowledge in school settings). One of us has elaborated elsewhere (Schubauer-Leoni and Grossen, 1993) on how the theoretical articulations between an experimental contract and a didactic contract are worked out in accordance with whether studies are weighted more heavily in favor of psychology or didactics. At this time, the state of research in these fields reveals use of a variety of paradigms featuring models with three if not four terms (questioner, questionee, the subject of questioning, and context; teacher, student, knowledge being taught, and environment). Nevertheless, the different focuses favored by this or that research project tend to emphasize some terms of a given model over others. Thus, for example, studies which concentrate on the effect of context on the answers of individuals can provide an alternative to theories which consider cognitive activities as definable in exclusively intraindividual terms. They nevertheless tend to lapse into the opposite sort of excess – namely, social reductionism. This is the result, on the one hand, of interpreting the behavior of the child as chiefly a function of the constraints operated by the context, and, on the other, of failing to consider not only the intersubjective constructions which translate these constraints but also the cognitive constraints which are specific to the task at hand. From another perspective, studies which analyze the construction of intersubjectivity between questioner and questionee often tend to underestimate the effects of context and institutional constraints in favor of the constructions which the interactive *hic et nunc* gives rise to. When such is the case, focus on interaction tends to lose sight of the object of cognition and its contents.

This inquiry into insoluble problems has also been exposed to such tensions, although it was undertaken with a view to overcoming certain kinds of reductionism, be they of a social or cognitive cast. With this in mind, we have attempted to specify the nature of the different kinds of rationality at stake, by bringing out the thinking processes which bear at one and the same time on: the cognitive operations which were activated by contrasting mathematical problems; the intersubjective situation involved in questioning; and the institutional framework serving as backdrop. When overlaid with public and private vectors, these different layers of rationality appear to offer access to levels of analysis which are necessary to a global kind of understanding of the psychological and educational phenomena at stake.

Chapter 7
Voice and perspective: hearing epistemological innovation in students' words

JERE CONFREY

I begin with a story of a fourth-grade classroom in which the teacher sought to introduce students to least common multiples (LCM) using rhythm. Two students were asked to volunteer. The teacher clapped out a steady beat. One student clapped every two beats, and the other clapped every five beats. After a few false starts, they succeeded in holding their rhythms. The class was asked to identify the beat when the children first clapped together. They listened and answered confidently "ten, every ten." The same exercise was repeated with one child clapping every two beats, while the other clapped every four. The class eagerly called out that "four" was the beat when the two children clapped together. The class tried two and three beats, but the clappers had trouble holding their beats, so, the class decided to break up into groups of five children. In each group, one child kept the steady beat, two children counted the two rhythms, and the other two listened for the unified clap. By then, many of the children had a conjecture for predicting the number of the first unified clap, "you just multiply the numbers together." Without responding immediately to their conjectures, the teacher posed two tasks to the groups. One task was to predict the outcome with a four-beat and six-beat, and to test their prediction. The other was to use the materials in the room to make a physical representation of their methods, showing all of the previous patterns including the four- and six-beat task.

The majority of the children found the representational task with classroom materials interesting and easy. A few began by trying to make piles of different sizes, but when their peers (the majority of the class) made lines of unifix cubes marking every second one in one color and every third in another color, they nearly all selected that method (see Figure 7.1). By clapping and using the unifix cubes, they guessed that 4 and 6 would meet first at 24 and were surprised to find

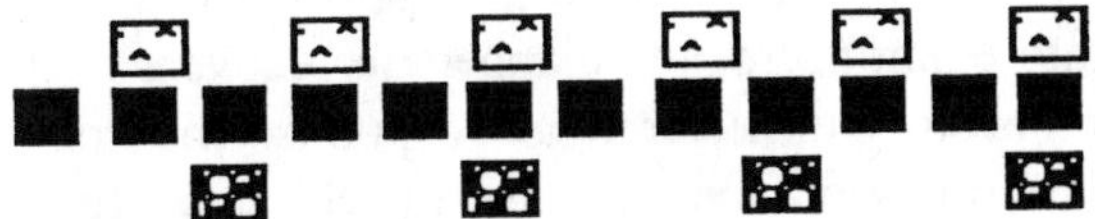

Figure 7.1. Most common model

Figure 7.2. Terry's model

that it had met at 12. The teacher used this as an opportunity to pose a challenge to the group. Is there a way to find the first unified beat while only looking at the numbers? All the children were actively and happily engaged, that is, all except Terry. Terry sat in her group in tears. No one would listen to her. No one understood her problem. No one understood her answer. And she was not willing to change her method, until she was given an opportunity to be heard.

Finally, the teacher reached her. She sobbed as she explained her method. She was using geometric shapes. She first put down five yellow hexagons. Then another five, separated by a space, and another five. She then put a red diamond on the second one in each group. She put a green triangle in every third one (see Figure 7.2). "But," she wailed, "they never meet!" It looked, at first glance, as if she had simply erred in her understanding of the problem. However, as she realized that someone was listening, she explained further. She pointed out that if the person clapping the steady beat just keeps going and a clapper gets lost, he or she can never figure out how to get back on track. Her way, she argued, the person counting the steady beat, "the counter" counts repeatedly to some number (she pointed out that any number would do) and starts over. She demonstrated with a count of five: one, two, three, four, five; one, two, three. . . . Each time the counter says two, the two-clapper claps, thus clapping every two, that is, every beat that is labeled two. Each time the counter says three, the three-clapper claps, thus, the other child is clapping every three. Yet, in her method, the pair of clappers never clap together.

As soon as someone had heard her method, Terry stopped crying. She admitted that her method was not the same as the other children's, but she simply had wanted someone to acknowledge the reasoning behind her proposal. And, she wanted a way to make it easier in the activity of rhythm counting for the clappers to recover.

I began with this story to illustrate a few points. The first is that in mathematics classrooms all over the world, children are genuinely engaged in thinking about the mathematics, and many of these children's inventions are not being heard. And, the result of not being heard is devastating to them. They end up feeling devalued and frustrated. And all too often, they abandon making conjectures and turn to the teacher to tell them how they are supposed to proceed. They learn to suppress their own creativity.

Most interpretations of constructivism recognize to some degree that the suppression of student invention is a problem. Most forms of constructivism express the essential qualities of ascertaining student's prior knowledge and encouraging students to be active in the process of learning. How, then, does radical constructivism differ from these other interpretations?

I want to suggest that differences lie in what happens with examples like the story of Terry. The radical constructivist is obliged to examine the student's invention for its epistemological implications, whereas for other constructivists, no such obligation exists. Typically, nonradical constructivists, while noting the rationality in Terry's approach, view it as "interesting," "alternative," or "partially correct," and they proceed on past Terry's method to reach their intended content, in this case, to find a numerical method for getting the LCM. The radical constructivist, however, is committed to evaluating the epistemological quality of proposals like Terry's.

This is because radical constructivism takes viability as a central requirement for knowledge. Constructivism is not just a theory of learning; it is a theory of knowledge. The claim that knowledge must be "viable" suggests that knowledge is not an accumulation of fixed truths, but that the *function of knowledge is adaptive and serves to organize experience*. Instead, it is constructed by the knower through her/his engagement in purposeful activity. Knowledge is the legitimized ways of making sense of experience that have proven to be viable from the perspective of the knower and which guide future actions. The demand for a knowledge to be viable was discussed as follows by von Glasersfeld (1982, p. 614):

> I have discussed the misleading connotation of "adaptation" and suggested that the term "viability" would be more adequate. From the organism's point of view, on the biological level as on the cognitive one, the environment is no more and no less than the sum of constraints within which the organism

can operate. The organism's activities and operations are successful when they are not impeded or foiled by constraints, i.e., when they are viable. Hence it is only when actions or operations fail that one can speak of contact with the environment, but not when they succeed.

How does this view of viability allow us to understand the story of Terry? First of all, the emphasis on viability and the rejection of access to a single reality leads to the *expectation of diverse points of view* in the classroom. Radical constructivists argue that the culture of the classroom must be changed to support diversity and to allow students the time, space, and mutual respect needed to articulate and clarify multiple points of view. However, though this perspective was introduced by radical constructivists (Balacheff, 1991; Bauersfeld, 1988; Cobb, Wood, and Yackel, 1991a; Voigt, 1985), it has been widely endorsed by nearly all constructivists. Thus, it no longer distinguishes the radical constructivist viewpoint.

Secondly, in addition to supporting the expression of diversity, radical constructivism commits one to examining Terry's proposal more deeply in terms of its epistemological content (Confrey, 1994; Confrey and Scarano, 1997). In order to do so, one needs a methodology to examine student thinking. The constructivist researcher is engaged in model building (Cobb and Steffe, 1983; Confrey, 1980) and is not describing structures in a child's head. The method by which one does this I have called "close listening" (Confrey, 1993) and was adapted from Piagetian clinical interviews. The principles for close listening include:

1. providing evidence in the student's words;
2. following the problem development carefully, trying to decenter from one's own perspective;
3. encouraging strongly autonomous expressions by students;
4. asking for clarification, rephrasing the statements in the student's language;
5. avoiding evaluative expressions except as they support articulation of method;
6. stepping out of the role of answer giver;
7. checking that the student remains emotionally confident with the interview and involved in the course of problem solving;
8. allowing the student to identify errors and contradictions;
9. providing resources to allow the student a variety of routes to proceed; and
10. conducting interviews for a long-enough duration to ensure that a fuller opportunity for expression is allowed.

When one applies ''close listening'' to the case of Terry, one is left with a fundamental question. Is Terry's method viable? Has Terry accomplished what she set out to do? How does her method relate to the problem as posed by the teacher?

To answer this question, one needs to examine what Terry's *problematic* was. I have introduced the term *problematic* to emphasize that this is not equivalent to the problem, as stated or written, but refers instead to the interpretation of the problem by the individual in relation to his or her purposes, goals, expectations, and prior knowledge. The problematic occurs during the period in which one notices a perturbation and is called into action. It is a roadblock to where one wants to be, a felt need for action, or a sense of disequilibrium. For a teacher or interviewer, getting a clear idea of the student's problematic is a slow process and does not occur instantaneously or completely; it is a progressive activity, with multiple periods of conjecture, clarification, reconsideration, and revision. It may be interspersed with periods of action and reflection by both the teacher/interviewer and student. Although Piaget certainly recognized the importance of the state of disequilibration in his clinical interviews, he did not address specific attention to the importance of trying to discern a student's problematic or of attempting to help a student articulate it more completely as an instructional method.

What is Terry's problematic? She wanted to find a way to allow the child who was clapping a rhythm to recover part-way through the counting exercise. One can easily see how her solution solves this problematic. Terry's prior knowledge and experience playing violin and reading music might also have influenced her problematic, in that she was familiar with measures as they are used in music.

Now, two interpretations of Terry's solution are possible. One can assume that she has fully transformed the problem. Instead of counting every two beats, one, two, one two, she redefined the task to count every ''two'' beats where ''two'' became the name of a beat in a sequence of five. Thus, a ''two'' came up every five beats. Thus, she has solved her problematic but created a conflict with her peers' results because her method does not lead to any time in which the claps coincide, while their method does.

Careful attention to a student's problematic and close listening gets one to a further investigation and a second interpretation. This is what is typically absent in most interpretations of constructivism. The questions are: Is there any common ground between Terry's solution and the solutions produced by the rest of the class? Is this just an isolated alternative conception, or might it shed some light on the understanding of LCM?

To answer this question, one might consider the role of the measure in conventional music notation. It seems that Terry is correct about the usefulness of a segmentation of the basic count; it allows a standard measure to align the downbeat across all the individual players.

When applied to the problem at hand, the idea of a measure seems to lead to a dilemma. For if the measure were based on a two-count instead of a five-count, then the "two" in each counted measure (one-TWO; one-TWO) would indeed represent a two-count in which every other beat was clapped, but there would be no three. And if the measure were based on a three-count instead of a five-count, then the "three" of each counted measure (one-two-THREE; one-two-THREE) would represent a three-count in which every third beat was clapped, but the clappers assigned to clap every time "two" was said would not be clapping every other beat. It seems as if there is no bridge between the class method and Terry's method, and her method, though understandable, becomes an isolated alternative conception.

However, suppose one restates the problem. How can we find a way for the keeper of the steady beat to assist both of the counters by providing a frequent way that they can correct themselves if they get offbeat while still retaining the meaning of a two-count as clapping every other beat and a three-count as clapping every third beat? Here Terry's method can be reconnected to the teacher's original intention. Suppose the counter uses the least common multiple of the two clappers' rhythm as the size of a measure, in this case, six. Then the two-clapper will clap regularly on the beats named "two," "four," and "six." And the three-clapper will clap on the beats labeled "three" and "six." And every six beats, the clappers get a chance to recover. Indeed, one can see that Terry's method can therefore lead to a measure as a means to creating a bridge between the two rhythms of the clappers. The teacher's challenge to the students becomes how do you find the shortest possible measure that allows each clapper to repeatedly clap on the same numbers.

Voice and perspective

In terms of the radical constructivist theory, how might we view such an interpretation? It is clear that the discussion has extended beyond the proposal of Terry, at least as far as she has worked it up to that point. And, it is also clear that it is not what the teacher intended to do with LCM. To describe such a form of analysis, which I am suggesting is fundamental work for the radical constructivist researchers, I have introduced a distinction labeled *voice and perspective.*

Close listening leads to the articulation of a model that we suspect may be operating for the student. I refer to the articulation of this model as *student voice* (Confrey, 1995). In the case of Terry, her proposal of segmenting a count and marking off the rhythm in terms of the count seems to be a reasonable description of student voice. Add in her dissatisfaction with the noncoincidence of the beats, her recognition that any valued count can be used as a measure, and her insight that measures will allow clappers to make corrections, and one gets a sense of student voice.

Along with the presentation of voice, there needs to be the recognition of and articulation by the interpreter of her/his own *perspective* and how it is changed during the process of interaction and interpretation. It is a discussion of perspective, of how the epistemological content of one's own mathematics is altered through interactions with students that is lacking in most nonradical constructivist writings. The introduction of "measure" suggests that in seeking an LCM, one is seeking a way to segment a third number line that can act to unite the other two. It does unite it by creating a quantity that can be measured integrally by both of the other two measures.

As one does an analysis of voice and perspective, one must keep in mind that they interact, and so no hard-and-fast line can be drawn between them. This interaction occurs during the original exchanges (in class or in an interview), for instance, when the perspective of the interviewer/teacher influences what voice of the student is heard. And the interaction recurs as one interprets the data. One heuristic is to view voice as embedded in perspective and try to disengage it, then reverse the relationship by viewing one's own perspective in light of the student's voice. As one learns to be more and more aware of this dialectic, one can come to see how frequently what is labeled as students' inadequacy is really the result of our own inflexibility in considering alternative perspectives.

An example from the postsecondary level

To demonstrate further the issue of voice and perspective, another example is provided. This example has been chosen because it demonstrates the need to bring in radical constructivist perspective not only to the elementary level, but to the secondary and postsecondary levels. There is a danger that reform in mathematics education will be limited to elementary school, as people assume the perspective of the trained mathematician is sufficient to recognize and encompass student voice. In our experience examining the development of the function concept, we find that modern mathematical training can limit one's ability to recognize legitimate diversity. Thus, I selected an example from an interview with a college freshman who was involved in a teaching experiment for eight one-hour sessions. This student had tested into the remedial mathematics section and did not feel successful in mathematics. He had been interviewed about his understanding of exponential functions through the use of contextual problems and multiple representations (Confrey, 1991; Confrey and Smith, 1994, 1995) twice a week for five weeks at the time of this final interview. Figure 7.3 shows his work, and references in the transcription describe what is written and when. The problem reads as follows:

An efficiency expert works in a factory which builds robots. The robot builds another robot in five minutes, and then that robot walks into a crate and is shipped off. The expert comes up with a great idea for a labor-saving device. He creates a robot which is programmed to build two versions of itself in five minutes. It then walks into a crate and is shipped off. He goes to the supervisor's office to explain to her that he has doubled the efficiency of the plant, and starts the robot off in order to be able to demonstrate his creation. She is in a meeting and he waits three hours. When he explains his invention, she looks up in alarm and rushes out into the factory. How many robots does she find? How many robots does the expert expect her to find?

The student, Dan, read the problem and then was asked for his interpretation. He replied:

Well, first, you have the robots. And one robot produced one robot every, every hour, and then that original robot was taken away. But then he increased efficiency by one robot produced two. And then that original, I think that original one is crated away too. . . . And he's gone for three hours. . . . So if he starts out with one, and that makes two with the first one and then that one is taken away and then each one of those produces two more in the second hour. And then the original two are taken away. Each one of those two produces two more, so that's eight. In three hours.

The interviewer drew Dan's attention to the statement ''the robot builds another in five minutes,'' asking him to reread it, and he replied:

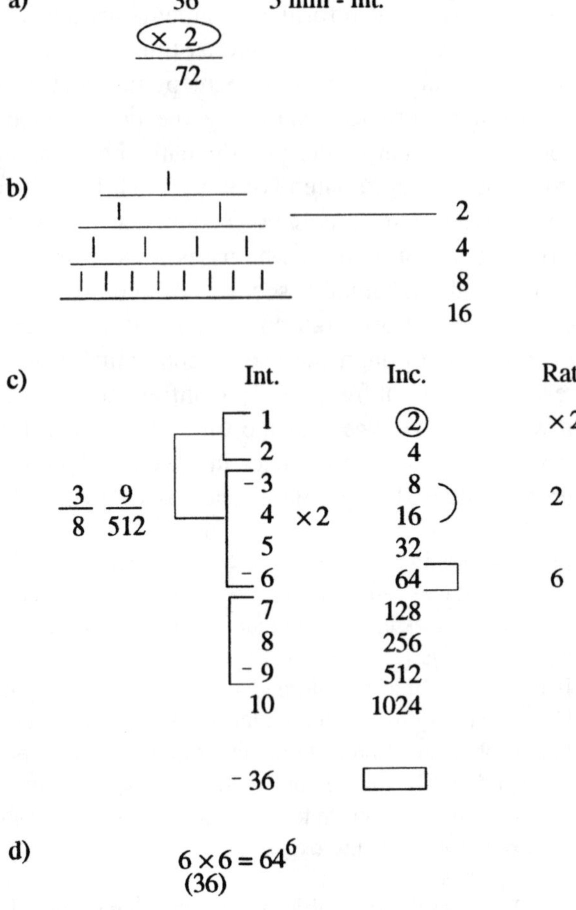

Figure 7.3. Dan's work

So, there's 12 five-minute periods in an hour. So then that's 12 × 3 which is 36, five minutes, 36 five-minute intervals. And, then with each five-minute interval, I'd have to find – just I'd have to find one five-minute interval from one robot five minutes later producing 2 and I have to find the rate at which they increase, they double. So, and then each one of those produces 2 more so the total is, so that produces 2 and then those 2 produce a total of 4, so whatever it is, it's squared, right?? (Okay, says the interviewer.) No, it's not squared. It's just times 2. Because after the first five minutes, there's at zero time, there's 1. After five minutes there's 2. After another five minutes there's 4 and after another five minutes, it's 8. So, it's times 2 every time.

Notice that after revising the original interpretation to allow for 36 five-minute intervals, Dan took quite a while to remake the initial problem to reach the previously known result that three intervals produce 8. However, the change in the problem's interpretation produced a change in his problematic, and he included in his restatement a challenge to find "the rate at which they increase" and then answered that challenge with "they double." His use of "interval" as a label on his first column was also noteworthy for the role it played in his development of a concept of domain where each individual entry represented the number of intervals, and a set of entries was also viewed as an interval, not as the name of a coordinate of a point or as a number. This issue resurfaced later when he sought to find a solution to the problem which depended on the fact that $6 \times 6 = 36$. The choice of doubling and squaring competed for a moment; and, as he rejected squaring, he also revised his doubling language to a use of "times 2." Eventually, the "times 2" language allowed a generalization to evolve more easily than if he had kept the language of doubling. Dan continued:

D: So then that would be after three hours, it would be 36×2, I would think it would be a little bit more, but $36 \times 2 = 72$. (He writes 36×2 on the paper and solves it). (See (a) in Figure 7.3.)
I: . . . what would you have expected?
D: Without going through, I would, oh, somewhere around like 200, 250, I don't know. . . . I'm not too confident with it just being times 2 every time. I think it should be more than times 2. (He sketches the tree diagram; see (b) in Figure 7.3.) But I mean we go from 1 to this to this to so that's $1 \times 2 = 2$ is $2 \times 2 = 4$ – so yeah, so it's times 2. It's just, something doesn't seem right. So I know that it's times 2 is right but it's 36, oh, all right, all right, . . . this answer here is just following one of these lines through, I mean. Something's not right here. Because all right this . . . the numbers work here. I don't know. That's right I guess. That's right.

One notices in this excerpt that Dan was working between the two representations on his paper, the tree diagram and the calculation. He had the calculation which said 36 times 2 is 72. And he kept convincing himself that it was indeed a "times 2" situation, so the representations supported each other. However, his tree diagram made him unsure of the "times-2" claim, because each branch was times 2, so for all the branches it seemed that it should be greater than times 2. He wrote in the totals for each row which confirmed the "times 2." This discomfort resurfaced later, but for now, he decided to let the calculation stand.

The interviewer asked what happened next in the tree diagram in an effort to help Dan produce his own contradiction with his prediction of 72, and they figured out the number of robots until they reached 1,024. He said:

> . . . so this is wrong. So what I would have to do is find out the rate at which they increase, . . . and then for some reason, it shouldn't be just times. It should be something to the power . . . of something. Um, 36^2 would be the right answer . . . (long pause). I think, . . . no, that's not right. The rate at which it increases here, each time, it's times 2.

Again, Dan redefined the problematic in light of his current efforts. He still wanted to find the rate at which they increase, but now he sensed that it was getting big too fast for a prediction of 72. Concurrently, he saw that every branch was "times 2." So, he tried squaring. However, his figures at the right of the tree diagram contradicted this conjecture.

He sketched a table (see (c) in Figure 7.3) and labeled the columns, "Int." (for interval) "inc." (for increase) and "rate." He listed the numbers 1 to 10 in the "interval" column and then 2 to 1,024 in the "increase" column. When asked by the interviewer what he wanted to know, he responded: "What's the interval? I want to know 36." He tried a ratio strategy of comparing across a row expecting to get 1:2 (1 to 2), confirmed it on 2:4 (2 to 4) and refuted it for 3:8 (3 to 8). Then he looked down the "Int." column and said, "So maybe if I do it by 6 because 6 × 6 is 36. . . ." (he marked a line by 6).

Dan has introduced a new representation: a table. It allowed him to name the columns and to extend the values. He resighted on his goal . . . to get 36. The column configuration led him to search for patterns and he tried applying ratio reasoning. Though his initial conjecture failed, he revised his strategy toward his goal: to "do it by 6 because 6 × 6 is 36." "Do it by 6" here means to move down in intervals of 6. In other interviews, he labeled this "creating a jump" and he used jumps to pose the question of how to move vertically in an "x" column while moving an "equal" distance down in a "y" column.

D: Somehow, um, all right. Three? (He marks a line by 3.) If the rate at 3, at the interval 3 was 8 . . . 3 is to 8 as 9 is to 512. (He marks a line by 9.) And because 3 × 3 is 9 and 8, 512 divided by 8 is (punches the calculator) 64. (Pause . . . Sigh . . .) 64 is the . . . the . . . the value for, for 6 here. (Pause) Three is to 8 as 9 is to 512.

At a glance this exchange seems thoroughly garbled. At first, it seemed that Dan was unable to recognize that the two ratios differed significantly. However, by following up on the relationship between 8 and 512, his attention was drawn toward 64 which led him to the following observation: ''When we are going from 3 to 6, we're doubling the interval. And then this (points to the 8) is being multiplied by itself. It's being squared (points to 64).''

He now had a conjecture that works to coordinate the changes in the ''interval'' and the ''increase'' columns. This is a significant moment in the interview, for it marks the beginning of his solution strategy. He also had equal intervals 3, 6, and 9 marked for attention on his paper which may have encouraged him to move down his paper to consider the interval from 6 to 9.

D: So, 3, all right. And then this here, 6 to 9, we're adding 3. So each time, we're adding, we're making a jump of 3 . . .
I: Each time we make a jump of 3 . . .
D: Each time we make a jump of 3, that's squared. Sixty-four squared is not 512. No, it's not, all right, no . . . ohh.
I: Three to 6, you added 3 but you also said you could think of this as doubling 3.

At this point, Dan had two frameworks competing to describe his movement down the left-hand column. He alternately saw it as adding a constant amount (adding 3) and as doubling. This is understandable since the move from 3 to 6 can be viewed either way, but the move from 6 to 9 can only be viewed as adding 3 again. The interviewer reminded him of his two different methods.

D: Yeah, so this is times 2 (he writes × 2 between the columns) and this is squared. So when I went from 3 to 6, when I added 2 to my original value, I took the answer for that value, which was 8 and squared it.
I: When you doubled your original value, you took the answer to it and squared it.
D: When I doubled, yeah, all right, when I doubled it . . . (he writes over the × 2) when I'm taking 6 and I'm multiplying it by 6, I'm taking my answer for 6, and square – uh, putting it to the sixth power. So on

6 × 6, which is equal to 36, I'm multiplying by 6 and then I take the answer for that, which is 64, and I'm raising that to the sixth power. Because here when I went from 3 to 6, I added, I multiplied by 2 and then I squared it.

I: I don't understand why you're changing it.

D: I'm not changing it. I'm now going from 6 to 36 and that's 6 × 6 is 36 and then I take the answer that I got for 6 and raise it to the sixth power. And then 64^6 which is 6.87×10^{10}. (See (d) in Figure 7.3.)

Again, at the beginning of this exchange, one can see the competition between the frameworks, and Dan now suggested adding 2, a hybrid of adding 3 and multiplying by 2. The interviewer chose again to restate his earlier conjecture. Dan now moved to a broader generalization, leaving the interviewer behind. He proposed using the fact that 6 × 6 = 36 and that 64 corresponded to 6 to claim that 64^6 corresponds to 36. After this exchange, Dan explained his correct conjecture more thoroughly and checked it again with two other examples. He argued that 2 × 2 is 4 and $4^2 = 16$ and that 5 × 2 = 10 and $32^2 = 1{,}024$. Both examples involved "multiplying by 2" and "squaring," so the test of his conjecture was narrow. He also demonstrated that he was able to return to the context of the problem and interpret it in light of his findings and expressed confidence in his answer.

Voice

The transcript sampled was from the ninth interview with the student, so there was a high comfort level with long pauses and little expectation for quick answers. The student took control of most of the interview, with relatively long passages where he was working on the problem out loud. The interviewer intervened at five significant moments: (1) she asked the student to state his interpretation of the problem; (2) she asked him to predict the next few values in the tree diagram so he could notice a contradiction with his prediction; (3) she asked the student to restate his goal when he seemed lost after making the table; (4) she called his attention to the two models, doubling and adding, which were competing; and (5) she requested that he clarify his conjecture which led him to check it. These are clarification and guidance roles and they have a significant impact on the course of the interview. It is this impact that has led Steffe to label these "teaching interviews," although such a label seems to diminish the importance of the student activity. Unlike ''clinical interviews'' which tend to be single episodes, these teaching interviews extend over significant periods of time. Perhaps a label of ''developmental student interviews'' would be more appropriate.

There are two other moments of interviewing that need comment. When the interviewer revised the student's additive statement (from a ''jump of 3'') to a multiplicative statement (''doubling 3''), she offered an overly direct prompt, despite the fact that it was a restatement of the student's utterance. Later, we see another point in the interview where the interviewer was left behind and scrambled to try and find the logic in the student's final conjecture. These kinds of moments are unfortunate, but unavoidable in the interview, and they emphasize the importance of interviewing in which the student feels confident and in control of the interview. The interviewer must take care to persist in asking the student to clarify her/his method.

Dan's problematic seemed to involve the idea of rate of increase. His first goal was to find the rate of increase; he uses this to claim 36 $\times$ 2 as his answer. However, this goal was revised into finding what goes with the interval 36 in his table; and finally, it was revised to figure out how to use the fact that $6 \times 6 = 36$ (for Dan, 6 intervals of 6) to find out what goes with 36. The development of the problematic evolves over the course of the interview as Dan moves into phases of operation, coordination of representation, and reflection.

Functions for Dan seem to be the coordination of ''intervals'' (which he often refers to as ''jumps'') with ''increases.'' The strength of this had become evident in earlier interviews. In this interview, that tendency had to mature into an ability to differentiate the operational structure he needed to create ''a jump of 36'' from the corresponding operational structure on the ''inc.'' column, based in raising to a power. He never saw the ''increase'' column as increasing powers of 2. Instead he saw that doubling and squaring co-occurred, hence ''times 6'' and ''to the power of 6'' should co-occur.

Throughout the interview, we saw doubling and ''times 2'' used alternately, both in terms of the rate of increase and in comparing intervals. Then, once Dan had settled on ''times 2'' to describe the rate of increase, he vacillated between describing the intervals in terms of multiplication or addition. Each language had advantages. Doubling was more clearly differentiated from adding, but the language of ''times 2'' was easier to generalize to ''times 6.'' Eventually, we saw Dan settle on describing the intervals multiplicatively and the increases as powers. He never resolved the question of how to go from 6 to 9 increments of five minutes. His move was to go from 6 times 6 to 64^6.

Operationally speaking, a key passage occurred when Dan tried out a proportional reasoning conjecture which failed to be a linear proportion but allowed him to cast about and find an alternative approach. Recall that he wrote: 3/8 and 9/512. And then he divided 512 by 8 to get 64. Because he had already defined his problem as using 6×6 to get to 36, he now had the equal intervals of 3, 6, and 9 marked for his attention. The 64 drew his attention to what was opposite 6 and then he quickly saw that as 3 was doubled, 8 was squared. Looking for operational structure in each column and coordinating that was essential in finding his successful conjecture.

He reflected throughout the passage, recognizing inconsistency, reformulating his goals, choosing the numeric answer as "good enough," and creating the language of intervals, jumps, increases, and rates of increases. His operational language also helped stabilize this approach. And, after the answer was achieved, he figured it on his calculator and checked with other problems to be sure his conjecture worked.

Dan's approach to functions has been found in so many of our student investigations that we have labeled the approach a "covariation" to functions and contrasted it to a correspondence approach. In a covariation approach to functions, students view functions as the coordination of two data columns. In the case of the exponential function, this approach allows one to view the exponential as the coordination of an additive structure in the domain with a multiplicative structure in the range (Confrey and Smith, 1994).

Perspective

This analysis of Dan focuses on the development of voice, since the voice of the student can be cast in terms of a covariation approach to functions that coordinates different representations and involves the constructs of interval, rate of increase, and increase. However, the issue of perspective is also particularly interesting in this problem as one considers how Dan seeks to use proportions, a topic that is central to a discussion of multiplicative structures (Vergnaud, 1983a).

At first glance, the proportion 3/8 and 9/512 seems ill conceived. However, in examining this transcript, we asked ourselves whether we could see a way in which it was productive. This constitutes the critical component of constructivist work: reexamining one's own understanding in light of the student data. In this case, it requires one to reexamine one's understanding of proportion. If one rewrites it:

$$\frac{3}{2\times 2\times 2} \quad \frac{9}{2\times 2\times 2\times 2\times 2\times 2\times 2\times 2\times 2}$$

one could read this as:

$$\frac{3\text{ (ones)}}{3\text{ (twos)}} \; \frac{9\text{ (ones)}}{9\text{ (twos)}} \quad \text{or} \quad \frac{3\text{ (ones)}}{3\text{ (twos)}} \; \frac{3\text{ of (3 ones)}}{3\text{ of (3 twos)}}$$

where the operation in the numerator is addition and the operation in the denominator is multiplication. In a certain sense (a logarithmic sense) the proportions are equal. Dan's notation no longer seems garbled but insightful.

With this interpretation, Dan could have generated this ratio by multiplying the 3 by 3 to get 9 intervals and raising the increase for 3 of 8^3 to get 512. The perspective that we find ourselves legitimizing is that proportional reasoning can be extended beyond additive structures to multiplicative structures to create a logarithmic proportion. In historical studies on the development of logarithms, we have found evidence of the use of such a model in the 1300s by Bradwadine (Smith and Confrey, 1994).

We are not claiming that Dan had this logarithmic proportion in mind; however, he might have glimpsed the possibility as he expressed his expectation that proportional reasoning would be productive. On the other hand, since he never expressed the repeated operation of times 2 notationally, its investigation may be primarily one of "perspective" rather than "voice." However, we claim that if we are to challenge fundamentally the narrowness of mathematics instruction, we must concurrently be willing to revise our own understanding of fundamental ideas and see the extent of our own unexamined assumptions. It is this kind of epistemological investigation that is characteristic of radical constructivist work.

Conclusion

In this chapter, I have argued that radical constructivist interpretations of constructivism differ from other interpretations in that radical constructivism is an epistemological theory based in viability. It is suggested that viability commits one to the expectation of and support for diversity in the classroom. Moreover, it obliges the radical constructivist to also reinterpret the mathematical meaning of concepts in light of the students' inventions. To do this effectively, the radical constructivist must learn techniques of close listening and follow these by the articulation of student voice and the examination of the changes in his or her own perspective. It is the ''voice-perspective'' relationship which makes radical constructivism capable of deep reform in mathematics instruction.

Chapter 8
Constructivism-in-action: students examine their idea of science

JACQUES DÉSAUTELS

Our ideas originate in the knowledge we had to start with. . . . You have to have had knowledge in order to have ideas and be able to observe.

A student

To uphold, as this student has, that: (1) observation derives from the frame of knowledge a person has developed, and (2) in order to know, a person must already have some knowledge, may amount to adopting a constructivist point of view on the production of knowledge. We should, of course, guard against reaching hasty conclusions on the basis of a single statement which has been removed from its overall discursive context. It is worth noting here, however, that this assertion was but one of the conclusions reached by this student following personal reflection on the process involved in producing scientific knowledge.

It was thorny questions such as these which provided the basis of a series of exchanges Marie Larochelle and I undertook with a group of thirty-five students in the first year of Cégep, a Québec two-year tertiary institution;[1] the starting point for the exercise consisted in the simulation of a number of conditions presiding over the production of scientific knowledge. Thus, it was not the discourse of accredited epistemologists which students were asked to reflect on, but rather the personal and collective cognitive processes which students themselves engage in when they attempt to solve bona fide puzzles. To borrow a metaphor, these students were called upon to engage in an in vivo, not an in vitro, type of epistemology, by means of a reflective, informed examination of their own epistemological framework.

As will be seen below, the way that participants went about accomplishing this demanding exercise shows to what extent criticism has been unfair to young people. According to some authors, who draw a rather superficial comparison with the youth of another time (read: their own), young people today do not master the rudiments of language, mathematics, and science by the time they have completed high school. In addition, they have purportedly developed negative attitudes toward knowledge, and they display only the shakiest sort of determination when confronted with the inevitable intellectual difficulties which emerge in connection with the appropriation of school knowledge. However, if the teaching context is made to undergo even the slightest shift; if students are seen as the actors of their own cognition, and not merely as reciters of other people's knowledge; finally, if this context is allowed to open onto a range of potentialities and is not used to relentlessly drive at one solution, and one alone (i.e., the "right" answer) – then these young people may well impress us, in terms of the enthusiasm and panache they bring to their work.

Details of the context of this simulation are provided below; space will also be devoted to examples of student discourse which attest to the epistemological virtuosity of participants. It is necessary at this point, however, to explicate the reasons justifying the integration of a constructivist approach to epistemological reflection within science teaching.

Representation and the relationship to knowledge

The first of these reasons is ideological in nature and is due to the fact that all approaches to science teaching convey, explicitly or implicitly, a certain representation of science. Students are presented with a certain notion of the nature of scientific knowledge and of the historicity and sociality of this knowledge, which is particularly important to the way students form their own notion. A good example of this is to be found in the point of view put forward by this high school senior, whom we interviewed in the course of a previous research project.

> Scientific knowledge is always the same thing. Scientific knowledge is F = ma. It's a formula, it's always the same. Whereas religious knowledge . . . can be affected by your family: if you are born into a Catholic family, you will believe in the Catholic religion. It depends on your nationality, it depends on what you've lived through, your environment . . . on society. [On the other hand, if scientific knowledge] is true, it is also true for the working class. I think an apple is an apple, and when it falls, it always accelerates at a rate of 10 meters per second squared: the Martians would find the same thing, too. (Larochelle and Désautels, 1991, p. 382)

Quite obviously, this student has, over the course of his studies, developed a representation of the nature of scientific knowledge as well as of its sociality and historicity, regardless of whether we intended this or were aware of this. From the outset, he imbues scientific knowledge with intemporality (''it's always the same''), although he is aware that his formulation does not refer to the present day, as is shown by his recourse to the anecdote concerning the falling apple to support his argument. Scientific knowledge is also granted a kind of ideological immunity, since, in contrast to religious knowledge, it is not marked by the sociohistorical conditions which were present at the time of its production, in particular, the conditions relating to social classes: scientific knowledge transcends all this. According to this student, such knowledge would also be universal, as is evidenced by the allusion to the ''Martians [who] would find the same thing.'' The object of scientific knowledge would, as it were, fit hand in glove with the objects of ordinary reality, and would, accordingly, describe their behavior with exactness – for example, the apple that falls to the ground. Furthermore, scientific knowledge in this view boils down to mere calculations and formulas, as is indicated by the references to numbers and the famous equation $F = ma$. To sum up, scientific knowledge is exact, true in the sense of standing in a relationship of likeness to reality (*adéquation*), transcendent, and universal, or, for all intents and purposes devoid of history, removed from society. This negation of the historicity and sociality of scientific knowledge constitutes a representation of these very same aspects nonetheless.

Admittedly, there is room for an interpretation of these statements that differs from my own. Nevertheless, this exercise has enabled me to reach a dual objective: to show that students do indeed produce representations of scientific knowledge and to provide an illustration of what we mean by representation. For present purposes, however, let us examine in what way the study of these representations is of ideological, hence social, interest.

When most students complete high school, they also end any contact they have or will have with the sciences in a classroom setting. Thus it is via the representations of science these students constructed during their high school years that they will interpret the discourses and social issues connected to the presence of science in our societies, as has been well illustrated in the work of Driver, Leach, Millar, and Scott (1996) and Ryan and Aikenhead (1992). It remains, however, that these representations embody relationships to knowledge and the producers of knowledge which render the student more or less capable of working out a critical position, or of ultimately becoming involved in action consistent with the social implications of scientific activity. How, for example, is the adolescent referred to above to become capable of criticizing the adage that scientific knowledge is neutral, it is only the uses of science which are potentially harmful? It would appear at the outset that, equipped with the attitude that scientific knowledge transcends the sociocultural conditions of its production, an informed skepticism is unlikely to be generated spontaneously. In addition, what sort of appreciation is the adolescent likely to develop of the social responsibility of scientists, when, in a certain way, the knowledge which they produce is also beyond their control? How is he to embark upon the examination of the ins and outs of theses having sociobiological or eugenic overtones, especially when these have received the support of scientists and experts? In contrast to politicians, do not these same individuals embody the same qualities (objectivity, neutrality, etc.) that are generally attributed to the knowledge they produce? In short, and for a variety of reasons, one is quite justified in thinking that ignorance of the relative, discontinuous, and historically located character of the development of scientific knowledge (Serres, 1989) will leave this student quite unprepared to gauge the limits of this type of knowledge and to appreciate the real worth of other knowledge forms and knowledge games. Will this student not indeed be prone to casting depreciative judgments on knowledge that has been developed within the context of other cultures or civilizations? In other words, how will he avoid equating the economic and technical hegemony of the West with the intrinsic value of scientific knowledge?

Questions such as these obviously have no meaning except in connection with a certain representation of the historicity and sociality of science. As we have elaborated elsewhere (Larochelle, Désautels, and Ruel, 1995), our viewpoint on the subject was and is of a piece with contemporary research in the history, sociology, and anthropology of science (Callon and Latour, 1991; Shapin and Schaffer, 1989), which has mapped out a representation of scientific knowledge and its production which is radically at odds with the somewhat triumphant representation passed down by the adherents of positivism. As Jenkins (1992) has stressed, the idea of an ahistorical, asocial kind of science, one which methodically leads on to objective truth, has now been relegated to the status of "ideological relic." One of the turning points in the challenge to this representation of science no doubt came with the publication of Kuhn's celebrated work (1983), which not only rendered the idea of continuous historical progress in scientific knowledge inoperative but also made it possible to envisage the sociality of science from a new angle. Indeed, the ''hard core'' of science is where the social character of science comes to the fore, since neither adherence to a paradigm, a change in a paradigm, or even the choice of criteria and norms for validating knowledge are entirely rational decisions. Such knowledge as is produced has no meaning outside of the context provided by a shared worldview, a view founded on postulates which are metaphysical and epistemological, aesthetic as well as ethical. Continuing in the same vein, with their ground-level approach, research and publications in the sociology of science (case studies, laboratory studies) have shed light on the conditions under which scientific knowledge is produced (Pickering, 1992), showing, for example, how the interpretation of experiments inevitably entails the negotiation of their meaning. In short, what these studies generally tend to show is that science is a social practice insofar as the conditions present at its origins and throughout its development are social. If, moreover, it is asserted that science is not only a kind of social production but is, as well, recursively productive of society, it must henceforth be viewed as a social problem, meaning, as Restivo (1988) has pointed out, that ''modern science is implicated in the personal troubles and public issues of our time'' (p. 209). Hence, major social stakes are involved in the adequate understanding of the scientific enterprise; it is for this reason that we looked into the representations students formulate concerning the nature of scientific knowledge and its production and ways by which to help them complexify these representations.

Epistemology and the appropriation of scientific knowledge

The second reason we think it necessary to integrate epistemology within science teaching relates to arguments of a pedagogical nature. Over the last twenty years, research in science education has helped shed new light on the problems arising in connection with science teaching programs. In particular, this research has enabled researchers in science education to rediscover, in their own way, one of the basic propositions of Piagetian constructivist theory, namely, that children do not wait until their first science classes to begin developing their own ideas of so-called natural phenomena. Even as youngsters, they construct their own explanations of phenomena occurring in their everyday lives, whether this be the fall of an object, suction of liquid through a straw, or the fragility of the neighbor's windows!

As we have examined in greater depth elsewhere (Benyamna, Désautels, and Larochelle, 1993), however, what took science educators aback, so to speak, was the discovery of the long lease on life which such explanations enjoy, however long schooling may last. To be sure, students make liberal use of words which denote a certain familiarity with scientific terminology (molecule, kinetic energy, etc.), but the core remains fundamentally unchanged, so that the "new words" become endowed with a kind of materiality which is scarcely compatible with the relational character of scientific concepts. The following excerpts from interviews with Cégep-graduates who have a concentration in science and who will also go on to do further studies in their field at the university level (Benyamna, 1987) offer convincing evidence of just this tendency. Thus, one of these students explains the transparency of glass with the claim that "glass particles don't have color, but [instead] are transparent"; another explains the spread of heat in the following terms: "Heat is conveyed by electrons." All of which gives teachers and researchers much food for thought: Is the problem one of teaching, one of learning, or one involving the accessibility of scientific content matter?

At first glance, were one to use scientific conceptions to gauge the worth of these students' conceptions, one might conclude that the latter represent a degraded version of the former, that they, indeed, are misconceptions, hence the proof of a learning problem. However, as numerous studies tend to show (Hills, 1989; Tiberghien, 1989), such an assertion would amount to ignoring the particularity of these conceptions, which serve to provide a kind of intelligibility to the scientific knowledge being taught, which, more often than not, has been stripped of all contextuality. It is exceedingly rare in science teaching that the conditions and rules obtaining in the construction and validition of scientific contents are presented in addition to the contents themselves (Sutton, 1996). Take only the example of the expression *scientific fact*: In the absence of any information whatsoever concerning the genesis of any one particular fact and the various operations which have led to its being endowed with the status of scientificity, what will be retained by students? How are students to give meaning to this expression? Will they not, indeed, tend to detach this fact from its original context (concerning which, moreover, they were not provided with any background) and classify it according to a frame of reference with which they are familiar (thus, by the same token, modifying the scope of this fact)?

In short, it is clear that students' knowledge can no longer be dispensed with in teaching. Whether in terms of its contents or organization, this spontaneous[2] knowledge serves as a basis for interpreting the information and events being taught, as research on the subject has shown. Students are neither tabula rasa nor some as yet unmolded putty. Rather, they are both actors and authors of their cognition: they compare, translate, symbolize, and transform. No better illustration of this is to be found than in the multiplication, indeed, the explosion, of studies on spontaneous conceptions. It is the examination of such conceptions which has given rise to major reformulations of the hypotheses and propositions used as a basis for teaching scientific laws, concepts, and theories, as is attested by the research carried out within a constructivist perspective (Driver, 1989). However, such propositions have their limits, which are in part due to the lack of consideration generally given to the epistemological dimension involved in the appropriation of scientific knowledge by students (Vosniadou, 1994). I should like to provide a succinct overview of this question.

I mentioned that students make scientific knowledge "easier to digest," to borrow the Moscovici and Hewstone expression (1984); that is, they assimilate this knowledge within their conceptual structure via a process of reconstruction, and they endow concepts with a kind of meaning compatible with the more or less tacit epistemological postulates which drive this structure. Thus the concept of light ray is likened to an ultrathin beam of light which may be perceived. Likewise, the concept of atom is likened to a miniature sphere of the kind which may be seen in the models of molecules on display in laboratories (Harrison and Treagust, 1996). In both cases, the underlying postulate holds that the sensory organs provide immediate access to reality and that explanation of a phenomenon is primarily a matter of describing that which is perceptible by the senses. Now, it is our hypothesis that for many students, beliefs such as these constitute a major stumbling block to appropriating the meaning of scientific concepts. Indeed, how is one to understand that heat is but one form of energy, that particles may annihilate one another during interaction; or that electromagnetic waves require no material support in order to be propagated? Such phenomena must indeed appear as even so many closed books if one is unaware of the postulates which habitually underlie one's own understanding of so-called material phenomena, when one is unable to conceive of other possibilities – in other words, as Piaget and Garcia have pointed out (1983), when one is unable to invent a problem where apparently there is none.

It is not my intention here to call into question or invalidate everyday knowledge. I am aiming instead at bringing out the contextual relevance of different forms of knowledge (Cobern, 1996). The explanations individuals usually construct are quite viable, in the sense that they are adapted to the goals an individual is attempting to reach. It is possible, for example, to tell someone to shut the door in order to keep out the cold (a concept which does not exist in science), so that the temperature remains at a comfortable level and heating costs are kept to a minimum. What is there to criticize in this way of thinking? Nothing, except that it is unsuited to the objectives pursued by scientists, who formulate questions that are unconceivable within the framework of everyday knowledge, arising as these do in connection with another system of epistemological referents. Whence the necessity, if one wishes to participate in the conversation of scientists, of understanding how the latter impart meaning to the notions and concepts they use; whence also the importance of epistemological reflexivity. Only when knowing subjects become aware of the postulates which underlie their usual ways of knowing, and when they place these postulates at some distance, as it were, and thus problematize their own knowledge will they become able to open themselves to other potentialities. Although this intellectual process of reflexivity is often associated with metacognition, it is distinct from the latter in that it does not involve the intellectual operations or strategies used in developing this or that bit of knowledge. Instead, reflexivity draws attention to "that which goes without saying" – that is, the unspoken assumptions or the unreflected aspects of thought which lead one to assert that something is obvious. It is this examination of what may be referred to metaphorically as the blind spot of a conceptual structure[3] which is a condition necessary for beginning that process whereby thought is complexified and autonomized (Varela, 1989). When such a condition obtains, it is possible at that point to make discriminations and grasp the notion that kinds of knowledge are viable according to the context of their production. Hence, it is not a question of evaluating the truth or falseness of either the common tendency of substantializing heat or the scientific tendency of dematerializing the same. Instead, it is the interpretation one makes of the context which will determine the appropriate signification.

Engaging in epistemological reflexivity along the lines I have just set out is an exercise which, assuredly, demands as much if not more intellectual effort than is the case with studying the contents of various scientific disciplines. However, in the educational setting we provided, the participating youths undertook this exercise with enthusiasm and panache.

The educational setting

Epistemological reflection can be integrated within curriculum by drawing on a variety of educational strategies. Our choice consisted in organizing a classroom simulation of a number of conditions involved in the production of scientific knowledge – in particular, the constructed, negotiated features of this knowledge – so that students would reflect on their own cognitive activity rather than on scholarly discourse on the subject. This was how we facilitated the students' task of questioning their own representations, so that they might surpass these representations. This does not imply that personal options were rejected, only that they were dialecticized. Specifically, students were to accomplish this goal by developing a capacity for critically reflecting on the postulates underpinning their own and others' strategies for constructing knowledge.

As part of this approach, we designed a computer program capable of generating a series of puzzles for which (true and false) answers could not be gotten from a textbook or an instructor (Désautels, Lauzon, and Larochelle, 1987). The puzzle to be worked out by our apprentice researchers involved the unexpected behavior of unknown entities emitted by any one of four emitters placed around an opaque square; the traces of this emission could be located on the screen. Thus, as may be observed in Figure 8.1, the traces left by an entity changed direction following possible interaction "beneath" (a reasonable postulate for sure) the black square, although it was expected to continue along a straight path.

Ultimately, it was the gap between the expectations of the researchers and what they actually saw on the screen that offered the possibility of formulating a problem for which a solution could be attempted. What did this apparent deviation mean? How was one to solve this puzzle? It was in a framework such as this that the students-cum-apprentice researchers were called upon to invent and test out a number of solutions. In addition, the plausibility of the solutions proposed was the subject of a debate among participants in a scholarly colloquium. That way, it was the students themselves who produced

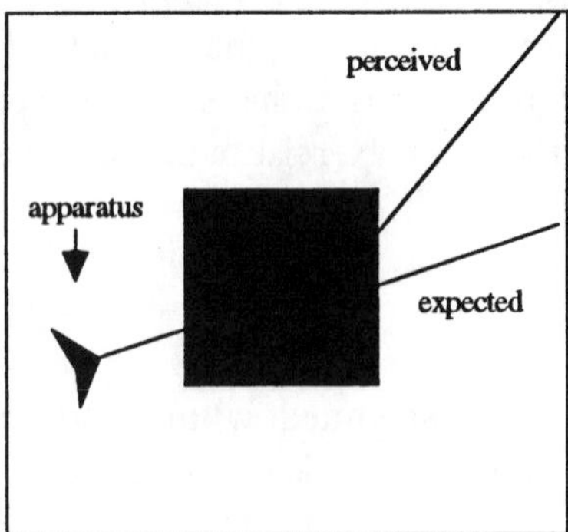

Figure 8.1. Potentiality-generating puzzle

the data upon which they based their reflection. They were aided in this process by the epistemological considerations to which we unceasingly drew their attention. Questioning in connection with epistemological issues could also assume a number of different forms. Thus we offered students two workshops devoted to reflection and knowledge production, the first bearing on inventive conceptualization (led by Professor Wilfrid Bilodeau) and the second on logical reasoning (led by the professor in charge of the course). On several different occasions, we gave students short, somewhat informal memos in question form to portray a number of problems and issues which their research activities raised. However, it was particularly during the team projects using the aforementioned computer program that we called on students to specify the implicit postulates they make use of for the purpose of: (1) constructing "scientific explanations" – for example, extending the paths in order to locate a point of impact beneath the square assumes that the entities continue along a straight path at the moment they disappear from sight; (2) formulating coherent lines of argument; and (3) developing awareness of divergences of opinion which debate brings into play. In addition, students were encouraged to keep an "epistemological journal," in which they wrote down their reflections concerning the production of scientific knowledge. In these, we added our comments in question form, thus enabling us to keep up a dialogue with each student concerning these thorny questions.

This strategy was implemented in a regular, required philosophy course offered during the first year of a two-year tertiary institution. The class met twice a week, for a total of three hours, over a twelve-week period. The group was comprised of thirty-five students, male and female, of whom the average age was seventeen years and five months. On average, they had taken six science courses at the secondary level and three at the tertiary level. At the time we conducted our research, seven students had opted for a concentration in the social sciences, three were pursuing a vocational track, and twenty had chosen a concentration in the pure sciences, while another five noted that they were transferring from one program to another.

Although the present discussion does not lend itself to entering into the details of how implementation of this strategy proceeded, the "metalogue" – that is, a conversation concerning "problematic subjects" (Bateson, 1981, p. 1) – provides an interesting metaphor for this process. There can be no doubting the problematical nature of the issues which were dealt with in class (truth, evidence, objectivity, models, postulates, etc.). Evidence of this complexity may be found not only in the point of view of the students themselves, as indicated by their statements, but also in the perspective of epistemologists of science, for whom such matters provide their daily bread and the subject of unending debate. In addition, the very structure of the dialogues which took place between the various actors involved in the research is intertwined with the problems this long conversation was prone to give rise to. Throughout this process, and in keeping with the constructivist orientation of the strategy used, we constantly confronted students with their own reflections and made no effort to impose the "right" point of view on them. This did not mean, however, that we refrained from suggesting avenues along which to pursue reflection. By focusing on their statements, actions, and lines of inquiry, our questions provided students with many springboards for their own reflection and avoided dictating the direction which such reflection was to follow. As a result, the students enjoyed the necessary autonomy for developing a model of knowledge production whose solidity they could adjudge by means of reflexively examining their research activity, which ultimately generated problematic subjects anew. Furthermore, since the outcome of these research activities could not be defined in terms of a right or wrong response, new problems accordingly arose in connection with the epistemological status of knowledge. The question remains, however, of whether this strategy is relevant in terms of the stated objectives. It is to this question that I shall now turn.

Student statements

Understandably, it is impossible to provide here a synthesis of the some four hundred pages of writings produced by the students in their journals. Instead, I will attempt to illustrate how these adolescents engaged in epistemology, and indeed how, by doing so, they developed a better-informed representation of science in action.

Generally speaking, after reading through the statements, one cannot help but notice the lack of familiarity with the kind of reflection at issue among a sizable majority of students, as the following excerpts illustrate. Thus, one student candidly admitted that she had never asked herself any questions about the production of scientific knowledge, whereas another classmate noted how she had once thought she knew everything there was to know on the subject. (Subjects are identified by a number at the beginning of each excerpt.)

S9 – I admit I had never thought of the process of production (of scientific knowledge). At first, I thought it was something like an inspiration from heaven. I quickly changed this simplistic interpretation of the process of production.

S12 – I thought I knew it all about the production of scientific knowledge, but the further we go along (in the course), the less I have the impression of knowing something about it and the more I discover things I never dreamed could exist.

Continuing in the same vein, the following comment offers a number of glimpses into the strangeness of epistemological reflection and how this reflection fills a person with no end of questions:

S26 – It is quite hard to ask yourself why you think something is so. This is because until now we've rarely been called on to ask ourselves such questions. Usually what we learn are previously established relationships. Now it's our whole way of reflecting on things which is thrown into question.

Once the surprise was over, how did the students tackle the problematic subjects that are dear to epistemologists? It is worth noting at the outset the multitude of problems which students reflected on, ranging from the role of metaphors in the production of scientific knowledge to the distinction between private and public forms of science, with concepts such as truth, objectivity, postulates, and so forth, undergoing examination in the process. It is at this point that I would like to present how a number of these problems were dealt with.

The workshop on inventive or metaphorical conceptualization sparked numerous reactions. Of the thirty-five students who participated in the experiment, twenty-two provided statements on the role of *metaphorization* in the production of scientific knowledge, emphasizing how the former should be seen as something more than mere figures of speech. Fourteen of these subjects characterized metaphorization as having a pedagogical or communicative function, in reference to the way in which it smooths out the difficulties engendered by abstraction.

S25 – It would be harder to understand all that, because oftentimes, we're dealing with things which do not exist – i.e., that can't be seen, touched, or smelled. The only thing we have left to define these things is in fact our imagination. And to make our imagination work, we have to rely on metaphors or something else that I can't put my finger on but which would have the same function as metaphor or would be related to it.

The other eight subjects drew on their own research activity to illustrate how metaphorical activity plays a constitutive role in the production of scientific knowledge:

S12 – Metaphors are indispensable because they allow us to create models of things that it would be impossible to discover otherwise. Metaphors provide the real basis of all conversation, hence of all human thinking. The production of scientific knowledge is obviously no exception to this rule. In order to arrive at some conclusion as to what was contained in the black square, we had to compare the deviations of the emissions with material things with which we were more familiar, such as the deviation of a ball of wood when it hits a wall, for example. We linked all the phenomena which we observed on our screen to things we were familiar with; hence, we continually used metaphors in order to understand.

This reflective insight into the role the imagination plays in the production of scientific knowledge can also be linked to recognition of the role of postulates in this same production, as is borne out in various forms by the statements of twenty-eight students. For example, some of the students offered a definition of the concept of postulate:

S19 – In our opinion, postulates are thoughts that don't require looking into. They are the underlying beliefs that we think we know but which have not necessarily been proven. Now, these postulates have to be properly identified and then reflected on with greater attentiveness.

For a number of students, reflection on the role of postulates led them, on the one hand, to realize the necessity of postulating in order to know and, on the other, to recognize the conventionality of postulates, in which the latter stand as neither true nor false.

S10 – Two parallels never intersect: this goes without saying, except that there's nothing to prove it. . . . It's more than clear that the evidence in and of itself cannot always be relied on. Every step along the progression has to be continually tested out because this [assumption] can never be true or false.

Following upon this realization, these students also arrived at a number of inferences concerning the consequences of adopting such a position for the production of knowledge. Thus, after having brought out the fundamental necessity of postulating the stability of the object of analysis, one student came to the conclusion that "obviously, this assumption implies that when the ray is emitted twice from the same point and in the same direction, its deviation will be exactly the same from one time to the next" (S12).

There were some students who adopted a position which recalls one of the propositions of constructivism. They recognized that knowledge is invented, and that this knowledge is based on previously held knowledge:

S9 – I do believe it's true that the way things are seen is created on the basis of the assumptions that people make and the ideas that people have. That is why, although the project was the same for everyone, each team approached the problem differently, in keeping with its own background. The approach is different because each person has his or her personal way of seeing things, which has been influenced by each person's experiences. Thus, it is we who create our way of seeing things, based on our assumptions. . . . [This is] because people don't analyze a phenomenon the same way; everyone goes at it according to their ideas.

Even in partial form, the results presented thus far provide clear illustration that these students performed epistemology by engaging in an examination of their own cognitive activity. One might wonder, however, whether, as a result of this process, they did not also develop a better-informed representation of the production of scientific knowledge. There is an abundance of indicators which suggest that this is in fact the case. First of all, many students were able to critically appraise their experience of learning science and, in particular, of school varieties of scientific knowledge. In particular, they mentioned that they have never been called on to reflect on the foundations of the knowledge which they have been presented with, nor have they been asked to relate these epistemological considerations to "science in the making," to use Callon and Latour's expression (1991). According to these students, such negligence warps not only the attitude they develop toward learning but also the type of relationship they develop with knowledge, as may be seen in the following excerpt:

S32 – All the courses I have taken are based on learning scientific contents that must be absorbed without questioning the basis of this research. Our critical capacity is reduced to nothing; we receive this information as though it were absolute truth. Once you're inside the system, I think you develop a liking for it because you become used to this sort of method that demands only some understanding and a little memorization; our curiosity gradually withers away, and I would go so far as to say that we become intellectually lazy, and that our interest declines, which could prove to be harmful at some point in the future.

These students have brought to light the dogmatism of science teaching and have identified the illusory nature of the representation of science which it conveys. In so doing, they have enabled themselves to bracket off and transform their notion of the production of scientific knowledge, and they have thereby developed a critical point of view. Illustration of this evolution is to be found in the following statement, which deals with the hypothetical and relative character of not only their own productions but of the production of scientific knowledge as well:

S7 – The same applies to science. Researchers are confident of their own theories, but they often forget that these are only assumptions for as long as nobody comes up with anything better, and so on. A conclusion that all teams arrive at wouldn't be a certainty either, since no one can ever see through the square; this [conclusion] will always be an assumption. On the other hand, postulates are quite useful, because there always has to be a starting point for our research. How else are we to begin?

The absoluteness of scientific truth was implicitely thrown into question on a number of other occasions, particularly in statements in which students identified the convention-bound character of scientific knowledge, as illustrated in the following excerpt:

S21 – In our research, as in the research of other scientists, we had to devise postulates, in other words, conventions among ourselves. These conventions had a determining influence on the results and on the model generated by the research. For example, by postulating at the outset that the ray continued along a straight line after having gone beyond the limits of the opaque square, we obtained a model which was completely different from that which would have obtained if we had begun with another set of postulates. An example such as this provides good insight into the importance of the postulates or conventions on which research is based.

On the other hand, some students took different cognitive routes to develop better-informed representations of the production of scientific knowledge for themselves. For example, in what appears to us as an example of epistemological reflection achieving "takeoff," one student proposed an emancipatory conception of research, one which integrates the concepts of error and detours and which, via a process of arborization, does not restrict itself to the idea of truth but instead opens onto that of the enrichment of potentialities:

S2 – Here is how I could describe [it]:

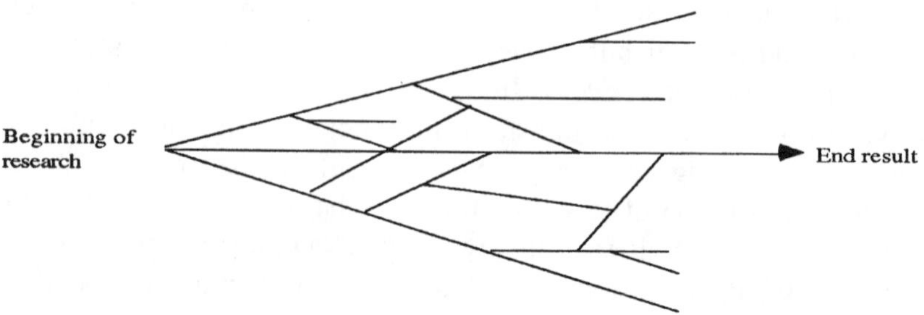

Figure 8.2. Student's conception of the research process

The arrow represents the shortest route to a result. The other lines form an infinite number of detours. As can be seen, one detour can lead to another and then lead back to the main path of research. But when all the detours are worked through, you may end up with a result which is unlike any other. Perhaps things would become complicated and entangled to the point of producing no result even. Or perhaps the paths or detours could make it possible to verify that it is in fact impossible to achieve a similar result. Or then again, these detours could spark new discoveries. So here, as with the other form of detours, the result will be research which is more solid, more thoroughly analyzed, and subjected to greater verification. One might conclude that these detours ought to be mentioned primarily in the research report and during a public conference.

Conclusion

In light of these statements, it is plausible to think that a good many students – two-thirds according to our evaluation – were able to construct better-informed representations of scientific knowledge. It is indeed plausible that once these students gained awareness of the constructed, relative character of this knowledge and were able to recognize the collective, consensual aspects involved in its production, they also acquired the basic intellectual tools which would enable them to develop a more *emancipative, critical* relationship to knowledge and its producers. This relationship may be described as being more *emancipative* for two reasons. First, from the moment that scientific knowledge is conceived as one knowledge game among others, it can no longer be invoked as a criterion by which to appraise the worth of other forms of knowledge, including one's very own. Secondly, scientists are no longer perceived as geniuses serving as mouthpieces through whom the secrets and commandments of Nature are revealed, but rather as people who, not unlike these students, imagine solutions to the problems they have invented and test these solutions by means of the collective implementation of the appropriate technical procedures. We have also described this relationship as being more *critical* because students have gained greater awareness of how a number of issues are at stake in the production of scientific knowledge, in particular the necessity of persuading one's peers of the solidity of one's research.

S8 – In my opinion, a scientist has to be good not only in conducting a research project, he or she must also be good at presenting it. What I mean is this: to begin with, you do a research project within a certain period of time and within all kinds of limits. You come up with a final result, which does not mean that research is over and done with or that the answer has been found. It is this result which the researcher believes in; he or she believes it is the best answer (or hypothesis). Now, I would compare this answer to a product that must be sold. . . . What I mean is that the experimenter must have certain aptitudes for communication in order to sell his/her product and to get across the message that this project is the best one.

Another issue, by no means a minor one, involves the image of scientists in society:

S9 – One other point: I don't think scientists stand to benefit from making known all the difficulties they have run into. This would detract from their status as scientists. Society needs heroes, and often scientists are put into a somewhat of a special category. They do research, so it doesn't serve them any purpose to mention they encountered a lot of difficulty during their work.

Thus stripped of its aura of transcendence, the production of scientific knowledge becomes, somehow, a more human experience, as well as a critical one. It is legitimate to ask, however, whether such relativist students will not indeed become prone to solipsism and turn away from science forever.

After working with these students for three months, and reading and rereading their journals, we encountered no evidence to that effect. Obviously, one may find traces of a rather fashionable sort of cynicism peculiar to adolescence or an occasional hint of ontological angst.

Generally speaking, however, these students did not adopt an absolutely relativistic position. More importantly, demystifying the production of scientific knowledge made science more accessible for some.

Moreover, in connection with research into spontaneous conceptions (among other topics), the question may be put as to whether the epistemological reflection performed by these students enables them to revise the materialistically tinted significations with which they habitually endow scientific notions and concepts. No answer may be provided to this at the present time. However, the majority of these students displayed sensitivity to how, fundamentally, scientific knowledge is model based and provisional in nature – that is, this knowledge is a map but is not itself the territory it purports to describe. Thus, there are grounds for believing that these students will demonstrate greater vigilance toward the relational aspect of the concepts made use of in such knowledge, for here, as elsewhere, these concepts are not to be taken for the thing itself!

Chapter 9
Constructivism and ethical justification

GÉRARD FOUREZ

From a constructivist epistemology to a constructed ethics

Several decades ago, most scientists believed that scientific results were the product of a rational, inescapable kind of logic that was central to the quest for ultimate scientific truth. In relatively recent times, the constructivist movement in philosophy and the sociology of science has given rise to a certain consensus which operates according to a different perspective. In this view, scientific theories are not conceived of as a reflection of reality itself or of some theory-derived idea existing in and of itself and governing the organization of the world. Science is increasingly perceived as a human production which occurs in history and which is pursued in accordance with certain finalities. This vision brings out the invented character of the construction of science, wherein the latter is conceived of as a body of representations which have been produced by human creativity in order to picture one's place in space and time and to communicate and act in the world, society, and history. By virtue of this development, science has become demystified and secularized and yet has avoided falling prey to a sort of disillusioned relativism. Science continues to be an enchanting (but not enchanted) cultural and aesthetic enterprise because human beings see in it one of the greatest achievements in which the mind is free to develop and recognize itself in the world. Thus, scientific development is dissociated less and less from the rest of human history. Science not only has a history, science must also be seen as occurring in History.

The evolution of ethics presents a parallel with that of the sciences. For a long time it was believed that, as with the "laws governing the material world," "moral laws" had been laid down by God, either directly or via the mediation of Nature. With the onset of secularization, moral law was viewed as an autonomous, imposed-from-without entity, which did not mean, however, that either God or Nature were invoked. Even among subcultures which have been heavily marked by free thought, there remains a vision according to which *Law* and, indeed, "duty" are given as categorical imperatives providing a structure to human action. Psychoanalysis has also set store in – that is, sanctified – the term *Law*. Furthermore, in everyday practice, ethics is still generally conceived of in terms of what is compulsory. Whether one is confronted with choosing a nursing home for one's elderly parents or deciding on a career track, the standard question remains, as ever: What ought to be done? If the issue arises of what limits should be placed on action, as, for example, in the case of experiments on humans, the question is: What may be done (about it)? Even if most people no longer think of themselves as operating with a heteronomous moral framework, many continue to think as if the answers to their moral questions were inscribed somewhere in a heavenly constellation of ideas awaiting discovery.

It is possible to establish a parallel between a nonconstructivist conception of science and the usual way of reflecting on ethics: in both cases, it is assumed that the answers exist independently of our human means of reflecting on such issues.

In science, constructivist perspectives have made it possible to conceive of the types of logic underlying scientific invention in new terms. Historians and sociologists of science have taken up scientific controversy, examining the justificatory strategies of actors independently of the relationship which they entertain toward a so-called scientific truth that has supposedly been demonstrated.[1] They have applied the principle of symmetry, wherein points of view that are held by scientists to be right are placed on equal footing with points of view which they hold (ultimately . . . or momentarily) to be wrong. From this perspective, the scientific basis of an argument does not derive from the argument's being more logical or well founded in terms of some absolute. On the contrary, the very purpose of scientific discussion is, in an open society, to debate each person's assertions and to do so according to criteria that are continually being subjected to challenge throughout history.

For constructivists, the rationality of scientific debates is based on a usually implicit kind of contract which, however, is consensually agreed upon in the context of scientific conferences or academic practice. By means of this contract, scientists establish an agreement as to the assumptions as well as to the principles and practices underlying research. Taken as a whole, these underlying principles and assumptions are generally termed a "paradigm" or "the matrix of a discipline." It serves as a basis upon which to work out an agreement over what, in a scientific discussion, will be considered relevant as opposed to irrelevant. Thus, scientific observation can only undergo closure on the condition that a whole series of elements are ignored which, were they taken up for consideration, would lead to observations without end. The notion of paradigm refers to these agreements between practitioners of the same discipline by which they are able to develop similar protocols of observation, come to an understanding of what they are doing, and define a particular area of objectivity. In other words, scientific paradigms are what make it possible for scientific debates to take place in accordance with socially instituted forms of rationality.

A fertile approach for the study of how science is constructed, this perspective may also be put to use in the study of ethics, beginning with the notion of paradigm.

From moral debate to ethical paradigms

If scientific practices are held to include scientific debate, it may also be said that rational ethics are rooted in moral debate. We engage in this debate whenever we ask ourselves: What will be done (or what will I, or we, do?); what do we (or I) want to do? These questions give rise to a debate having a certain rationality, provided that there is sufficient agreement concerning the contexts, situations, values, and issues which are brought into play. Thus it is possible to view this set of assumptions, on which a certain consensus exists, as forming an "ethical paradigm" of the situation. Thus, in order to hold a debate bearing on the ethics of slavery, a minimum degree of agreement is required concerning notions relating to liberty, dependence, property, social institutions, humanity, and so forth. In order to debate organ transplants, some consensus should exist over notions such as the chances of survival, the psychological impact on the patient, the consequences for the family, the costs of the operation, health, the quality of life, and so forth. As in the case of science, the notions and values providing the basis of an ethical paradigm always remain somewhat hazy and are linked to the myths and founding narratives which structure our representations.

Just as it is possible to study the historical emergence of scientific paradigms (for example, in our time, the paradigms governing molecular genetics or cybernetics), so it is possible to identify the emergence of ethical paradigms such as have occurred in connection with slavery or organ transplants. In the case of organ transplants, in particular, one need only compare the "freewheeling" debates of the 1950s with the types of exchanges now occurring among hospital staffs. Forty years ago, it was primarily a doctor's "best judgment" which held sway, in the almost total absence of any organized, critical reflection. Today, in a number of milieus at least, debate has taken on a decidedly interdisciplinary cast and draws on firmly established traditions. Participants know what types of questions are worth raising or not; in short, a new type of rationality has come into existence in accordance with an implicitly accepted paradigm.

The notion of an ethical paradigm enables us to adopt a constructivist angle in the study of moral debates. It is possible, in other words, for historians, epistemologists, and sociologists of ethics to examine the way in which modes of moral justification have been constructed at different times. Constructivist hypotheses have made it possible to investigate how scientists translate the situations they study in terms of the paradigms they are working under and to explore how scientists attempt to justify their position. Such investigation has been performed without regard to the ultimate value of the arguments advanced by these scientists (Latour and Woolgar, 1988; Latour, 1989) or concerning the truth of their theses. Similarly, we have been witness to an innovative development in ethics involving the study of justification which, on the basis of constructivist assumptions, has shown how moral justifications have developed historically. The recent model developed by Boltanski and Thévenot provides a groundbreaking basis for this approach which warrants further examination.

Boltanski and Thévenot: "on justification"

A study of justification without assumptions about the ultimate value of moral systems

Boltanski and Thévenot (1991) used an approach toward ethics which has become standard for the social study of science. Using a methodology familiar to anthropologists, they examined how ethicists work, without attaching too great an importance to the idea which the latter have formed of their own work.[2] From this perspective, they consider the notion of justice not as a property in and of itself, but rather as the outcome of a process of moral justification. Instead of claiming that an action is morally right on account of a series of properties inherent to it, this point of view holds that an action is morally right when, in terms of a certain problematic, the actors involved agree to bring the debate over ethical considerations to a close.

In the constructivist perspective they adopt toward ethics, Boltanski and Thévenot inquire into the specific ways by which people arrive at an agreement as to what is right. The authors set out to "seriously consider the imperative of justification, on which the possibility of coordinating human behavior rests, and to examine the constraints which bear on an agreement over a common good" (Boltanski and Thévenot, 1991, p. 53). Such an approach does not lead to relativism. Instead it is concerned simply with looking into the way people justify their actions in a variety of contexts and with "pursuing all the consequences of the fact that people are confronted with the necessity of justifying their actions – not in the sense of inventing rationalizations, after the fact, in order to disguise hidden motives, as when one comes up with an alibi – but so as to perform deeds in a way that makes it possible to submit them to a justificatory trial (*épreuve de justification*)" (ibid., p. 54). Hence, it is a question of finding "under what conditions a principle of agreement is held to be legitimate" (ibid., p. 55). Such an endeavor is to be engaged in "without availing oneself of the facility afforded by a transcendental approach": at issue, then, is not a "critical reflection concerning the categories of knowledge," but instead "an analysis of disputes" (ibid., p. 427). Or, in other words, the authors aim at discovering how, and in what precise social and ideological contexts, arguments become acceptable – or, as Ricoeur (1979, p. 87) has stated, are capable of halting the search for "whys" in justificatory processes. Just as in the case of the sciences, where, within precise paradigms, arguments can be identified which make it possible to bring discussion to some form of closure and to produce scientific justification, agreement, and assent, so too Boltanski and Thévenot elucidate analogous procedures which occur in the case of moral justification.

A plurality of "orders" of justification

On the basis of their analysis of the ways by which judgments are legitimized in the political philosophy of the "commercial or merchant order," Boltanski and Thévenot (1991) systematize such procedures into a kind of "political grammar" which they then confront with contexts other than that described in the case of a predominantly commercial society. They present half a dozen such "orders," or spheres, of justification, with each one being viable in certain contexts. For the authors, these orders deserve the attention of our contemporaries because they convey expressions of the common good on which today's society functions (ibid., p. 34). They do not claim, however, that "taken together, these orders cover all orders of society which could be constructed." Thus, their analysis is in no way aimed at presenting all possible forms of ethical and political construction, but is instead meant to bring out a number of forms which, in our Western experience, serve to frame our justifications in the present time.

The orders to which attention is devoted are: commerce or trade; the home; industry; inspiration; opinion; and civic or public affairs. All six orders represent socially instituted legitimation structures[3] to which ethical and political justifications refer. These structures are not necessarily compatible; as will be seen, our exercises in ethical reasoning are generally negotiated between and within these orders. Thus, for example, someone who possesses "greatness" in the commercial or merchant order will not necessarily be "legitimate" in another order, such as the inspirational order.

Thus, the commercial-merchant order brings together individuals via rare goods which are sought after by all. This order "rests on two pillars: the common identification of marketable goods, trade of which makes it possible to define the direction given to action; and, the common evaluation of these goods by means of prices, which makes it possible to adjust diverse actions" (ibid., p. 60). This order thus conveys "a principle of agreement and an analysis of human nature which is intended to explain the way by which everyone can adjust to this principle" (ibid., p. 61). This principle of agreement, in other words, "the fair price," is linked to a vision of a human being who is free and who enjoys security, in a system in which the coveting of goods is presumed to lead to the cooperation of individuals (ibid., p. 67). According to these two authors, this order finds a typical expression in the philosophies of Adam Smith and David Hume.

From the notion of "greatness" to the concept of "city"

Thus, an order defines a conception of humanity and society which is based on what Boltanski and Thévenot call "states of greatness" (*grandeurs*) – that is, forms of the common good which are recognized as legitimate within that order. These states of greatness enable humans to distinguish between that which, with respect to this order, is legitimate or not, between that which is great and that which is abject. However, that which is considered ''great'' in the commercial order could prove destructive, occasionally at least, in the domestic order. And, empirically speaking, we discover that we do live in different orders. Sometimes, for example, a person will discover that he or she is pursuing objectives that have been defined by the commercial order while at other moments, that which in his or her estimation confers ''greatness'' on him- or herself will be family qualities originating in the domestic order.

Boltanski and Thévenot have thus devised a series of interpretative hypotheses concerning life in society which enable them to define what they have termed ''models of the city.'' Such models ''are constructed upon an order of greatness, provide a foundation for various constructions of political philosophy, and offer guidelines for defining the ordinary meaning of the right and just'' (ibid., p. 96). According to these authors, we may speak of a city when we accept a series of axioms which found a sociopolitical and moral order (ibid., pp. 96–102). These axioms attempt to formalize the manner of functioning of discourse which responds to the imperative of ''justification,'' and they thus serve to found an ethic. They may be summarized as follows: (A1) the principle of ''the common humanity'' of a city's members; (A2) a principle of ''dissimilarity,'' according to which some members may be considered as possessing more or less greatness depending on whether their actions are more or less legitimate in this city; (A3) the possibility of attaining various states of greatness, ensuring by the same token that members share a ''common dignity''; (A4) the possibility of ordering states of greatness according to a ''scale of values''; (A5) the existence of means by which ''committing oneself'' to the pursuit of a state of greatness may be accomplished, in acceptance of the costs and sacrifices implied therein; (A6) the belief that the pursuit of higher states serves the ''common good'' of the entire city. Such a definition of the city is not inclusive of every type of justification or every scale of values. ''City'' does not comprehend, for example, an order of justification advocating eugenism or one that would originate in the company of thieves, because the former does not satisfy (A3) (common dignity), and because the latter fails to satisfy (A6) (a common good).

These axioms give rise to justifications which often extend beyond the frame of reference to which ethicists are accustomed. Hence, in the commercial city: people are not goods (A1); differences in wealth distinguish states of greatness (A2), and these states are ordered (A4); every human being has the right to become rich (A3), but must, in exchange, accept sacrifices (A5); and, finally, the pursuit of wealth (at least as this is set forth by Adam Smith) is presumed to work to everyone's advantage (A6).

Six cities

There are several cities; that is, there are several registers of justification, several spheres of justice, and several ways of specifying the common good. Moreover, we intuitively recognize that a person who acted in the domestic world according to a business ethic, or vice versa, would find him- or herself poorly justified.

Boltanksi and Thévenot provide definitions for six cities. We have already touched on the "commercial or merchant city." The "inspirational city" (ibid., p. 107) – whose emblematic figure is, in their view, Saint Augustine – is characterized by a quest for total acceptance of grace. Grace may be understood in the classic Christian meaning of the word or, analogously, in connection with other kinds of inspiration or spiritual search, such as are to be found in art, poetry, and science. The "domestic city" (ibid., p. 116) is characterized by the placing of an individual within a social or familial body. That which confers greatness upon each individual in this body is a person's capacity to hold his or her rank within a universe which, fundamentally, is organized into a hierarchy or system and which occasionally is viewed as the expression of a divine or cosmic plan. In the "city of opinion," greatness depends solely on other people's esteem (ibid., p. 126). It "is related to the constitution of conventional signs or marks, which, by condensing and manifesting the force generated by the esteem which people bear toward one another, makes it possible to establish an equivalence between different individuals and to calculate their worth" (ibid., p. 127). In Hobbes's view, individuals hold power only by virtue of the authority invested in them by others. In accordance with this order, persons whose eminence is recognized by only the few possess little greatness. As for the "civic city," which is related to the thought of Rousseau, it makes out excellence "when citizens renounce their singularity and detach themselves from their particular interests and thus concern themselves exclusively with the common good" (ibid., p. 138). In this sphere, "for morally right relationships to develop between people, human interactions must be mediated by a relationship to a second-level totality'' (ibid., p. 240); interpersonal relationships must be mediated by the relation to the globality of the social body. Finally, the ''industrial city'' is founded, as with the world of engineers, on ''the natural objectivity of things'' (ibid., p. 152). In this scheme of things, an ethic is ''conceived of as a system of functional rules which ensure harmonious relations between two types of beings, the individual and society'' (ibid., p. 153). The notion of utility is related to work, the production of material goods, and the satisfaction of needs. The foremost political capacity of this city resides in the ability to administrate (as exemplified in the thought of Saint-Simon).

The denomination of city is appropriate for these approaches to social reality because a city is the institution which organizes the history of human beings. Each of the cities presented above constitutes a system of reference for ethical and political justifications. They are not necessarily compatible with one another, however. Indeed, one city may contradict another: what is right in one city may not necessarily be right in another. These moral systems and these cities are institutions which are created by human beings, for human beings, over the course of human history. It is possible to compare these moral orders, which can be viewed as being constructed, with scientific disciplines, which can also be considered as constructions of the world that are produced by humans, for humans.

These cities also provide a locus in which to conduct trials (within moral debate as within experimental science) of justifications which are put forward for action. In such trials, everyone will be forced to become involved.[4]

Each city comes bearing its own world

The trial which is set in motion in the process of justification ''cannot be reduced to a debate of ideas. The justificatory trial involves people – bodily – in a world of things serving as supports; indeed, in the absence of this world, there would be no basis for subjecting a dispute to a trial'' (ibid., p. 166). It is in this way that each city calls forth its own world into existence:

> That which enjoys existence within the purview of one city will be unknown within another: the world of inspiration comprehends demons and monsters for example, whereas the domestic world comprises household pets, which are unknown in the civic world, as are children, the elderly, etc. Objects,

which in one order of nature, constitute instruments serving to set off the greatness of individuals are given no consideration in another world. (ibid., p. 166)[5]

In ambiguous or obscure situations, people rely on the typical objects of the world in which they are located – for example, a testimonial for a loyal servant in the domestic world, a rigorous expert evaluation in the industrial world, a national assembly in the civic world, the tribute paid to an inventor in the world of opinion, and so forth (ibid., p. 173).

Each world is structured around a common higher principle which makes possible: a kind of equivalence between individuals; a definition of states of greatness; a notion of the dignity of persons; a repertory of the subjects, objects, and apparatuses relevant for a given city; a formula of adherence and commitment; a relationship to greatness; a set of relations which are said to be natural between individuals (obviously varying from city to city); a harmonious figure of the natural order; a typical testing procedure; a mode for the expression of judgment; a form for evidence or proof; a sense of both the normal and the moral; and a state of pettiness or abjectness in the city (ibid., pp. 177–81).

In a parallel with the world of laboratories in experimental science,[6] these worlds are the subject of presentation, use, and mobilization in our society. Boltanski and Thévenot have shown how this is so by means of their analyses of a number of contemporary publications, which were used as guides to these various worlds. For the world of inspiration, they took a textbook for businesses that was written by a counselor in creativity. In this work, the author draws a clear distinction between creative situations and those constructed in accordance with other worlds (by opposing, notably, creativity with school routines, which, according to Boltanski and Thévenot, fall within the scope of the industrial world). Given the genre of his work and its intended audience, the author is nevertheless forced to make a number of ''compromises'' with this selfsame world of industry.

Each of these worlds is quite specific and takes shape with its own cast of characters, objects, actions, and supporting frameworks. What is an individual to make of good manners, etiquette, rank, title, residence, introductions, signatures, formal announcements, gifts, and flowers in the industrial world, to take but this example? Instead, we are confronted with performance, the future, the functional, the reliable, breakdowns, energy, experts, specialists, superintendents, operators, tools, graphs, lists, plans, standards, mastery, cogs, commands, optimization, instrumental action upon things and people, realizations, and so forth (ibid., pp. 200–62).

The conflict of worlds; compromises; and challenges to trials

Just as, practically speaking, no set of concrete phenomena can be explained entirely within the framework of a single scientific discipline, so also "in a differentiated society, each person must, on a daily basis, deal with situations belonging to various distinct worlds" (ibid., p. 266). Choices cannot be justified in terms of the coherence of one city or world alone.[7] Whenever persons and things which belong to different worlds are brought together in the setting of a justificatory trial, different figures of criticism come to the fore.[8] A universe in which several different worlds meet "offers actors the possibility of escaping one form of trial and of falling back on some outside principle in view of contesting the trial's validity or even of reversing the situation by pursuing a valid trial in another world" (ibid., p. 267). Such a process may come to the fore when, for example, an employee on the verge of being laid off shows his employer the family photo sitting on his desktop. The possibility then arises of contesting the very principle of a trial and of invoking another world so as to turn the tables (ibid., p. 269). The model put forward by Boltanski and Thévenot "thereby allows for the possibility for criticism, which deterministic constructions are unable to account for" (ibid., p. 267). It is in this way that one world stands in criticism of or denounces another: Thus, "a person who is brimming with energy and ideas in the world of inspiration will be muddleheaded in the domestic world" (ibid., p. 289).

It is in this context that the notion of equity takes on meaning: "A judgment is deemed equitable whenever it takes into account the existence of worlds which are external to the nature of the trial" (ibid., p. 285). Criticism and equity presuppose a goal – that is, a common good reaching beyond specific worlds.[9]

The multiplicity of worlds entails compromises in which "the actors agree to parley, that is, to suspend the disagreement, without settling the dispute by recourse to a trial in one world only" (ibid., p. 338). (This process can be compared to interdisciplinary work.)

> The parties to a compromise renounce clarifying the principle of their agreement, concentrating only on maintaining a disposition that is oriented toward

the common good. . . . Compromise holds out the possibility of a principle which is capable of making judgments compatible that are otherwise founded on objects belonging to different worlds. It aims at a common good which goes beyond the two opposed forms of greatness by encompassing them both. For example, promoting "techniques of creativity" presupposes reference to an unspecified principle which would place industrial routine and the tapping of inspirational resources at the service of the same common good. (ibid., p. 338)

Compromises, as with the results of most interdisciplinary research, are essentially fragile. However, they too may solidify – that is, become socially stabilized and entrenched (as in the case of some scientific concepts and interdisciplinary approaches – e.g., biochemistry or geography).[10] "Whenever a compromise becomes entrenched, the objects or persons whom it has brought together become difficult to separate from one another" (ibid., p. 340), as in the case, for example, of "workers' rights," a notion falling within the confines of both the civic and industrial worlds. And in the same way that a well-stabilized interdisciplinary approach becomes a quasi discipline (Fourez, Englebert-Lecomte, and Mathy, 1997) possessing its own criteria (such as is the case with molecular biology), "a solidly entrenched compromise will evidence a form of trial which occasionally presents similarities with disputes occurring in a single world" (ibid., p. 340). Such is the case with "the rights of labor" since, as was stated by Saint-Simon, "economic interests form the unique substance of common existence, hence they must be organized on a social basis" involving a kind of civic-industrial society. In all likelihood, that is how new cities come into being.[11]

Overlapping a number of worlds, figures of compromise indeed abound: the initiatory relation between master and disciple (inspirational-domestic); the act of protest (inspirational-civic); the passion for rigorously executed work (inspirational-industrial); inalienable property (commercial-domestic); the efficiency of good habits (industrial-domestic); the surveying of opinion (industrial-opinion); the effectiveness of public service (civic-industrial); methods of doing business (industrial-commercial); and so on (ibid., pp. 356–407).

Surpassing justification: from relativization to pardon

Justification, a basis of rational dialogue and human communication, could eventually become locked within a most confining universe. In addition, attempts at stabilizing compromises often produce the opposite effect, creating discord, since exploring the bases of the agreement "causes compromise to be seen as a simple assemblage having no foundation – which amounts, in other words, to denouncing it" (ibid., p. 408). It is at this point that forms of agreement and social coexistence that surpass justification come into play.

Compromise has been characterized by the objective of a common good. There are other types of agreement, however, which do not satisfy this clause. They refer instead to a reciprocal arrangement: "You do that, and that suits me; I do that, and that suits you." Boltanski and Thévenot term these private agreements "arrangements," in the sense that they cannot be justified in relationship to a city (ibid., p. 408).

Arrangements are not the only means by which to extricate oneself from disagreements without becoming totally involved in the process of justification. It is also possible to "agree that nothing matters" (ibid., p. 412). This type of relativization may represent a response to the fear of undergoing the trial, "but may also be a means by which to quietly break a path toward another world by avoiding disagreements" (ibid., p. 422). "Relativization presupposes the active connivance of people in bringing contingency to the fore and focusing on it so as to avoid any generalization that might risk bringing back the tension occurring between incompatible principles" (ibid., p. 413). Relativization thus creates an unstable situation, and that is why "it is often a figure occurring in the interim between trials of different kinds" (ibid., p. 413).

Relativization is not relativism, even if the former can lead to the latter. Relativism is a situation in which, "by bracketing off the constraints of the city, actors adopt a position of exteriority on the basis of which the din and toil of earthly existence may be subordinated to a general equivalent that is not the common good" (ibid., p. 414).[12] "Relativism is thus distinct from relativization in its claim to denouncing the common good from a general point of view. . . . It takes hold of the essential consideration in a given situation in order to undercut the common good, yet does so without deriving its basis from some alternative principle" (ibid., p. 414). Relativism denounces but does not elaborate the position from which denunciation is proffered; it assails the very possibility that a common good may exist, to the point of contesting the reality of any form of sacrifice and at the price of lapsing into a radical, self-destructive nihilism (ibid., pp. 415–16).

Relativism "may attempt to develop an alliance with science" (ibid., p. 417), when the latter, in its positivist version, claims to free itself of values. This option cannot, however, represent the totality of the scientific enterprise, since in order for the latter to prove its validity, it must grapple with reality, make predictions, and be subordinated to some determination serving to specify its project. Thus, the tendency of technocracy is to indicate constraints which are treated "as a determination which acts upon individuals but which, however, remains indifferent to any role that the will of actors might play" (ibid., p. 417). The constraint of justification is thus externalized and deemed an "illusion or a deception, as is demonstrated for example by the most common uses of the term 'ideology' " (ibid., p. 418). Thus, technocracy tends to leave less and less room "for the justifications that people give of their actions" (ibid., p. 420). It credits people with the capacity of losing their illusions with respect to their justifications and of developing awareness of a reality which science has supposedly revealed to them (ibid., p. 420).

In opposition to this, the constructivist model of Boltanski and Thévenot, with its focus on situations of trial and negotiation, makes it possible to "register new phenomena" which do not fit within the frameworks of technocrats and to "describe operations of justification, denunciation and compromise, while managing to avoid oscillating between an attitude of disillusioned relativism and grandstanding accusation" (ibid., p. 421).

The starting and ending points of the justificatory dispute

The preceding analysis has focused on the moments when the ethical or political debate becomes intense, that is, in situations of dispute or trial. But how does this debate get set in motion, either between individuals or in personal reflection? It is not possible to reflect on this question without examining the interconnections of affectivity and forms of rationality. Obviously, mention should be made here of experiences of failure, of foul-ups and suffering, all of which reveal an expectation which has gone unsatisfied and a need to identify the persons or objects who can be counted on to meet it. When a snag or foul-up is not corrected rapidly, "one may attempt to circumscribe it by forcing the course of action back on track, without examining the circumstances" (ibid., p. 428). This is what occurs during fits of rage and invective in response to some emotion, thus bringing out the difficulty of returning to reflection. At that point, the only way to avoid violence is to become involved in forming a shared or common judgment. However, this operation can only be had at a price: the reduction of divergent interpretations within a common framework (and it is the fear of this cost which makes such rage understandable). "The crisis is thus a paradoxical moment in which, in contrast with the moment of action, the question of the agreement on reality occupies all minds," but in which, "in the absence of such an agreement, a sense of reality is lacking." It is at this point that debate is opened, with its "rhetorical exigencies" and the demands that are entailed by the "scientific search for truth" (ibid., p. 430). "The dynamic of the process – with its criticisms, its trial mechanisms and the repeated impetus that it imparts to the inquiry – delineates situations and contributes to the objectivity of beings (persons and things) which have been invoked as proofs" (ibid., p. 431). The image and the model of the city is what makes it possible to analyze this process by means of reconciling two requirements: (1) the order necessary to performing an action in conjunction with others; and (2) the common humanity of the actors involved in the moral debate. This dual requirement is constructed in accordance with the objective of a common good.

Debate may undergo closure and stabilize – and must do so in order not to become pathological – around an accepted judgment (the ethical equivalent of scientific results). But this judgment may always be brought forward for debate whenever a party claims that the justification has unduly reduced the complexity of the situation. Hence, the judgment which is delivered has a "conventional character to it, in the sense that everyone knows that the accounts or descriptions can neither sum up past action in its totality nor encompass all of the potentialities contained in actions yet to come" (ibid., p. 433). The force of law will follow upon the judgment.

There is an alternative to the judgment, and that is "pardon" (ibid., p. 434). In this option, actors give up the evaluative process and "devote themselves to a process which focuses solely on the persons involved and which foregoes the placing in perspective and totalization of past actions" (ibid., p. 434). With its focus on unique individuals, pardon does not admit of generalization. "Thus, action recommences after pardon, although the consequences of the crisis have not been brought out and although the lessons to be drawn from the inquiry, or the judgment (as the case may be), have not been made use of" (ibid., pp. 434–5).

Another way of leaving room for the human dimension of the relationships involved in the quest for a common good consists in not treating every action as a trial, as is expressed in the notion of ''tolerance.'' It is tolerance which, ''by putting off the moment of trial, sets aside the will to knowledge, which pushes for inquiries and brings judgment to bear'' (ibid., p. 435). ''Tolerance makes it possible to understand the position of actors who bear the weight of being right in isolation, without bringing it out into the open by a remark or an excuse'' (ibid., p. 435). In addition, it accredits people's demands that situations not be reduced to categories of analysis and legitimates their desire to keep their options for action open. Thus, ''a pragmatics of reflection ought to account for the passage between, on the one hand, moments of involvement in action and slackening of reflection, which are manifested in tolerance or localized accommodation and, ultimately, the forgetting[13] entailed by pardon, and, on the other hand, moments in which action is thrown into question (as occur in the crisis) and reality is fixed by means of the inquiry'' (ibid., p. 434).

Constructivism in science and ethics

By way of concluding this foray into a constructivist perspective on justification and ethics, it is fair to claim that it is increasingly difficult to consider constructivist approaches in science and ethics in isolation from one another: ''Crisis and judgment are moments during which actors make public, and verbally deploy, their action. It is during such moments that they attempt to use language to generalize and to piece together facts, and do so in a way which offers parallels with the approach taken by science'' (ibid., p. 436). In both types of practice, ''actors inquire into reality and put what is found to obtain to the test, and are thus able to discard contingent phenomena in favor of that which holds in general and, as a result, bring out the relationships which link the local to the global. By taking an objective distance toward action and by pursuing the objective of truth, they will bring descriptive languages into play'' (ibid., p. 436).

That is why a constructivist approach to science teaching must consider the connections to be made with a constructivist approach to ethics. Therein lies, moreover, a theoretical basis for the perspectives which may be grouped under the heading of ''Science, Technologies, and Societies.'' In keeping with the orientations presented above, such a foundation would show: (1) how it is impossible to construct the sciences without having some awareness of the way in which they constitute a mediation in the social construction of a certain common good; and (2) how, whenever the goal is to construct a human city, the quest for such a common good is contingent upon agreement over the objectivity of a given world.

The perspective which has been outlined above also provides a conceptual framework by which to approach the teaching of ethics wherein the socially constructed character of ethics is delineated more clearly. Such a framework would also avoid the twin pitfalls of an overly psychologistic relativism and a dogmatism which fails to take into account the historical and social components of ethical discourse.

Chapter 10
Social studies, trivial constructivism, and the politics of social knowledge

STEPHEN C. FLEURY

In most departments of psychology and schools of education, teaching continues as though nothing had happened and the question for immutable objective truths were as promising as ever.

von Glasersfeld, 1989, p. 122

The growing popularity in mathematics and science education of the body of ideas known as constructivism is a hopeful sign of renewed interest in educational theory and practice in the United States. This is especially fortunate for social studies education, which has been bereft of significant developments in these areas in recent years. Recent research programs of social studies educators are showing promise, but the nearly exclusive attention on the development of historical understanding fails to address the need for a broader and more comprehensive social knowledge (Ashby, Lee, and Dickinson, 1997; Barton, 1997; Barton and Levstik, 1996; Brophy, VanSledright, and Bredin, 1992; Seixas, 1997, 1994; Thornton, 1997). May (1992) observes that no one has proposed the ''radical restructuring'' of social studies for studying the social, scientific, and technological issues that riddle the contemporary world; she asserts that a postmodern approach is needed to ''promote an ecological, moral, cultural, pluralistic, and spiritual perspective, an 'ethic of caring' and a critical pragmatism''; and laments that social studies educators have instead ''been guilty of rationalizing and simplifying the most intriguing and complex human endeavors and problems'' (p. 81).

Constructivism is a postmodern theory of knowledge with the potential to transform educational theory. Its present popularity in science and mathematics education, however, is no assurance of its enduring influence on education in general or social studies in particular. One need only recall how Piaget's work has been previously misunderstood and effectively misused to bolster narrow curricular ends (Egan, 1983). Constructivism could meet a similar fate in our contemporary educational and political climate. The historical tendency of educational psychology in the United States to decontextualize educational theories of their cultural and political basis could trivialize the profoundness of a constructivist theory of knowledge, especially for social studies education. This thesis is further strengthened by the significant and mutually supportive roles played by science and social studies education in supporting a positivist theory of objective realism as the basis of social knowledge. The significance of this analysis lies in the potential that constructivism has for revitalizing education for a democracy. The failure of social studies educators to seize this opportunity would be unfortunate.

Constructivism

Constructivism is a range of ideas about the production of knowledge and its construction by groups and individuals (Driver, Asoko, Leach, Mortimer, and Scott, 1994). Its relatively recent appearance in educational literature is an outgrowth of developments among linguists, cognitive theorists, and philosophers of science. Cobern (1993) traces the present impetus for constructivism, in part, to the cognitive research of Novak (1977) and Driver and Easley (1978), Berger and Luckmann's work in the sociology of knowledge (1967), von Glasersfeld in cybernetics, as well as others in anthropology, cultural studies, and social interactionism. Von Glasersfeld (1989) explains that "a different view of knowledge has emerged" as an alternative to the traditional epistemological paradigm which was reported by Kuhn (1970) as being seriously "askew" (p. 121). He credits this different view to ideas contained in Giambattista Vico's epistemological treatise of 1710. Written in Latin and remaining virtually unknown for two hundred years, Vico's treatise, according to von Glasersfeld, foreshadowed many of the ideas of cognitive construction later elaborated by Baldwin and Piaget in the twentieth century. It may surprise many contemporary educators that Piaget was working with far more sophisticated ideas than simple stage theories.

Two philosophical principles characterize constructivism. Both are important. The first is that knowledge is actively built by a cognizing subject. This idea has become common currency in education and is highly espoused by educators in the field of child development and curriculum theory in support of the popular concepts of assimilation, accommodation, equilibrium, and developmental stages. Piaget spoke of developmental stages in reference to intellectual operations that could be used by an epistemic subject in order to construct knowledge (Piaget, 1950, 1961, 1970, 1971, 1972, 1983). The educational tendency in the United States has been to reify these theoretical descriptive constructs as "learning stages," inappropriately rendering them as prescriptions for curriculum development and instruction (Egan, 1983). Many theoretical issues remain problematic about these constructs (Hendry and King, 1994), but it is probably safe to say that the concepts of assimilation, accommodation, equilibrium, and learning stages are as much a part of teacher preparation as are behavioral objectives and unit plans.

An important point to make is that the construction of knowledge has traditionally been viewed among mainstream educators as an individual's personal action, with little consideration given to the influence of social context and environment on cognition. The idea of social constructivism is becoming more commonly accepted in the United States, in part with a broader familiarity of the Russian theorist Lev Vygotsky (1978, 1962) and Jerome Bruner's (1996) increasing attention to the cultural basis of learning.

A second foundational principle of constructivism has largely been ignored by most American followers of the Piagetian tradition, namely, that the function of cognition is to organize one's experiential world, not to discover an ontological reality. Curricular interpreters have made little of this epistemological challenge of Piaget's constructivism, and especially of the fact that Piaget was primarily concerned with developing a theory of knowledge by examining the process of knowledge development, and was not concerned with prescribing an educational theory.

Contemporary attention to this epistemological implication of Piaget's (and Vico's) thoughts comprises the substance of "radical" constructivism, a label von Glasersfeld (1984) applies to differentiate it from discussions of constructivism that omit an epistemological challenge to Western philosophical thinking. Von Glasersfeld (1989) emphasizes that it is "the *construction* [emphasis his] of the individual's *subjective reality* [emphasis mine] which . . . should be of interest to practitioners and researchers in education and, in particular, to the teachers of science" (p. 122).

Two questions loom and, subsequently, a third. Why has this important characteristic of constructivist thought been virtually ignored until recent conversations in mathematics and science education? Why should teachers of science "in particular" be interested, any more than teachers of any other subject matter? What might be the implications of constructivism for social studies knowledge?

A challenge ignored?

The philosophical importance of Piaget's constructivism may have been overlooked because many of his original works were not translated into English. Or, perhaps many educators are familiar with Piaget through secondary rather than primary sources. In any case, it is abundantly clear now for scholars with access to the full range of Piaget's work that he understood knowledge is constructed by individuals within a social context. An exemplification of this point is taken from *Psychogenesis and the History of Science* (1989):

> [Action] does not take place only as a result of internal impulses (except for the first part of the sensorimotor period). It is not generated exclusively in centrifugal fashion. Rather, in the experience of the child, the situations she encounters are generated by her social environment, and the objects appear within contexts which give them their specific significance. The child does not assimilate "pure" objects defined by their physical parameters only. She assimilates the situations in which objects play a specific role. When the system of communication between the child and her social world becomes more complex and enriched, and particularly when language becomes the dominating means of communication, then what we might call direct experience of objects comes to be subordinated, in certain situations, to the system of interpretations attributed to it by the social environment. The problem for genetic epistemology here is how to explain in what way assimilation remains, in such cases, conditioned by a particular social system of meanings, and to what extent the interpretation of each particular experience depends on such meanings. (Piaget and Garcia, 1989, p. 247)

This passage shows that Piaget was critically aware of properly using the concept of "epistemic subject" when explaining how the child constructs knowledge in context. He refers to this concept, which constitutes the "natural" way to conceive of knowledge at a certain historical time for an individual in society, stating that it is transmitted like language from generation to generation, and functions like an ideology.

When asking himself how the concepts or beliefs of a social group act upon the cognitive development of an individual, Piaget says:

As we noted above, any adult subject has already an elaborate arsenal of cognitive instruments enabling her to assimilate – and hence to interpret – the data she receives from the surrounding objects, as well as to assimilate the information transmitted to her by her society. This latter information refers to the objects and the situations already interpreted by the society in question. Following adolescence, when the fundamental logical structures that will constitute the basic instruments for her future cognitive development have been fully developed, the subject has at her disposal, in addition to these instruments, a conception of the world (*Weltanschauung*) which determines her future assimilation of any experience. (ibid., p. 252)

This does not seem to be the Piaget taught in most schools of education.

There is another more profoundly serious aspect to why the full philosophical importance of constructivist thinking has lacked a significant impact on educational theory and practice. Both radical and social constructivism deny the existence of an objectivist, ontological reality whose essence can be disclosed by a "correspondence theory of truth." This metaphysical and epistemological denial effectively opposes the basis of knowledge for science and social studies education, as well as the knowledge which helps structure the organization of schooling itself. If constructivism becomes widely accepted among educators, it will implicitly threaten the ability of education to uphold stable views of reality, views that are condoned by, and instrumental for maintaining, the dominant culture.

The constructs which organize modern schooling and its content depend on a general acceptance that they, in fact, describe an objective world as it exists. For example, "grade levels" are taken to represent natural, conceptual developmental levels of students; "adolescence" is considered a natural, distinctive, and genetic growth phenomenon (rather than a socially defined construct of modern industrialized cultures); and labels such as "at risk" and "learning disabled" are believed to represent a student's inherent limitations. Constructivism would, by accepting the potential viability of alternative views, alter the dynamics of cultural politics enacted through the educational system.

Von Glasersfeld (1989) explains how the sacrosanct notion of "truth" changes with constructivist thinking: "[The] word *knowledge* refers to a commodity that is radically different from the objective representation of an observer-independent world. . . . Instead, knowledge refers to conceptual structures that epistemic agents, given the range of present experience within their tradition of thought and language, consider viable''(p. 124).

Replacing ''truth'' with ''viability'' pits constructivism against the objectivist philosophical position that undergirds most school practices and theories. In education literature, the prevailing theory of knowledge is usually referred to as positivism, and while there is no ''unified conception,'' Stanley and Brickhouse (1994) describe ''key positivist assumptions [that] have been targets of criticism'':

> Among these are: (1) a naive realist ontology that assumes the existence of a single tangible reality that can be broken into segments to be studied independently; (2) a correspondence theory of truth in which ''truth'' is defined as knowledge that matches reality; (3) a universal conception of scientific language and method; (4) a verificationist method of justification; (5) the assumption that theory and observation (as well as the observer and the observed) could be kept separate; (6) the assumption of value-free method and the separation of facts and meanings; and (7) the temporal and contextual independence of observation. (p. 390)

Each of these assumptions has been questioned, modified, critiqued, or rejected by philosophers of science over the past century. Positivist tenets remain a dominant influence in Western industrialized culture, however, especially in the organization and teaching of knowledge.

Science education provides an example of the influence of positivism on school practices. Duschl (1988) argues that the factually oriented, textbook-driven classroom climate of most science classes is related to the prevailing positivist views of teachers. Authoritarian pedagogical practices provide few opportunities for student inquiry. Even in laboratory classes, students usually experience the ''discovery'' of predetermined knowledge by using a linear and highly simplistic verification methodology. These teaching practices convey to students that research methods are objective and that proof is thereby obtained. The scientific method is ''a myth of what never really existed'' (Hurd, 1994, p. 110), yet becomes an authoritative epistemological tool in science education by being embedded in science textbooks and established early in science courses as leading inevitably to a conclusion (Moyer and Bishop, 1986; Stake and Easley, 1978). Through such instruction, a series of logical problems are created from a theory of knowledge perspective. Faulty reasoning is fostered by teaching the logic of scientific confirmation, itself a logical fallacy (Popper, 1968). ''Confirmation bias'' is systematically condoned in classrooms by considering selected evidence and ignoring disconfirming evidence. Most often, we fail to involve students in testing for results. It is relatively easy to see how the practices and methods of traditional science education both promote and depend upon positivist assumptions about knowledge. The emphasis on using an authoritative scientific method to gather what appears to be neutral, objective, and noncontroversial truths about the world is consistent with the positivist assumptions identified above.

Each semester I query my college students on their perceptions of the nature of knowledge of school subjects. They clearly associate science with objective and factual information (real) and social studies with opinions and personal values (subjective). They believe these subjects involve two different realms of knowing, oblivious to the underlying positivist premises that unify these school subjects around the goal of citizenship. The perceived separation, of course, is provided by historical, personal, political, and arbitrary curricular practices (Grossman and Stodolsky, 1995). Popkewitz (1991) assists in constructing this argument: "The significance of modern pedagogy is its tie to problems of social regulation; pedagogy links the administrative concerns of the state with the self-governance of the subject. The forms of knowledge in schooling frame and classify the world and the nature of work, which, in turn, have the potential to organize and shape individual identity" (p. 14).

A certain form of citizenship education results from the way students construct social knowledge through the school subjects of science and social studies. School science teaches students a "scientific method" for discovering and testing facts, but discussions of the diverse human values and assumptions involved are neither encouraged nor valued. In an inverse fashion, social studies instruction usually allows for the discussion of opinions and values, but does not offer students an epistemological means for resolving disagreements or contradictory conclusions about different views of reality. In the complementary way that these two school subjects "frame and classify the world" to maintain a false fact/value dichotomy, students are prevented from relating issues of social knowledge to issues of social power.

History may truly be a "primitive epistemology" (Cornbleth and Waugh, 1995). The failure to provide students with a means for testing their views and beliefs about personal and social realities may account for much of the student disdain for social studies. The assumption that an objective historical reality once existed implies to students that truths in social studies can only be known after one sees how things eventually turn out. In this manner, an *ontology* of history becomes the de facto *epistemology* of social studies knowledge, with a concomitant sense of inevitability.

In the history of the field of social studies, many social studies educators (Lawrence Metcalf, Alan Griffin, Shirley Engle, Edger B. Wesley, James Shaver, to mention but a few) have condemned the tenacious hold of a traditional version of history on the curriculum. Its patriotic values, glorified images, and sanitized conceptions of the world are passed generationally through the content and teaching of social studies. In 1979, Shaver found that most social studies teachers believe their main role is to socialize students into the status quo of society, a role that ten years later, Leming (1989) argued is the most credible one for social studies education. Leaders in this field continue to advocate and promote a critical orientation to the study of history and society, but educational and governmental leaders at local, state, and national levels have successfully reasserted the use of a traditional history curriculum (Cornbleth and Waugh, 1995).

Many historical approaches could promote a more critically oriented social studies – that is, intellectual history, cultural history, social history, a Black Studies perspective, and Feminist studies, but these approaches potentially conflict with the political socializing function of the public school curriculum. Originally a subject of social philosophy, history has struggled to evolve from a literary endeavor to an increasingly scientifically oriented subject in the late nineteenth and early twentieth centuries (Handlin, 1979; Reichenbach, 1951). While history has not been as successful as other social science disciplines in adopting and applying empirical methodologies for studying the social world (Ross, 1991), its moralizing message has nevertheless remained important within the mission orientation involved in the formation of public education (Popkewitz, 1991).

In *Contradictions of Control* (1986), McNeil poignantly illustrates how a defensive use of history in the social studies curriculum brings about a form of social control. The chronological structuring of history allows social studies teachers to employ particular models of social knowledge for establishing both content and classroom order. For example, teachers omit knowledge that is potentially controversial, a move to prevent conceptual disruption in the classroom. Providing students with lists and outlines about important subjects is a way to fragment and simplify the social world, effectively objectifying reality and concealing complex social relationships. And, according to

McNeil, students are often informed by teachers that certain topics are very important to know about, but the content too difficult for them to master. This action of mystifying knowledge places the teacher in a controlling role as "expert" who relates only what students "need" to know.

McNeil's analysis shows that like science education, social studies practices reinforce objectivist and positivist assumptions about the nature of knowledge: The teacher's expertise is premised on his or her having a fuller picture of reality; lists and outlines of subject matter knowledge represent aggregate pictures of an objective world; and facts and values are treated separately by avoiding attention to inherent contradictions, assumptions, implications, and relationships. A form of "confirmation bias" is at work, whereby only selected and supportive information is examined. And a fact/value dichotomy exists, separating the physical from the social world. With students deprived of opportunities to examine complex social dynamics and explore the uses and limitations of social knowledge, social studies become a form of disempowerment of their abilities to reason, judge, and act on their social world.

Context of educational reforms

Science educators are responding to the profound effects of the changing understanding of the nature of science on science teaching. Education literature is alive with theoretical and practical developments on conceptual change theory and constructivist teaching approaches. Since 1989, three international conferences of philosophers, educators, and scientists have been held to discuss the history and philosophy of science in science teaching. However, one might question the likely success of a radical reform such as constructivism in an isolated subject area without an equally enthusiastic reconsideration of the beliefs involved in all of schooling.

The fundamental philosophical changes entailed in constructivist thinking require an intellectually receptive environment. Skepticism abounds over whether the present reform environment in the United States can be accurately described as "intellectually receptive" (Berliner and Biddle, 1995; Bracey, 1996; Cornbleth and Waugh, 1995; Good, 1996; Smylie, 1996).

The organizational techniques and practices of public schooling are based on a legacy of industrial organization and management principles, principles reflecting the influence of logical positivism on social knowledge in the late nineteenth and early twentieth centuries (Apple, 1990; Kliebard, 1987; Popkewitz, 1991). By all appearances, recent educational reforms simply reinforce these practices and principles, providing reason for reform critics to question whether school administration and teacher preparation programs are able to reconsider assumptions about knowing and schooling. In *The Moral and Spiritual Crisis in Education* (1989), Purpel writes:

> The recent flurry of educational reports do not, for example, reflect or propose anything approaching a fundamental reconceptualization of the schooling process much less anything in the way of serious social/cultural critique. Instead they suggest relatively minor reforms directed at amelioration rather than transformation. It is indeed ironic that these reports are highly critical of the intellectual excellence of schools and yet themselves offer relatively superficial responses to the roots of the problem they identify. (p. 3)

Amid the educational reform phenomena occurring in the United States within the past fifteen years, ''constructivism'' is anomalous because of its seeming emphasis on student-centered learning and especially because of its challenge to the epistemological foundations of our prevailing social knowledge. Since the governmental release of *A Nation at Risk* in 1983 by the President's Commission on Education, subsequent reform proposals and legislation have presumed that inquiries into matters of learning – either about its processes or the substance of what should be learned – divert scarce human and material resources from the needed efforts to hold students and teachers accountable for teaching and learning standards. Political muscle has transformed national educational priorities from a culture of knowledge creation to one of standardized knowledge. For example, financial support for basic research and educational innovations was diminished and diverted toward the creation of a federal office for monitoring and publishing educational statistics for comparison purposes (Clark and Astuto, 1986). Questions of who should decide learning and teaching standards have been overridden by the din of warnings from those who cry that an impending national, even worldwide, disaster will result if the United States continues to lag behind other industrialized nations in terms of mathematics and science test scores, the hours and days its citizens spend in schools, production of industrialized goods, and measures of worker efficiency.

With the publication of *What Works: Research about Teaching and Learning* (1987), the U.S. Department of Education condescendingly reported research findings that coincided with common sense; *whose* common sense to use as a measure was ill-defined. Best-selling books, such as *What Do Our Seventeen-Year-Olds Know?* (1987) by Ravitch and Finn and *Cultural Literacy: What Every American Needs to Know* (1987) by Hirsch, complemented the cooperation of government officials and academicians in relating the educational crisis to a fundamental deterioration of core Western values. America's educational problems became defined as caused by a half century of overindulgence in progressive educational ideas (such as inquiry methodologies and conceptual learning) and not enough attention to what President Reagan's Secretary of Education William C. Bennett labeled the "Three Cs: Choice, Content, and Character." With a convergence of both political parties, an association of state governors, and the largest teachers union in support of the federal educational policy known as *Goals 2000*, later to become *America 2000*, the transformation of educational activities from epistemological interests ("what are the best ways to learn?") to essentially ontological concerns ("how to ensure learning of established views of the world?") was complete (Good, 1996; Smylie, 1996).

As part of the larger reform efforts in education, social studies reforms have been particularly effective in quietly redefining social studies to mean the teaching of history (Fleury, 1989). A group of conservative scholars and educators, forming themselves as the Educational Excellence Network and positioning themselves in key organizational roles, have been influential on curriculum policy making at state and national levels. Calling for a reassertion of history as the core of social studies, outspoken leaders such as Diane Ravitch and Chester Finn have favored a canon of Western knowledge (Cornbleth and Waugh, 1995). The pressure exerted through political lobbying and academic writing has had a powerful effect on how the field of social studies is perceived by social studies teachers. Although social studies theoreticians in higher education resist an explicit canon of Western historical knowledge as the core of social studies, they have contributed to a considerable increase in research and writing on the topic of history and historical understanding as a basis for social studies. The era of the New Social Studies, which began in the 1960s with an emphasis on the social sciences as *a way of studying* social behavior, has been widely abandoned in a rush to enforce historical standards.

One result of the contemporary marginalization of the social sciences as *a way of knowing* is that mainstream social studies represents a truncated version of social knowledge. By neglecting to focus students' attention on how we know in multiple forms, intricate relationships are concealed between issues of knowledge and issues of social, political, and economic power. Questions concerning "who gets what kind of knowledge?" and "how do they end up with it?" are rarely, if ever, connected to questions of "how are social institutions and practices preserved or changed?" One effect of preventing students from actively constructing social studies knowledge is the perpetuation of what Parenti (1991) has called a "social orthodoxy." Students spend many school hours superficially "covering" events in America's past but gain few disciplinary links for understanding their present situation in society. This is overwhelmingly apparent in social studies textbooks which are the primary instructional tools of history instruction (Loewen, 1995):

> Textbooks seldom use the past to illuminate the present. They portray the past as a simpleminded morality play. "Be a good citizen" is the message that textbooks extract from the past. "You have a proud heritage. Be all that you can be. After all, look at what the United States has accomplished." While there is nothing wrong with optimism, it can become something of a burden for students of color, children of working-class parents, girls who notice the dearth of female historical figures, or members of any group that has not achieved socioeconomic success. (p. 3)

Traditional social studies are valuable for the political socialization of students because of the disciplinary moralizing (values) purposes of history. In a complementary fashion, school science contributes to the political socialization function of schooling through its disciplinary factual orientation.

Science and cultural politics

Mathematics and science are considered high-status knowledge in our industrially oriented society because of their technical uses. This status is evident in a number of examples in education: the federal support of these subjects in the aftermath of Sputnik, the public attention given to international comparisons of student achievement in mathematics and science, and the level of public and private grants for technical projects in institutions of higher learning. The value of this technical knowledge, however, depends on its scarcity as well as its utility. Apple (1990) argues that the processing of scientific knowledge through schools creates and maintains its scarcity. His argument is drawn upon the work of Bourdieu and Passeron (1977), Young (1971), and Bernstein (1977) among other sociologists of knowledge to show that the transmission of culture through schooling is instrumental in determining who gets what kind of knowledge in society.

Schools assume the *habitus* (i.e., cultural rules) of the middle class as natural. This assumption of normality in education effectively filters in favor of middle-class children. These students have more "cultural capital" in the form of linguistic and other social advantages. By "taking as natural what is essentially a social gift" (p. 33), school knowledge implicitly screens for social class. The cultural filtering of schools allows some students to "naturally" achieve and not others, depending on their possession of cultural capital. Here the relationship between cultural and economic capital is important.

Efficiency, in a capitalist economic system, is based on an organization's ability to maximize profit. Organizations function at their greatest efficiency when society's unemployment rate is around four to six percent. The cost of full employment in a society would erase the profits normally accrued by businesses. In other words, the value placed on economic efficiency and the value placed on the distribution of work opportunities clash. When it comes to an economic decision about employing all workers or maximizing profits, the choice for efficiency is obvious.

Consider a similar model for viewing scientific knowledge as a cultural commodity. A certain production level of scientific and mathematical knowledge is needed to keep the economic system operating efficiently. Our educational system ensures that a sufficient amount of scientific and mathematical knowledge is generated, but it also assists in its regulation by preventing too many students from acquiring it. Widespread distribution of scientific and mathematical knowledge would render it far less valuable as a commodity. As long as schools produce enough technical knowledge to keep our industrial engines running, our economic system can thrive on lower levels of mathematics and science achievement among students from the lower classes, as well as among women and minority students. Apple (1990) states: "Like poverty, poor achievement is *not* an aberration. Both poverty and curricular problems such as low achievement are integral products of the organization of economic, cultural and social life as we know it" (p. 33).

Apple's analysis provides an important link for understanding how science education contributes to the school's role in maintaining social and economic inequalities. The application of certain teaching methods, the assertion of subject knowledge standards, and the use of certain types of testing excludes and allocates who learns scientific knowledge. The organizational and conceptual principles responsible for these school practices are premised on a sense of objectivist realism that undergirds most modern institutions. One can foresee the resistance likely to besiege a radical social constructivism as a movement in education. The social roots constructivism will pull up are philosophical, economic, cultural, and political, as well as educational.

Social studies, scientific understanding, and constructivism

The efforts of science education researchers in examining epistemological and educational considerations are striking when compared to research in social studies education. This is not to say that social studies educators have ignored the topic of cognition or its implications for the curriculum. There has been ongoing interest in higher-order thinking abilities (Newmann, 1991; VanSickle and Hoge, 1991), and some highly substantive and impressive theoretical works that encourage us to reconsider our traditional assumptions about learning theory (Byrnes and Torney-Purta, 1995; Levstik and Pappas, 1992; Torney-Purta, 1991). These developments, however, do not relate cognitive theories to fundamental challenges about the nature of knowing that are currently being debated in philosophy and science and mathematics education. As it appears, constructivist ideas come in a trivialized form.

For example, Byrnes and Torney-Purta (1995) and Torney-Purta (1991) emphasize schema theory. Schema theory is constructivist in nature, but its emphasis on the individual's active learning process omits consideration of the social context of learning and leaves unchallenged the assumption that an objective social reality exists about which to actively learn. The intentional use of schema theory to change a learner's "misconceptions" or "naive concepts" implies that a true concept exists which corresponds to an objective reality.

Levstik and Pappas (1992) challenge the global inclusiveness of Piaget's stage theories. They marshall support to argue that a learner's development through stages is domain-specific – that is, dependent upon an individual's previous knowledge and experiences with a particular type of knowledge. Levstik's and Pappas's analysis has Vygotskian and constructivist overtones in showing that historical understanding can occur for learners at an earlier age than our conventional curriculum tenets establish. Their exclusive emphasis, however, on narrative scripts and cultural frameworks, important and useful as they are, implicitly places historical understanding at the center of social studies knowledge.

Historical and scientific understanding

The meaning of social studies knowledge has been under political attack during the past decade by educational reformers who wish to assert a primary role for history and geography. Leming (1992) forcefully blames the intellectual leaders of the social studies field for failing to "articulate a view of the purposes of the social studies" that would "gain the support of teachers, the general public and the political establishment" (p. 308). He argues that in order to regain an effective voice about the direction of social studies, social studies educators need to follow two "fundamental principles." The first is to acknowledge that social studies are a discipline that lacks expertise. By this, he means that no empirical evidence has established that experiencing social studies education is related to increases in higher-order thinking or improvements in active citizenship behavior. Yet, he points out, these are the two most commonly stated goals of social studies education.

The second principle is that social studies educators need to accept that education is a conservative activity, especially social studies.

The implications of these principles seem clear to Leming if social studies educators wish to reclaim their field. First, social studies educators should establish only the objectives that educational practices can deliver. Secondly, they should define citizenship in a way that the public and the profession can perceive it as "developing loyalty and commitment to our nation and its core culture and democratic values." Leming prescribes that the "development of an accurate knowledge of our American history, our tradition and the social world" should be *the* goal of social studies (p. 310). Leming's arrogance might deter many social educators from examining his conclusions. This would be unfortunate. His authoritarian admonishments (he might refer to his views as merely "realistic") could inadvertently start us on a reexamination of the relationship between *how we know* and the democratic goals of social studies education.

The debate over whether history or social science is the proper content of social studies is often superficial. C. Wright Mills (1959) pointed out years ago that it depends on *what kind* of history and *what kind* of social science is being discussed. Thornton (1990) echoes this idea in his thoughtful response to recent history reform proposals: "The content the teacher chooses to emphasize, how that content is presented by the teacher, what the teacher evaluates, and so forth, determine the curriculum that counts – the curriculum that students actually experience" (p. 57). Citing Herman (1977, p. 54) he continues to explain that: "School children are very interested in social studies questions, but they generally dislike the instruction they receive in the subject" (p. 57).

The need for social studies teachers to thoroughly understand the nature of the content is an opportunity for a constructivist proposal – a proposal that asks social educators to reconsider scientific understanding as an important basis for social studies knowledge.

The last foray of scientific understanding into the social studies was during the 1960s and 1970s era of the New Social Studies. Whelan (1992) describes the common perception of the New Social Studies as being a vision of "cool, scientifically trained students discovering the truth about history and society" (p. 8). This, of course, was not the vision of all social studies educators who were involved. In 1982, Shaver expressed his disappointment: "Trying to be 'scientific' often without substantial efforts to understand science or its relevance to the study of human behavior, has resulted in structures that often unreasonably bind and blind us in our work" (p. 13).

The idea of teaching a social science that would enable students to aggregate empirical facts in order to discover the reality of the social world is not philosophically different from teaching simplistic notions of historical causation through the use of chronology. Both are highly positivistic and deterministic, and neither allows learners to be involved in the social construction of knowledge. Both methodologies assume that a right conclusion awaits students at the end of inquiry, or as Walter Cronkite would say at the end of his evening television newscast, "And that's the way it is."

The theoretical work of Banks (1995) in multiculturalism, epistemology, and the social science disciplines, contains highly significant and profound developments for social studies education. Banks observes that mainstream social studies instruction inadequately reflects the way contemporary social science knowledge is "constructed and reconstructed." He argues that while the mainstream social science influence of the 1960s and 1970s was framed in an objectivist and positivist paradigm, contemporary social science knowledge is being "challenged" and "transformed" by scholars of color and feminist scholars. He appeals for social studies educators to close the "wide gap between the transformations taking place within the social science disciplines and the ways that the social studies are taught in the schools.'' For this to take place, students need to understand how knowledge is constructed:

> This process consists of the methods, activities, and questions teachers use to help students understand, investigate, and determine how implicit cultural assumptions, frames of reference, perspectives, and biases within a discipline influence the way knowledge is constructed. When the knowledge construction process is taught, teachers help students understand how knowledge is created and influenced by the racial, ethnic, and class positions of individuals and groups. (p. 14)

The epistemological tools of a constructivist philosophy of science are too important to be relegated to a secondary position within an ill-defined historical version of social studies. Hestenes (1992) says that ''the main objective of science . . . should . . . be to teach the modeling game'' (p. 732). This modeling game could also be the main goal of social studies education.

The objective of helping students create viable cognitive structures for making sense of their social experiences can contribute to a social theory of education for democracy. The constructivist need to negotiate knowledge within a social community ultimately requires democratic social practices. The tenets governing the process of doing this kind of science are the virtues of democracy: a search for workable truths, personal humbleness in the power of evidence, toleration for different perspectives and interpretations, and an acceptance of the tentativeness of what is held to be true at any particular time (Bronowski, 1965).

Helping students to construct viable structures for understanding their social worlds could be the missing expertise of the social studies. But this reform could be very dangerous. Once provided opportunities to develop their epistemological tools, students might come to understand how schooling provides only a limited number of students the social knowledge and skills necessary to run our most prized economic and political institutions.

Chapter 11
Practical knowledge and school knowledge: a constructivist representation of education

YVON PÉPIN

Constructivism as a general theory of education

It is customary to associate constructivism and theory of knowledge. That is probably one of the reasons why this approach in education has retained a cognitivist cast until now. Research has borne principally on the examination of the cognitive processes at work in intellectual development and the constraints operated by these not only on teaching but on learning particular school subjects. All the same, the import of constructivism for education is much greater than this. Research conducted in other contexts has provided clear illustration of how this approach holds promise for the pursuit of educational objectives other than those associated exclusively with cognitive development or schooling (see, for instance, Gergen, 1985, 1995; Mahoney and Lyddon, 1988; Watzlawick, 1988).

Such is the thesis of this chapter as well. I would like to show how the constructivist point of view makes it possible to develop a vision of the whole of educational phenomena which is comprehensive and penetrating and which, at the same time, is both viable and even fertile. This kind of vision would embrace education as much in terms of its psychological, developmental, socioaffective, and psychopedagogical aspects as of its cognitive and didactic aspects. By the same token, I would also like to show what occurs when the constructivist approach is widened to include all educational phenomena: It is possible at that point to contextualize and delimit application of the approach in relation to more specific problematics involved with schooling and teaching – two areas that, after all, form only a subset of the entire educational field.

Indeed, if certain aspects of constructivism provide a most interesting theory of knowledge, the approach also offers a global perspective on the meaning of the human adventure, on the way human beings impart meaning to their whole existence in order to survive and adapt. If the ultimate goal of every educational enterprise is to somehow contribute to this very adaptation and survival of a human being in his or her entirety, and not simply make do with developing those skills and kinds of knowledge presumed to be important and necessary, then constructivism may very well present us with a new, refreshing educational landscape to contemplate because of the radical ways it redefines the issues.

Thus I will first attempt to outline the main features of this shift in perspective in terms of processes of human adaptation and development. The constructivist approach derives all its strength from its description of education as this occurs independently of the intentions of actors, who, to borrow a well-worn expression from the school of Palo Alto, "cannot not educate or not learn!" Accordingly, I will temporarily leave to one side the formal or informal intention of educating or learning in order to show how otherness – that is, what has gone unmastered and uncontained or proven impossible to assimilate according to preexisting schemas – forces human beings to learn, that is, change their ways of perceiving and behaving (i.e., adjusting) in the world. It is this same process which explains why it is that, in everyday life, people only learn when they have to learn, that is, whenever their modes of adaptation and previous knowledge fail or become problematic.

Once imported into the field of intentional education, this change in perspective creates a certain discomfort. Constructivism is incompatible with several beliefs which generally provide the basis of formal education or schooling. As a rule, these beliefs appear as received truths, and amount to ever so many assumptions, exempt from all critical examination, concerning the different operations and possible goals of education, the processes involved, and useful ways of acting. From among the goals and operations whose feasibility is practically never called into question, I will examine in particular those relating to the transmission of knowledge, the reduction of the gap occurring between what the student knows and what he or she ought to know, and, finally, the preventive accumulation of knowledge which is to be used at some future time. Constructivism does not declare these missions impossible, but it does require us to operate a radical revision upon them.

Finally, in the last portion of this chapter, I will reintroduce the formal intention of educating or learning, but now as simple elements of the interaction between educator and student, who both learn by attempting to adapt to one another. What is it that is learned whenever we attempt to adapt to someone who is attempting to educate us? What viable constructions may we develop in a context such as this? As will become apparent, the constructivist perspective on informal education and the development of practical knowledge holds great interest for a reexamination of the processes of formal education, in terms of both success and failure. It will also become more apparent how a split develops and takes root between school knowledge on the one hand and practical knowledge which to develops independently on the other. The result of such a situation is that formal education alienates all the motivation and cognitive energy that enable individuals to adapt.

In the conclusion, I will indicate a number of conditions which might well make it possible to reconcile school knowledge and practical knowledge.

A constructivist appraisal of adaptation and learning: the transformation of practical knowledge

It is a hypothesis of constructivism that living beings survive and adapt to their existence by providing forms to the flow of experience which they are capable of manipulating. In this view, the world, as such, has no preestablished form and hence does not admit of direct perception or knowledge. In order to perceive or know the world, we are obliged to provide it with a form which is suitable to us. The visible world does not exist as such but assumes a form when it is constructed by the eye. Or again, the audible world does not exist as such but is the form the world takes on when it is known by the ear. Thus we are only able to survive and adapt to the extent we succeed in providing a *viable form* for our experience and we manage to contain and harness this experience within the structures of knowledge we impose upon it. In other words, these structures that we put out into the world are, in the final analysis, nothing more than the reflection of what, at every moment, our human faculties enable us to make of it. "There is no world except that experienced through those processes given to us and which make us what we are" (Varela, 1988, p. 341). In order to adapt, we must fashion this world after ourselves, humanize it in effect. Failure to do so would prove fatal to us.

Knowledge as a vital, global activity

It is this entire process which constructivism calls cognitive activity or knowledge. More than simply representing a conscious cerebral or intellectual activity, knowledge is that basic vital activity the scope of which corresponds to what existentialist philosophers have termed being-in-the-world (*Dasein*). Knowledge is "the search for *fitting* ways of behaving and thinking" (von Glasersfeld, 1988, p. 39) for this being-in-the-world, globally but also locally, or in terms of the situation at hand, depending on the goals being pursued.

The fact that the world as such cannot be called on as witness or arbiter in evaluating the different ways of knowing and constructing it, leads constructivists to substitute the criterion of viability for that of truth. Now, this criterion is radical: Knowledge which is nonviable will prove fatal if it is a question of survival, and it is synonymous with failure if it is a question of some other goal. The simple fact that this knowledge makes it possible to survive or reach the desired goal signifies that it is viable, regardless of whether or not it appears erroneous from some other perspective. However, survival or success do not in any way stand as proof that some particular knowledge is truer or provides a better description of reality than another: the only conclusion one may be permitted is that one is dealing with an effective, functional way of constructing the world. Several viable versions of reality or a given reality may coexist, and "no one in particular can have a claim to better understanding in a universal sense" (Varela, 1988, p. 320). On the other hand, the verdict of failure allows of no appeal, thus prompting von Glasersfeld to remark that "the 'real' world manifests itself exclusively there where our constructions break down" (1988, p. 38). Failure means that the world will not submit to the form we wish to impose on it, at least whenever it is a question of achieving a particular goal.

Learning in terms of the success or failure of practical knowledge

The preceding considerations serve to underscore the fundamentally assimilative nature of knowledge: we constantly attempt to create the world in our image, to contain it within the structures we have available to us and which indeed are part of our make-up; we continually attempt to deny otherness, to "produce sameness with that which is different." And all knowledge which manages to do this enjoys such status that we end up believing that the world is indeed as we perceive and construct it – that is, to a great degree stable and permanent. In that sense, failure to contain and master experience is the main agent involved in the transformation and evolution of our knowledge – even knowledge bearing on ourselves – and cognitive equipment. Failure forces us to accommodate ourselves, that is, it involves us in deconstructing and reconstructing the world as we know it and ourselves along with it. Piaget maintained, moreover, that intelligence organizes the world as it organizes itself (1971a, p. 311), and a major portion of his work consists in showing how cognitive equipment which is invested in the world in order to know it proceeds from an assemblage of reflexes all the way up to the articulation of formal operations. The nature of the world which is known to us also changes as our cognitive equipment undergoes change.

This means that we literally cannot learn – that is, change our way of understanding the world or a particular phenomenon or our way of behaving toward it – unless our previous knowledge fails to lead us where we wish to go. If such a failure does not occur, the only thing we learn is that our current way of constructing the world is viable and produces the desired results. The knowledge being made use of is thus reinforced and possibly "reified." In terms of cognitive activity, failure (and the necessity of accommodating) is a kind of catastrophe which we attempt to avoid at all cost since this signifies the nonviability of the self in the immediate world. Doubtless that is why we organize, most often unconsciously, our knowledge into systems of "self-fulfilling prophecies" which are extremely difficult to invalidate (Carson, 1982; Watzlawick, 1988a).[1] The subjective recognition of failure to master experience and achieve goals which have been presumed (just as subjectively) to be important is crucial with respect to learning and the evolution of practical knowledge. Thus, at every moment of existence, we continue to be who we are and to know what we know, while at the same time we become "other" and know "other-wise," according to our capacity to contain our experience (Mahoney and Lyddon, 1988, p. 209; Maturana and Varela, 1987). Importantly, this implies that all knowledge which persists and is perpetuated is knowledge which, until that time, has proven viable and adaptable for the person who has developed it.

This also brings out how new knowledge cannot develop in a void but instead requires the alteration of previously existing constructions. There is no constructing a phenomenon unless it has already figured in the field of experience. By the same token, for experience to be perceived, it must have undergone construction previously. If no prior construction of an object of knowledge were present, there would be nothing to ''deconstruct'' or reconstruct with greater viability. A new construct, and the way it may be constructed, depends on what has already been constructed (von Glasersfeld, 1988, p. 31). In Fourez's words, ''learning means giving up one representation in favor of another, more promising one'' (1996, p. 24). There is no such thing as a tabula rasa! There is no starting all over again!

Hence, the kinds of knowledge with which constructivism is concerned are practical and experiential types of knowledge, which either do or do not serve the capacity of the persons who develop them to approach the world *viably*; I am referring here not only to students but also, and above all, to individuals, or organisms who organize themselves. Also, it is these same individuals who alone are capable of relying on their awareness of mastering and more or less containing their experience to evaluate this very viability in light of the goals they pursue. As long as the world they have constructed is ''practicable,'' a world from which unforeseeable or insurmountable problems are absent, or as long as they are able to behave as though that world were true, there is absolutely no reason to learn anything else or understand things any differently. At best, one can only refine and solidify the current construction.

The construction of others and their knowledge

Finally, I must devote some space to the unavoidable necessity of constructing the other who constructs the world and us as well. The presence of others, their own ability to behave as though their constructions were true, and, consequently, their intrusion into our experience through the effect of their behavior on our feeling of adapting more or less successfully are all factors requiring that we construct others in some manner or another. The processes involved in this construction are similar to those which were previously touched on. It is still a question of containing and mastering the experience we have of others so that we may survive, reach our goals, achieve our projects. Success reinforces previous constructions and failure forces us to make novel distinctions or to reconsider our representations more or less globally. And, in a certain way, we have here the stuff of conflict – the conflict of constructions, the conflict of knowledge – since the viable forms given to experience by this or that person are likely to be incompatible in varying degrees: what is viable for one person may, in practice, turn out to be a source of failure for another! In other words, others must be constructed, known, "understood" in a way making it possible to adapt to others and to contain the effect of their behavior. From this perspective, it is possible to describe human interaction as the contextual, yet perpetual, affirmation, testing out, and negotiation of the respective worldviews of partners, who, so doing, co-construct their reality. However, it is not necessary that the aims and knowledge of those involved be identical in order for interaction to be viable, let alone bearable. The notion of "pragmatic agreement," which was developed by Dionne and Ouellet (1990, chap. 3), makes clear just how interaction of this kind is possible without having to assume or even aim for common consensus or understanding: it is only necessary that interaction enable each partner to construct (and deconstruct and reconstruct) the behavior of the other in a way that is viable for him- or herself.

As for other people's knowledge, we take this under consideration only if, in terms of our own knowledge, it offers some utility for our projects and serves to resolve our problems of survival and adaptation – in short, only if, from our point of view, it is capable of constituting practical knowledge. If our own knowledge poses no problem for us, then other people's knowledge is for all intents and purposes lost on us. However, problems that do arise may derive from the practical necessities of interaction and communication and not from the object of knowledge being dealt with. It even occurs that we are obliged to develop a language or a formal kind of knowledge concerning an object, but that this knowledge will not at the same time correspond or contribute to our practical knowledge of this object. If, out of necessity or personal determination, I intend to interact with psychoanalysts on the subject of mental reality, it is in my interest to become acquainted with the formal discourse of psychoanalysis, even though it is of absolutely no help in resolving the problems that this reality poses for me and even though, practically speaking, I use a different construction.

The preceding considerations appear to me to translate the essence of the constructivist approach, which resides in its capacity to cast a different light on the educational enterprise as a comprehensive effort at fostering human adaptation. It is at this point that I would like to examine a number of areas of incompatibility which arise whenever this approach is brought into contact with the everyday received truths of education as these appear in a school setting.

Constructivism and received truths in education

The perspective I have just elaborated upon leads me to reconsider and call into question a number of propositions we take for granted – that is, received truths which provide a basis for most teaching programs. I will limit myself to identifying and critiquing only a number of the most salient examples of these.

Knowledge can be transmitted

The belief that it is possible for a subject to understand and assimilate some precise bit of knowledge which has been mastered by another subject is without a doubt the main basis of our customary representation of education. Accordingly, transmitting knowledge becomes the major practical problem that several works are specifically dedicated to solving. In concrete terms, this basis is translated into programs and courses in the following way: a corpus of knowledge is established beforehand, which students are to master, if all goes well! The educator is supposed to master this knowledge, and his or her teaching approach will consist in implementing a variety of means designed to enable students to understand what he or she understands, so that they are able to reproduce this on their own. Knowledge that is taught or explained in this way is considered as existing by and of itself, removed from all context, as though it embodied properties of "reality" or something outside oneself, which the educator has appropriated and which students must appropriate in turn. Only rarely do educators specify the context and particular problem that gave rise to the production of knowledge, the difficulties which accompanied legitimation of the latter, or the problems encountered by those who produced it. If, on the one hand, all school knowledge is practical knowledge for those who produce or use it, the concept of transmitting knowledge, on the other, presupposes that knowledge can be acquired without being practical.

Constructivism holds that human beings construct their knowledge in the very process of adapting and that knowledge only has meaning to the extent that it resolves problems encountered while attending to various goals or the accomplishment of various projects. Knowledge is irremediably a construction by one or more subjects. The subject who constructs his or her knowledge has an interest in doing so only to the extent that he or she is tangibly confronted with the problem this knowledge is supposedly able to resolve. Even when this is the case, there is nothing which suggests that the knowledge he or she has developed in order to deal with this problem will conform to the knowledge he or she was supposed to learn. In terms of the subject's goals and prior constructions, by which a particular experiential universe is determined, a different kind of knowledge may be just as viable for this individual, if not more so. What is more, the subject has no direct access to the teacher's knowledge. Inevitably, it is the subject's construction of this knowledge, on the one hand, and the subject's relationship to the teacher, on the other, that provide the necessary basis for imagining and even inventing what the teacher thinks and understands. In this context, an exact correspondence is a slim possibility.

Thus, at the outset, there is nothing in constructivism that is capable of explaining how knowledge can be transmitted from one subject to another; or how knowledge can be conveyed effectively and correctly; or how to make sure that a student is learning the precise bit of knowledge on his or her own. Indeed, it is the very viability of this received truth in education that is called into question.

Education can and ought to involve reducing the gap between what the learning subject knows (or does not know) and what he or she should know, with the first term always being corrected in favor of the second term

A goodly part of the educational enterprise, as this is habitually represented, consists in narrowing the gap between what the subject knows or does not know and what it is he or she should know. Daignault (1985, p. 23) even asserts that "teaching is the third world of knowledge," meaning that the energies which go into teaching are, for all intents and purposes, exploited in favor of the promotion and hegemony of knowledge which is developed elsewhere.

It is occasionally presumed that students know nothing or that they have no prior representation of what one would like to represent to them. In other instances, attention is concentrated on diagnosing students' naive or spontaneous conceptions in order to show them to what extent they have erred with respect to "true" knowledge (Larochelle and Désautels, 1992, p. 10). Knowledge is taught because it is held to be true or at least important, regardless of its viability in resolving the problems experienced by those to whom it is taught.

In effect, school knowledge is generally considered as something acquired once and for all, or as embodying the intrinsic properties of the phenomena being studied – two examples of the ''substantialist logic'' denounced by Moscovici and Hewstone (1984) – or again as truths upon which all future knowledge is to be based. This relationship to knowledge, which constructivists have described as realist, permeates most teaching practices and class content. Thus, students' practical knowledge is constantly gauged against a standardized kind of knowledge which is dictated by the state of knowledge in a given field, bound in course and program objectives, and supported by the methods used in evaluating learning progress.

The constructivist critique of this received truth in education is radical on more than one count. First of all, it challenges the notion that this realist sort of knowledge can exist, and it asserts that all knowledge is a hypothesis which has proved viable in accordance with certain goals. It also takes issue with the notion that the gap between the spontaneous knowledge of students and school knowledge can be narrowed through a process of correcting the first variety according to the terms of the second. Besides, how is it possible for school knowledge to enjoy a power of attraction such that it could invalidate practical knowledge which had proven viable up until that time![2] The only correction possible must be of the subject's own doing, in a process of self-regulation resulting from a subjective realization of the failure of his or her knowledge to master a situation or achieve a goal. In short, the key to the correction and the development of knowledge resides in practical knowledge and not in school or formal knowledge.

Along the same lines, but at a different level, the constructivist perspective denies the possibility that nonknowledge can give way to knowledge. All new knowledge must necessarily be constructed upon prior knowledge, either consolidating the latter, complexifying it, or deconstructing it. Students are not ignorant: they know or believe something other than what one would like to teach them, and these beliefs and this knowledge are as yet viable. Students are not unmotivated, but they are motivated by other goals than those which the educator would like them to pursue.

The complexity and heterogeneity of human desire is such that the viability of a form of knowledge, taken with the latter's potential for success or failure, can only be appreciated subjectively. Subjects only change or adapt their knowledge if it threatens their survival or creates problems for achieving their goals. For as long as it is possible for subjects to assimilate experience in terms of what they know, they will continue to think whatever it is they think, and no truth, howsoever established it may be, will keep them from doing so. And, in fact, throughout history, the production of new knowledge (including the original institution of the scientific enterprise itself, including the elaboration of the constructivist position itself) has provided frequent testimony of the often difficult rebellion of their creators against a set of "established truths" which threatened their survival or hindered them in the pursuit of their goals (Feyerabend, 1979; Kuhn, 1983).

To sum up, for constructivists the only knowledge possible for subjects is practical knowledge of a kind which enables them to survive, accomplish their projects, or come to terms with their desire – regardless of the value other perspectives place on this knowledge.[3]

It is both possible and desirable to accumulate knowledge now for use in the future

As we have just seen, the way in which education is usually envisioned assumes that something new can be learned without our previous knowledge of this thing meeting with failure or appearing problematical in the slightest. By the same stroke, knowledge acquires a preventive connotation, in that it is assumed that the subject's mastery of knowledge guarantees that he or she personally will never have to resolve the problems of survival and adaptation which forced other subjects to produce it. A number of formulations of the concept of basic education even advance the claim that it is possible to provide students with all the basic knowledge necessary for tackling any and all problems characterizing various scientific and professional disciplines, suggesting that such an approach fosters versatility, maximizes the range of available choices, or prepares for interdisciplinary work. We are dealing here with a kind of knowledge to be stored away for future use – that is, "just in case" the subject runs into some problem it might prove useful for, knowledge that could help subjects avoid solving for themselves problems others have solved before them. In other words, we are dealing with "school" knowledge which has not yet become "practical" knowledge.

From a constructivist point of view, it is possible to construct and foresee future experience only on the basis of our current construction of past experience. Knowledge functions according to the principle that what is yet to be is of a piece with what has been, and that what is to be known must be assimilable to what is now known. Knowledge is thus viable only in terms of the apprehension that our present schemata allow us to have of a future experience, with the possibility that this apprehension may turn out to be irrelevant at some later time. Thus it is impossible to develop any kind of knowledge in the present moment which is to become useful later on, unless it is useful now for understanding current experience or for surviving or achieving current goals. A person cannot develop knowledge unless he or she has personal or at least analogous experience to which such knowledge may provide form. [4] There is no such thing as experienceless knowledge that can be implemented whenever the targeted form of experience occurs.

It is clear, then, that the constructivist perspective offers no room for a kind of education that is conceived of in terms of transmitting knowledge, reducing the gap which separates students' knowledge from established knowledge, or acquiring knowledge which will prove useful only at some later time.

Rupture and alienation of practical and school knowledge: a constructivist interpretation of current practices

In order to bring out several of the consequences of this constructivist interpretation for education, I first ought to show how this perspective sheds light on a number of phenomena to be observed in current practices. To do so, I will attempt to answer a few, very simple questions: How might a student construct an educational universe of the kind described above in such a way as to survive, adapt, and reach goals within it? What is it possible to learn during interaction with the schooling system and with all persons whose objective is to transmit knowledge, reduce the gap between our knowledge and ''real'' knowledge, and help us develop knowledge which might come in handy only at some future time? What kind of knowledge in and of this context is viable?

The construction of the school world

The first thing one observes is that, for students, the main focus of cognitive activity consists in constructing the overall meaning of the experience which they are undergoing at school. This is where they encounter practical problems; it is here also that all their practical knowledge will continue to develop: their knowledge of themselves, their educators, the rules of the educational and social game, and fitting ways of behaving – in short, ways which enable them to survive and adapt in this context. School knowledge – that is, the knowledge for which schools have been primarily instituted – represents only a minute fraction of what subjects are required to construct in order to adapt to schooling.

There is no guaranteeing that students will construct school reality the way educators want them to. This construction can assume all manner of forms – some of which are startling to say the least – which vary according to the previous knowledge students have of themselves, adults, and social systems such as the family, and which also reflect the capacity of this knowledge to assimilate and contain schooling experience. Failure to do so will trigger transformations in these structures by which students apprehend the world, hence setting in motion changes in the very world they know. Knowledge that is viable at home or in the street is not necessarily viable at school; where viability does not obtain, knowledge must undergo change or complexification.

The construction of the educator

Students are thus obliged to construct one crucial representation – that of the educator. In a less formal context, this figure is someone who simply has knowledge that may be useful to assuring their own survival and to achieving their own goals. This occurs "naturally," and they spontaneously turn to such figures, whose authority they have judged for themselves. Then, even the formal or school-type knowledge of such natural educators can be drawn on to develop and transform practical knowledge.

In the formal context of school, however, the authority of the purveyors of knowledge is no longer worked out in terms of a student's own appraisal, nor does it depend on his or her own goals; instead, authority acquires an institutional definition. To confront this new situation, students must construct viable ways of thinking and interacting with individuals whose knowledge, by definition and independently of their own evaluation, is superior to their own, and who behave toward them accordingly. These individuals have the power to reward and to punish, and the effects of their behavior can threaten a student's feelings of adaptation or imperil the achievement of his or her goals. One solution to this problem consists in learning (more or less successfully) to know what it is that educators want students to know, oftentimes because failure to meet educators' expectations might well represent a threat to students' adaptive processes. In other words, a student can learn the rule of three or the plural possessive of James, not because he or she is faced with a concrete problem of calculation or communication, but because failure to do so could produce problems in terms of relations with the persons who are attempting to teach these things. The lessons learned involve not mathematics or language but human relationships, because, in terms of practical knowledge, the problem lies in human relationships, not in mathematics or language. What students learn, then, is that it is in the interest of their own welfare to learn whatever it is that supposedly knowledgeable people want them to learn; once learned, this lesson will apply for all school subjects. It is as though, to a certain extent, a context were created in which: (1) a split occurred between interpersonal communication and communication with the object; (2) the underlying motivations to be grasped centered more on adaptation in personal, interpersonal, and organizational terms than on the object of knowledge; (3) bridging the two levels of learning (a form of communication concerning the object) was an impossibility. Thus, school knowledge would be practical knowledge inasmuch as it constitutes ways for students to successfully enact their own presentation of self. Often in this context, the relationship to instituted authority is what is systematically constructed – a kind of knowledge which can be quite practical indeed!

The construction of knowledge

What is also learned is that practical knowledge – that is, the kind of knowledge, precisely, which enables individuals to look after themselves in everyday situations – has very little value in formal terms and does not necessarily enjoy consideration on the part of the institution. The result is a distinction, or rather a split, between school knowledge and practical knowledge, most often occurring at the expense of the latter. Knowledge and beliefs that are viable or useful in everyday life, even within the school setting, are qualified as unknowledge or irrelevant knowledge, hence unusable for constructing formal or school varieties of knowledge at some future time. School knowledge, which students develop for purposes which have absolutely nothing to do with the goals for which it was constructed, is no longer of any use in transforming practical knowledge, which escapes formal education and goes on to develop independently. Such an outcome obtains because, in the course of events, it is forgotten that the subject who constructs his or her knowledge remains the final judge of its viability.

At that point, it is not surprising that by the end of our studies, and throughout their duration, we represent knowledge as something external to ourselves, as something foreign which can only be appropriated and mastered with the utmost difficulty: this knowledge is not our knowledge! What is more, we cannot even picture it as knowledge which someone else has constructed for purposes of his or her own and which may resemble or differ from our own. It becomes exceedingly difficult to imagine how some other project could produce different knowledge, or to throw into question the point of view which informed this other person's knowledge. What will we have learned, then? Probably a relationship of submission and powerlessness toward established knowledge; the inability, at least in part, to picture ourselves as the legitimate producers of knowledge; and even an atrophied capacity for dialectically and productively evaluating and criticizing the knowledge being proposed to us.

The construction of the self and the relationship to school knowledge

In research bearing more directly on education, even of a constructivist variety, it is frequently forgotten that schooling takes place in a context of communication in which the partners construct themselves and, more generally speaking, the world they must adapt to, even as they direct their attention to specific, primarily discipline-based objects of knowledge.[5] It is forgotten or ignored that the construction of a relationship to mathematics, science, philosophy, et cetera, is but a subset of the overall construction of a relationship to the world whose viability is the only thing that really matters.

Thus, a number of students quickly learn that they are not particularly good at the game involving any or all varieties of school knowledge and the disciplines upon which these are based. One viable way of constructing this situation consists in declaring oneself incapable (e.g., lousy in mathematics, ungifted for English, unsuited for history, or, generally speaking, not bright enough to get through college) or to declare the knowledge being dealt with or school itself irrelevant: "What good are biology, integral calculus, or Thomistic philosophy if I want to be a carpenter? My uncle is a businessman who has done very well even though he never finished high school!" In contrast with this, other students learn that they are quite strong and become accomplished performers, indeed virtuosi, in the game of impressing the educator so as to produce enjoyable situations for themselves and feel as though they have adapted. In both cases, students develop viable representations of their experience of schooling: the first group depreciates the very school knowledge which has depreciated them, the second group pursues the opposite tack. In terms of practical knowledge, they have learned the same structure; they have even learned to fit into the appropriate positions, which otherwise are located at poles opposite from one another – that is, which embody success or failure in school, either totally or specifically. It is practical knowledge of this kind – that is, these limiting but viable constructions of self and various types of school knowledge – much more than exposure to a more or less general or basic form of schooling, which reduces well-roundedness or adaptability in terms not only of educational and professional direction but more simply of the interest a student will take in knowledge, even of the school variety.

I think it important to emphasize here how school or formal knowledge is diverted from the very ends for which it was constructed – that is, as a way by which someone constructs some problematical aspect of reality in order to make it less of a problem and to be able to deal with it. Most school knowledge is not of a kind to cause students problems, subjectively speaking. Instead, they are faced with the extremely concrete – that is, practical – problems of social integration and school success or failure (and all the psychosocial difficulties accompanying this). Characteristically, those who fail in this department react by picturing failure, or themselves, as a matter of no great consequence: such is the price of adaptation!

To the extent that the imposition of school knowledge is undertaken without regard for practical knowledge, and even to the detriment of the latter, it is no surprise, from a constructivist perspective, that formal education, as habitually conceived of, has proved to be such a difficult and frustrating endeavor for those who are involved in it. If knowledge and learning are seen as the activities of a subject who is attempting to come to terms with his or her own experience, then ignoring the constructions which he or she devises in this process can only proceed at the cost of triggering numerous perverse psychosocial effects which, more often than not, go unnoticed in educators' own constructions of teaching. Teachers call on students in a setting in which the latter can only know something other than what one would like them to know. Teachers lose sight of what determines whether students take an interest in knowing and learning.

Guideposts for a constructivist praxis in education

Inasmuch as consistency is an objective, it is important to recall that the constructivist perspective is itself a construction whose value, compared to "alternative" constructions, resides primarily in the viability which it holds for its adherents. In this context, any prescription merely acquires the status of a proposal, whose utility will be worked out in accordance with the judgment of those to whom it is addressed. It is with only this intention in mind that, by way of conclusion, I will present a certain number of guideposts for use in charting a constructivist praxis in education and outline several general implications for a constructivist approach to teacher education as well as for a constructivist approach to educating . . . constructivists.

The constructivist education of students

The first thing that must be understood is that the better part of students' cognitive activity is not directed toward assimilating various types of school knowledge but rather to ordering their overall experience and to constructing their own relationship to that which is other – including school taken both as a whole and in terms of its specific and situational aspects. The subject constantly strives to construct the world in both situational and overall terms, in such a way that he or she may integrate that world and assume a viable position within it. From this perspective, a problem with mathematical or linguistic knowledge does not necessarily imply a problem with mathematics or language, and there are many possible ways of grasping and solving such a problem. Hence it is important to take into consideration how this problem with a particular variety of school knowledge is part and parcel of a student's entire efforts at adaptation and worldview construction, a problem of practical knowledge to be sure. In other words, in what way is a "learning problem" for the student not in fact a problem of practical knowledge?

When the question of students' practical knowledge is brought to the fore, several typical problems of teaching and didactics – for example, intellectual development, aptitudes, motivation, discipline, et cetera – appear in a different light. Students are neither unable nor slow to learn; they know something else which is more or less compatible or at odds with what one would like them to learn, and this something else happens to still be viable for them in their own context, perhaps more so than in the case of what one would like them to learn. The student is undisciplined only in relation to a kind of discipline found in a school setting: the practical knowledge that this choice of behavior is based on is undoubtedly viable in other contexts, or perhaps for accomplishing other goals within this selfsame school context. What usually is diagnosed as a lack of motivation for school in general or a school subject in particular appears as motivation for something else. And all this practical knowledge, all this cognitive energy, can be mobilized for educational ends. By taking an interest in this practical knowledge, teachers can stimulate students to develop their discursive awareness of this, confront them with it (without disqualifying it in the name of school knowledge, however), and invent strategies to produce failure and so trigger its transformation and development. In the end, all future learning can only be a transformation or a complexification of this previous conception.

The idea of producing failure in practical knowledge is crucial in this context. If all knowledge is the deconstruction and reconstruction of previously held representations subsequent to the subjective recognition of nonviability, educators have no choice but to produce failure in students' knowledge and to do so according to criteria that the students themselves recognize. Students can incorporate school knowledge within their practical knowledge only to the extent that the problems of viability which they encounter and perceive as such prompt them to ascribe authority to the former type. If all school knowledge is a kind of practical knowledge for those who are confronted with the problems giving rise to its production, students, on the other hand, are not necessarily in the same situation. Whence the necessity of imagining in what ways students' experience presents problem areas for which this knowledge could, through structural analogy, become viable, directly or indirectly; whence also the possibility, when the need arises, of strategically triggering such a situation, bearing in mind students' current goals, whatever these may be.

The constructivist education of educators

I must emphasize that the preceding comments apply equally to the education (and knowledge) of educators as to that of students. In order to survive and achieve teaching (or other-type) goals in the school context and, in addition, master their experience of school and students, educators must construct a viable representation of these phenomena, taken as a whole and in terms of their situational aspects, and develop practical knowledge in connection with this. Now, this practical knowledge is as prone to success and failure as students' knowledge. Some individuals fail radically and either voluntarily give up teaching or are asked to do so. In accordance with the logic set forward by von Glasersfeld (1988), it is possible to infer that "educational reality has manifested" that it could not be constructed the way such individuals had been attempting to do so; reality only manifests itself there where our constructions fail. The others survive, which, in keeping with the same logic, makes one surmise that their practical knowledge is viable, whatever other point of view (even constructivist) one might take on this. These survivors all encounter teaching problems which, taken as a whole or in situational terms, require that they call into question and transform their practical knowledge in relation to various educational goals which may be more or less ambitious.[6] They, too, learn and develop their practice only to the degree that failure to reach certain goals has obliged them to do so. They, too, must, as part of their overall adaptive process, construct not only the reality of their teaching practices – including the school knowledge which they are to teach and their knowledge of students and educational psychology – but also the practical problems of their own knowledge in this context – that is, the demands that are made on them, the ways by which they are evaluated, and the institutional and interpersonal constraints operating upon them. If many teachers have not changed their practices, despite all the learned discourses which have insisted on this necessity, that is because the practical knowledge they have of education is still viable in their context, perhaps more so than all the school knowledge which educational psychology, didactics, and assorted philosophical, epistemological, and ethical considerations on educational reality is capable of offering them. It is ultimately they who are the judges of the viability of the different kinds of school knowledge they are offered in preservice or in-service teaching programs. From that point of view, the problem of educating teachers is analogous to the previously described problem of educating students.

The constructivist education of constructivist educators

Constructivism in education has itself become a kind of school knowledge in several teacher education programs. As such, and as is the case with all other forms of school knowledge, it may or may not become practical knowledge for those who come in contact with it or who are taught it. It is of practical value only to the extent that it proves viable for mastering and solving the practical problems of the pre- or in-service teachers to whom it is proposed, and in accordance with their own evaluation.

The constructivist perspective is not adopted, let alone taught, either for ontological reasons (i.e., because it offers a more accurate description of the "nature" of discipline-based knowledge, understanding, human learning, or education) or for ethical or moral reasons (i.e., because it corresponds more closely to transcendental educational values), but rather for pragmatic reasons (i.e., because, according to our own evaluation, it enables us to deal with our experience better). It is far from obvious that constructivist knowledge concerning education also constitutes practical knowledge for education.

Part IV
The mediating role of teachers and teacher education

Chapter 12
Sociocultural perspectives on the teaching and learning of science

KENNETH TOBIN

Teaching and learning can be viewed as forms of enculturation into a community of practice. Usually teaching and learning are considered to occur in classrooms, which can be regarded as evolving communities of practice in which the discursive practices (e.g., talk, writing, cognition, argumentation, and representation) of participants are constantly changing in response to the interactions of a teacher and students, not only with one another, but also with social structures, such as conventions and norms (e.g., McGinn, Roth, Boutonné, and Woszczyna, 1995; Roth, 1995) and power relations (Bourdieu, 1991). Learning in such communities, it is argued, is most effective when the cultural resources of participants are acknowledged as capital for learning, teachers and learners can access a shared language, and power is equitably distributed (Tobin, 1997).

In a community that is learning science one might expect to see students engage in ways such that the discourse of a class would become more sciencelike over time. Discourse, as it is used here, refers to a "social activity of making meanings with language and other symbolic systems in some particular kind of situation or setting" (Lemke, 1995, p. 8). For instance, if science can be regarded as a form of argument in which emerging conceptual understandings are related to evidence and their fit with canonical science (Kuhn, 1993), then one might expect a form of discourse that involves students routinely in arguments over the efficacy of the warrants for knowledge claims. Social interactions using a shared language enable the teacher and learners to communicate and test the fit of their knowledge with others' representations. When the fit reaches an acceptable level it is concluded that a consensus has been achieved, in the sense that personal constructions bear a family resemblance to the constructions of others with whom negotiation has occurred. However, efforts to test knowledge claims share a potential problem, that theories not only illuminate experience and facilitate meaning making but also obscure potentially productive ways of making sense and increase the likelihood of retaining initial conceptualizations. One way to address this problem is for those who know and can use their knowledge to meet their goals to teach others in the community who are motivated to learn.

This discursive orientation in teaching and learning science does not appear to have discernible effects yet on what occurs in schools. For instance, many teachers conceptualize science as transmission of facts to students and implement the curriculum in whole class settings through the use of lectures and independent activities that employ worksheets and textbooks (Gallagher, 1993; Tobin and Gallagher, 1987). In other words, positivism still seems to permeate the teaching and learning of science; as Aikenhead (1996) has emphasized, "The 'taught' science curriculum, more often than not, provides students with a stereotypic image of science: socially sterile, authoritarian, nonhumanistic, positivistic, and absolute truth" (p. 13). Generally speaking, two forms of positivism tend to be used as referents by participants in science classrooms. The first assumes that knowledge passively mirrors a world out there, unmediated by ontological, theoretical, and political assumptions. A second type of positivism requires knowledge to be formulated in terms of causality, arrived at by testing, rejecting, and improving hypotheses, through the use of if/then statements. The knower can then be regarded as a passive agent who acquiesces to the pregiven nature of what exists out there. Beliefs such as these can be used to sustain a curriculum that emphasizes how to learn about the facts of science and to solve standard problems algorithmically (Tobin, Tippins, and Gallard, 1994). Furthermore, they can also contribute to sustain a perspective that life can be no other way; that it is what it appears to be. Agger (1992) noted that positivism, as ideology, has led to the domination of class, race, gender, and nature.

Although my history as a teacher, teacher educator, and researcher was grounded initially in positivism, in the past fifteen years my evolving referential system has become increasingly social. I regard teaching and learning as cultural phenomena that take account of the knowledge, interests, and values of individuals as well as the cultural capital of different minority groups and characteristics of the discipline to be taught and learned. The extent to which teaching and learning in a classroom community are productive depends on the *habitus* of participants, a set of dispositions that incline individuals to act and interact in particular ways (Bourdieu, 1991; Lemke, 1995). As students and teachers enact a curriculum, their roles are adaptive to the interactions of the community and its associated constituent cultures. Accordingly, interaction is a critical analytic unit for understanding teaching and learning. There are many viable ways to think about action and, although I regard it as a holistic concept, I find it useful to consider action in terms of four components, a behavioral set and an associated set of beliefs, the actor's goals, and the context of the action. Each of these components is inextricably linked with social phenomena. Interactions occur when individuals act in the presence of others and thereby perturb their actions or when they participate independently in an activity but utilize social constructions such as language in the process of thinking, writing, drawing, and so on. Individuals do not exist as separate entities and only know in terms of the cultures in which they have lived their lives. Thus, meanings are grounded in sociocultural processes.

The remainder of this chapter consists of four sections in which sociocultural perspectives are used to illuminate issues associated with the teaching and learning of science. Examples from my professional history are used to illustrate the role of theory in making sense of experience, learning from concrete experiences, the significance of coparticipation in learning science, and science as a form of symbolic violence for students. Implications for the practice of science education are presented in a conclusion that acknowledges that the perspectives I have employed in this chapter are useful in bringing certain issues into the foreground but, in so doing, push other issues into a background of obscurity.

Theory and making sense of experience

1, 1, 2, 3, 5, 8, . . . Two thoughts flashed through my mind as the seminar speaker revealed a sequence of numbers on an overhead transparency. The first was my vulnerability for being questioned since I was seated in the front row. That threatening thought focused my mind on likely candidates for the next term in the sequence and, having figured that out, I began to generate other possible questions that might be directed my way. I had experienced unexpected questions all too often and did not like to provide solutions in a public forum when I was unprepared cognitively. My second thought was one of excitement since I enjoy searching for patterns in number sequences.

The speaker revealed some of his favorite patterns in what he described as the Fibonacci sequence. He was interested in squaring any term and then comparing the result to the product of the terms either side of it. I was fascinated with an early example that suggested a Fibonacci-like family could be obtained by beginning with any two terms and summing them to generate the third and successive terms in a sequence. As the seminar progressed I began to construct several number sequences and examine their properties. I looked with interest at examples the speaker had used to show characteristics of the Fibonacci sequence, and my excitement grew as I saw similar patterns in the sequences I produced. The speaker provided applications of the Fibonacci sequence in science (e.g., spirals, petals, pine cones) and art. Golden numbers, convergent sequences, . . . Time out! I was hooked and wanted to learn some things for myself. The seminar, initially an inspiration, had become a source of frustration. I was motivated to learn and was being distracted by attempts to teach me. Although there were journals, websites, and number theory texts that could be used as resources for learning more about Fibonacci-like sequences my motivation was directed toward generating and testing some of my own ideas.

As I walked away from the seminar, images of a mathematics activity undertaken in a French-speaking elementary school in Montréal flashed into my mind. The class consisted of nineteen children from all elementary grade levels, brought together because they could not yet speak French proficiently. My experience in the school was as a visitor accompanying a colleague involved in a longitudinal study of language and mathematics learning. I was accepted by the teacher, the students, and my colleague as a participant observer with limited proficiency in the speaking of French, the language of instruction.

The students were arranged in an open rectangle such that they could collaborate on their tasks in groups of two or three. On this occasion, the assigned task involved the use of toothpicks to construct triangles, each side of a triangle comprising an integral number of toothpicks. Students were provided with round toothpicks, construction paper on which to display the different triangles that were built, and adhesive tape to secure the toothpicks. For a given number of toothpicks students were to use them all to build a permissible triangle. All students appeared to learn that the simplest triangle could be constructed with three toothpicks and that no triangle could be built with sides comprising a total of four toothpicks. In addition, most students learned that different triangles could be constructed with the same total number of toothpicks (e.g., seven toothpicks could produce permissible triangles having sides of 3, 3, 1 and 2, 2, 3). There was no limit on the number of toothpicks that could be used and students tried many permutations.

When I heard about the focus for the activity I made sense of it in terms of a search for patterns relating the number of different triangles that could be constructed for a given number of toothpicks. Using my knowledge of Euclidean geometry, I translated the task into a problem of generating alternative permutations of integers which, for a given number of toothpicks, would comprise permissible and different triangles. During the class period, I never attained my goal of identifying a viable pattern. However, over a period of approximately eight months, as I intermittently used the activity as an example of teaching and learning science and mathematics, I focused on possible ways to arrange the data and tested the viability of different patterns. Now, my newfound knowledge of Fibonacci numbers and their seemingly ubiquitous applications to natural systems encouraged me to compare a Fibonacci-like sequence to the data generated from the activity (i.e., 0, 0, 1, 0, 1, 1, 2, 1, 3, 2, 4, 3, 5, 4, 7, 5, 8, 7, 10, . . .).

In my search for a pattern I re-presented the data in a variety of ways. Initially, I disaggregated the data for each number of toothpicks into equilateral, isosceles, and scalene triangles. Then I separated the data for even and odd numbers of toothpicks. My activity attracted the attention of colleagues and in almost every instance they attempted to divert me from toothpick geometry to something that was even more interesting to them. Even though their desires to teach me were strong, I persevered because my motivation to construct a viable pattern was stronger. After several hours of intensive effort I gave up on the Fibonacci sequence and generated and tested alternative patterns, all the while making sure that the sequence itself was a correct representation of the number of permissible triangles. My determination to force fit the Fibonacci sequence prevented me from observing two simple patterns; however, it also strengthened my resolve to solve the problem. Finally, I decided to ignore 0, collapse equilateral and isosceles triangles into one category, and examine the permissible triangles for even and the odd numbers of toothpicks separately. That arrangement of data enabled me to see a pattern and to link the sequences for even and odd numbers of toothpicks. The four sequences of permissible isosceles triangles, I_o and I_e, and permissible scalene triangles, S_o and S_e are:

I_o: 1, 1, 2, 2, 3, 3, 4, 4, 5, . . .
I_e: 1, 1, 2, 2, 3, 3, 4, 4, . . .

S_o: 1, 1, 2, 3, 4, 5, . . .
S_e: 1, 1, 2, 3, 4, 5, . . .

At this stage I regarded the problem as solved and my interest in further analysis diminished (at least for the present time). What is salient about this vignette is that even though I regarded this activity as extremely interesting and used it many times to illustrate issues pertinent to learning mathematics and science from the manipulation of materials, I was not motivated to solve the initial problem I set for myself during the class period. However, the seminar on Fibonacci numbers rekindled my motivation and led to a more intensive effort to find a pattern to describe the data. Having made a commitment to solve the problem, my engagement became much more focused and prolonged, and until I identified patterns to fit the data, the search for a solution became my highest priority. Although my attempts to use the Fibonacci-like sequence as a template for the data were futile, they were motivating and caused me to correct errors in my data and explore alternative ways to present the data. Without the incentive to carefully generate and test the data and then to explore ways to display it, I would not have solved the problem I had constructed. In addition, without the faith that a pattern existed, I would not have persevered for the time taken to reach a solution. The vignette is an example of the necessity of considering affective and cognitive dimensions of learning conjointly. My experience in attaining a satisfying solution to a problem also reveals the levels of complexity involved in making sense of experiences. Knowledge of the Fibonacci sequence catalyzed my search for patterns while obscuring other relationships in the data. However, without my efforts to organize the data to fit the template of the Fibonacci sequence, I would not have had opportunities to connect other patterns to the data. The link between what is known and making sense of experiences has obvious implications for the teaching and learning of science and mathematics.

Learning from concrete experiences

In addition to my personal experiences with toothpick geometry there are insights to be gained from an analysis of the roles of the teachers and students during the activity. It was not easy to make triangles using toothpicks and the other materials provided, particularly as the number of toothpicks increased. Each toothpick had to be rolled into position, held, and secured with tape. Pressure on the construction paper caused some toothpicks to roll away, making it difficult to secure toothpicks in place while maintaining a triangular shape with approximately straight sides. Accordingly, it was difficult to use toothpick models to test the viability of given configurations. Realizing this, one student searched through her possessions, produced a stick of glue, used her fingers to cover the sides of the toothpicks with glue, and rolled the toothpicks into place to form a triangle. Thereafter, the students who had the glue and the knowledge of how to use it possessed a technology that enabled them to quickly build triangles and try different permutations. Thus, access to resources empowered the group with respect to the knowledge they were able to construct and an emergent discourse in which they could engage. Given the limitations of learning from these materials, it was not surprising to find that one group of students built a model for a triangle with sides of 2, 1, 1 and argued for its viability. This might have been a teachable moment, in that the experience of this group may have provided a context in which students would be interested to know the generalization that, for a triangle to be permissible, the sum of any two sides must be greater in magnitude than the third side.

If they were pursuing different goals than mine, the relationship between the combined length of any two sides and the third side of a permissible triangle might have little relevance to teachers and students involved in toothpick geometry. There is a tension between students pursuing a learning agenda shaped solely by their own interests and one constrained by a need to learn specific canonical science. Because a diversity of motivation to learn, interests, and capabilities characterizes any social setting, variation can be expected in the optimal time for students to learn given ideas. One way to address this diversity in a learning community is for those who know and can do to act as learning resources for others. But what is to be taught and learned? Although it can be asserted that students should decide what they want to know and when they need to know it, or the converse, teachers and students can negotiate curricular goals and jointly monitor progress toward their attainment. In this way it is possible for personal interests to be pursued in conjunction with goals that reflect canonical science. However, if those within a community are to participate in this manner, attention should be given to the roles enacted by teachers and learners, equitable access of participants to discursive resources, and associated power interrelationships.

The knowledge of the teachers was not a visible part of the community and neither was the knowledge of the most able students. Students worked together to produce triangles on their construction paper, and, as issues arose, they negotiated ways to proceed. Is a 4, 3, 2 the same as a 4, 2, 3? Can one be transformed into the other? My limited French would not allow me to ask those questions in ways that the students could understand and I was tempted to set up a demonstration to create a perturbation. The teachers consciously constrained the task environment and opportunities to learn by providing materials, initiating verbal interaction, and adopting roles that encouraged students to engage within their groups, not telling them if they were right or wrong, and generally leaving them to figure out what was and was not appropriate. However, the teachers' roles raised questions in my mind because the social aspects of learning were not maximized. For example, as interesting triangles were produced, I wanted to bring them to the attention of others and encourage students to observe and learn from others' actions, not just from those in their group. The social construction of knowledge was limited by a tendency of students to remain in their own groups and for teachers not to disseminate information about the accomplishments of others. The teachers' roles were facilitative of learning but appeared to consciously suppress their own expertise. In contrast to the way they enacted their roles, I wanted to be more of a core participant, to build my own triangles and engage in discussions about what was and was not permissible about building triangles. Furthermore, I wanted to encourage students to look at others' triangles as they were presented on the construction paper and discuss the variety of approaches and solutions of different groups.

The following vignette describes a similar experience based on research undertaken in a third-grade classroom in which children were building castles with easy to find manipulatives (Tobin, 1997a).

Hold it! Hold it! Oh no! Ana you've got to hold it while I connect the roof on. Michael was agitated with Ana. They had been working on building a castle for three days now and still the walls would not stay up. They had planned a good castle and the drawings looked fine, but the materials Ms. Roberts had given them to build with would not work. Ana was feeling grumpy about this whole activity. It was not her fault that the stupid walls would not stay up. Every time she held it up the pins came loose. Why couldn't they use glue anyway? "Castles are not made out of pins and straws!" she retorted. Ms. Roberts was pleased with the activities. The students were busy and they were doing science. Furthermore, the activities in which they were engaged involved manipulatives, oral language, drawing, writing, social studies, and literature. The idea of building castles arose from their studies of Germany. It was neat that students were problem solving. As a facilitator, she perceived her role as closely observing her students, learning from listening to them, and making plans to assist them to meet their goal of building a castle.

The vignette describes an activity that is consistent with a hands-on, minds-on metaphor in which the teacher's role is conceptualized as facilitator. However, even though there is extensive hands-on activity, communication, and problem solving, the development of scientific ideas is absent. Scientific knowledge does not reside in the materials to be mysteriously released during hands-on activities. On the contrary, scientific knowledge needs to be co-constructed in interactions in which students and the teacher interact verbally using a shared language. For example, the knowledge that a structure could be made rigid through the use of triangular braces is a reasonable goal for the activity previously described in the vignette. However, in this case it is unlikely that students would construct that understanding and, if they did include triangular braces in their structure, would they associate their inclusion with increased rigidity of the structure? In addition to providing a context for rich conversations in which those who know science can mediate the learning of those who do not know, manipulations of materials provide an important grounding for what is known. To facilitate the learning of science it is essential that the teacher infuses scientific discourse activities and provides a scaffold into the languages of the child and of science. This does not imply a return to the days of teachers transmitting facts in lectures or the principal learning resource being a textbook. What is significant is that students talk science in ways that connect to activities they have experienced directly and to their other studies and lives outside of school.

Recent research has focused on the links between the actions and interactions of students and the emergence of a discourse that was consistent with canonical ways of knowing science (Roth, 1996; Roth, McRobbie, Lucas, and Boutonné, 1997). For example, during a thirteen-week investigation of a fourth/fifth grade classroom, Roth (1996) explored the questioning strategies of a teacher who was successful in promoting student-centered activities without compromising canonical content knowledge. In the initial weeks, the teacher's questions were frequent and focused on connecting the language of students and their classroom practices to concepts of engineering science. The most visible aspect of learning, aside from the development of tool-related practices, was an increase in the extent to which students talked about topics related to the design of structures. When the teacher introduced items from canonical engineering discourse, it required mediational efforts on her part to assist children to appropriate the discourse. She used questions to provide a scaffold between what students knew and had done and where she wanted them to go with their thinking and learning. The teacher's questions were invitations for individuals to speak about what they had done and learned and to interact with others in student-centered discussions. Throughout the unit, the emergence of a shared language was facilitated by the teacher who ensured that ideas originating with students were communicated with the rest of the class, usually in whole class settings during which teacher questions enabled students to appropriate terms previously introduced by others. As the unit progressed, the teacher decreased the frequency of her questions and there was a higher incidence of self-sustaining discussions in which students interacted with one another independently of the teacher. The teacher's role became less central as students included engineering-related issues in their designs and provided longer and more complete accounts of their work and plans. In assuming a less central role, the teacher enabled students to increase their contributions to whole class discussions, ask more questions, and become less reliant on the scaffold of teacher questions.

In a study of laboratory activities with a group of twelfth-grade physics students, Roth, McRobbie, Lucas, and Boutonné (1997) described how the phenomena which students constructed were diverse, different from, and often incompatible with, canonical accounts of science. Students frequently constructed understandings that were not those of canonical science because they lacked the necessary language and physical actions and employed interpretive frameworks that produced understandings that were not scientific in character. The authors concluded that students who do not yet know scientific principles are unlikely to see what their investigation is intended to show, for the principles that are to be exhibited are prerequisites to observing the phenomenon to be experienced. Hence it is improbable that students will construct scientific knowledge in laboratory activities unless they possess an appropriate interpretive framework and receive guidance from someone who already knows the science. The study has obvious implications for the conduct of school laboratory activities which are often regarded by teachers and students as the critical ingredient of a science course yet appear to be unproductive activities for learning canonical science (Lunetta, 1998; Roth, McRobbie, Lucas and Boutonné, 1997; Tobin, 1990).

Coparticipation, power, and the learning and teaching science

If students are to learn science as a form of discourse, it seems necessary for them to be able to diversify their language resources as they practice science in settings in which others who know science assist them to learn by coparticipating in activities (Roth, 1995; Schön, 1985; Tobin, 1997). Coparticipation implies the presence of a shared language that can be accessed by all participants to engage the activities of the community with a goal to facilitate the learning of others. Alternatively, interactions among participants can facilitate the development of a shared language and additional discursive resources. Within an evolving knowledge community, concern is shown for what is known by learners at any given time and how they can represent what they know. A teacher can structure activities in which students engage such that they can use their existing knowledge to make sense of what is happening and build new understandings on a foundation of extant knowledge. The focus of the teacher on the representations of the learner is what is most critical about a coparticipatory environment. The mediating role of the teacher is focused not only on what students know and how they can represent what they know but also on the identification of activities that can continue the evolutionary path of the classroom community toward the attainment of agreed-upon goals. In such a setting, students have the autonomy to ask when they do not understand, knowledge claims that make no sense are clarified, and discussion occurs until such time that a learner is satisfied that he or she now understands. Students do not feel that they cannot understand and that their only recourse is to accept what is said as an article of truth based on a faith that others understand the warrants for the viability of the claim.

The standards for accepting knowledge as viable can be negotiated within a community. My experience as a teacher and researcher is that most students regard authority as the arbiter of what is or is not viable. Accordingly, for many learners, the voices of science, as represented by teachers, books, and resources such as videotapes, can be more powerful than common sense and other forms of personal knowledge. I reject the romantic notion of rugged individuals working alone to test the internal coherence of new ideas and extant knowledge or of empirically testing the viability of their knowledge. Although I acknowledge the value of individuals engaging such activities, as most students endeavor to make sense of phenomena and test the viability of what they know and can do, usually they will need and seek the assistance of others and might accept certain ideas on faith, at least in the short term. For any individual there needs to be a balance of what can be understood in terms of its fit with other knowledge, what can be tested empirically, and what is accepted as true on the basis of the voices of science.

Power within a community needs to be distributed in such a way that all students have equitable access to resources to enhance their learning. In essence, this means that all participants have the autonomy to coparticipate in the discourse of the community. If someone speaks, then an individual should have the freedom to comment on what was said or to ask questions. Of course there are very many possible verbal moves after another person has spoken. At issue is whether a person is able to participate authentically in the practices of the community. There are several scenarios in which coparticipation does not occur. For example, perhaps a teacher is using a form of discourse that is inaccessible to the learners. If that is the case, students might not raise questions because of a fear that they do not know enough to ask a question, or they might not coparticipate because the teacher does not provide opportunities for their participation. In each instance, the power of the teacher is constituted in a form of discourse that cannot be appropriated by the students, leaving them with little recourse other than rote learning. How then can a teacher avoid discourses that disempower learners? One way to address this potential problem is for teachers to become more reflective on their practices and build interpretive frameworks to enable them not only to recognize power differentials,[1] but also to realize that students can assume a shared responsibility for their own learning. In this sense, a critical element of an instructional strategy is to allow students to practice in a coparticipatory way using their discursive tools and thereby render their performance visible to themselves and others. What students can and cannot do can be rendered visible to the student him- or herself and for the critical review of others by encouraging students to speak, use gestures, and write. Students also could have opportunities to write questions that need to be answered and, when necessary, to interrupt the flow of delivery by asking questions orally. Within each classroom, the power-sharing needed to facilitate coparticipation should be tailored to reflect the cultural histories of participants in the community.

The diversity of science classrooms around the world and even within a given city in the United States of America cautions against a monolithic view of the form that coparticipation might take in different contexts. For example, in circumstances of limited proficiency in the use of the language of instruction, such as occurs in cities such as Montréal and Miami, or in schools where many dialects for a given native language are spoken, the form of negotiated language and its appropriation can take on features that reflect the specifics of the students' language proficiency, the cultural capital of the students, and the cultural history of classroom teachers. Schön (1985) described coparticipation in the following way: "As the two persons approach convergence of meaning, their speech becomes more elliptical, they use shorthand in word and gesture to convey ideas that might seem complex to an outsider; they communicate with greater confidence; they finish one another's sentences, or leave sentences unfinished" (p. 64).

Schön's description of the conditions associated with the convergence of meaning awakened me to a whole new realm of possibilities. After many years of undertaking research on wait time, I had grown comfortable with the logic of verbal interaction based on one speaker at a time and attentive listening (Tobin, 1987). If learning is to occur, silence is needed, I have always argued, so that individuals can think things through and be reflective about what is and is not known. Making connections requires time and freedom from the distractions of others. Although two decades of research on teaching and learning suggested that many students learned in conditions in which teachers and students maintained average wait times of between three and five seconds, Schön's case study of learning to become an architect was consistent with my professional experience. Several years ago, as I walked on the veranda of a school in Costa Rica, I was struck by the noise emanating from the classrooms. My observations of several classrooms confirmed that, in comparison with situations in other countries, there was more verbal interaction occurring at a whole class level, and my impression was that students often were speaking simultaneously, filling the pauses between words with their own oral texts. From my own cultural perspective, it was too noisy to be conducive to learning and, as teacher or learner, I would seek more silence. Whether or not simultaneous speech is tolerable, facilitative of learning, or an inhibitor of learning depends on the cultural history of the learner. In this instance, teachers and students appeared comfortable with simultaneous speech and a classroom environment that to me seemed noisy. This experience reinforces the notion that the practices of classroom communities reflect the larger culture in which schooling occurs and cautions against a one-size-fits-all notion of educational research that all learners will benefit from average wait times of three to five seconds. Grand narratives such as these, based on research in an era when many educational researchers sought them out and tested them with a positivist set of referents, may be used as a guide to reflect on teaching and possible directions for change, but they should not be regarded as guaranteed formulae for success.

Science as symbolic violence

Bourdieu (1991) uses the term *symbolic violence* to describe the problems of peripheral participants within a community concluding that their cultural capital is not valued and is seemingly ''worthless'' in the context of scaffolding which is insufficient to permit them to learn to use the discursive resources of the community. In a process of progressive devaluation, symbolic violence occurs when individuals encounter situations in which their cultural capital is not viable. A common example of symbolic violence occurs when students are unable to use their own language resources to make sense of science. This happens most frequently when the focus of a curriculum is on coverage of the subject matter, often relying heavily on the chapters of a textbook. In such circumstances the teacher may focus on content coverage and only attend to the extant knowledge of students when mistakes are made, and only then to correct those mistakes. Scaffolds are not provided to enable students to employ their cultural capital in authentic ways as they learn to participate. In such circumstances, students may not understand the scientific meanings of terms and, when provided opportunities to clarify their understandings, feel that they do not know enough to ask sensible questions. Their personal language resources are not helpful in bridging the semantic space between their own discourse and that of science. Of course language is more than words, and the gap also reflects differences in the habitus of participants in the scientific communities and those populated by students. Because students in these circumstances have difficulty in being successful, they can begin to regard their cultural capital as having little worth in this community. That is, the practices of the community are such that individuals learn to devalue their cultural and linguistic capital.

The potential for science to be a source of symbolic violence exists for all students but is strongest for those who do not belong to the majority culture for whom the curriculum tends to be tailored. Accordingly, the potential for symbolic violence is greatest for students who have a different language from the majority (e.g., speakers of Spanish, Haitian Creole, Ebonics, etc.). For example, students may have experienced symbolic violence if the teachers in the toothpick geometry activity had insisted they use syntactically correct French to express their ideas about triangles. Furthermore, enforcement of the canonical view that 2, 1, 1 was not a permissible triangle could also result in symbolic violence for those students who had built a model and argued for its viability.

Students from different cultures may also experience symbolic violence when their habitus does not enable them to meet their goals within a sciencelike community. One clear example includes those who do not employ positivism and its associated objectivism as referents for making sense of experience. The roots of positivism permeate science and science education and have done so since the birth of modern science and the time of Leonardo Da Vinci (Ihde, 1993). Students who view the universe in alternative ways may not feel comfortable with the positivist underpinnings of Western modern science and the way science is taught, and they might experience symbolic violence because of inconsistencies between their own beliefs and practices and the postulates and habitus of science. The most common examples involve religious beliefs but these may be only the tip of the iceberg. Feminists such as Butler (1990) and radical ecologists such as Bowers (1993) have provided examples of communities utilizing more connected ways of knowing and making sense, and Japanese science educators, such as Kawasaki (1996), have questioned the value of Western modern science because of its lack of connection with nature and spirituality. These concerns are consistent with the efforts of critical theorists, such as Marcuse (1969), who have endeavored to interconnect the cognitive and imaginative aspects of science.

Belonging to a different culture is a source of disempowerment for minorities because the habitus associated with life in their home culture is no longer viable for them. One does not flow into a new culture but has to learn new routines, and this takes time. If we relate this concept to the context of learning science it seems to me that teachers can do a great deal to make it easier for learners by being aware of their cultural capital in the process of learning science. Instead of allowing the inevitable disempowerment arising in the failure to co-participate and the symbolic violence of realized failure, teachers might be pro-active in identifying the discursive resources that can shape goals, actions, and interactions of peripheral participants in a community.

Conclusions

A sociocultural perspective on teaching and learning rejects the overly simplistic appeal of a one-size-fits-all approach to enacting a curriculum and cautions against technical adherence to rules about what does and does not work in promoting the learning of science. The theoretical frames used to make sense of experience illuminate and obscure. Accordingly, when considering educational practice, it is often desirable to employ a ''bricolage'' of theories to selectively illuminate and obscure particular issues. The approaches to teaching and learning that are advocated in this chapter are supported by a variety of sociocultural perspectives, each of which is consistent with radical constructivism. From a radical constructivist perspective, cultural capital constitutes a foundation for learning that illuminates learners' efforts to make sense of experience in terms of what is already known. A dialectical relationship between radical constructivism and sociocultural phenomena situates individual sensemaking in a community of others, each of whom is a potential teacher and learner. A challenge for all participants is to enact a curriculum in ways that acknowledge that learning involves co-constructions of knowledge in a milieu saturated by the cultural histories of participants. Efforts can be made to enhance the learning of science by increasing the quality of social interactions that focus on what participants know and can do.

The realization that learning environments should be safe was apparent as the seminar on Fibonacci numbers commenced. My fear that I would be asked a question that I could not answer was not a positive force in driving inquiry. On the contrary, even though I searched for a solution and quickly found one, my search was distracted by the concern that I could be asked to respond to a question I could not answer. Accordingly, my thoughts concerned issues of self-esteem and not wanting my lack of knowledge to be visible within this particular community. That experience draws attention to the need for learning environments to be safe in that learners are willing to reveal what they know and can do without feeling insecure about being unable to succeed.

The knowledge of students can be used as a template to make sense of experiences. Because it captured my imagination, the Fibonacci sequence became a source of motivation for me as I endeavored to apply it to data that I had framed from an investigation. The process of testing whether or not there was a fit between the data and the theory required me to manipulate the data and re-present it in many different ways. Several significant issues emerge from this example. My extant knowledge was a source of motivation and capital for learning, the analysis of data was an imaginative process that is critical in testing the fit between theory and data, my commitment to the elegance of the Fibonacci sequence obscured other possible solutions that fit the data and also were elegant, and my quest for a solution to the problem began when my interest and imagination were piqued to an optimal level and concluded when the challenge of the problem "drained away." There are two emphases that I consider important here. First, that teachers should be aware of the significance of the links between the cognitive aspects of problem solving and imagination, motivation, and interest. Second, at some times I was inspired by the teaching of a colleague and at other times frustrated by his efforts to teach me. For a given learner, there will be times when teaching is needed and welcomed and other times when it becomes an unwelcome constraint. If coparticipation is occurring, a student could have the autonomy to indicate those occasions when additional input is welcome and when time is needed for private reflection and engagement. Providing the learner with autonomy to codecide when teaching is or is not appropriate is a possible solution. In the example of the Fibonacci sequence, I learned some of the most interesting and potentially useful knowledge at times when I was highly motivated to pursue my own activities. The power to decide when mediation should occur is best left to the contexts that arise when coparticipation occurs.

Significant issues for teachers to consider include how individuals can maximize their own learning, the social transmission of knowledge, and the evolution of a discourse that is canonical. Because of the diversity of contexts in which science is taught and learned, it is imperative for teachers to identify and use all available resources to support the development of a learning community in which those who know and can do assist those who want to learn. The theoretical perspectives used in this chapter have highlighted potential pitfalls of hands-on science and laboratories. If manipulatives and laboratory activities are to continue to have a role in the learning of science, it is evident that teachers will have to carefully include them in a curriculum where they contribute to an evolving discourse. Even though there are challenges in developing canonical science from hands-on and laboratory activities, the examples from this chapter suggest that it can be done when effective mediation is provided by teachers who know when to provide scaffolds and when to fade into the background.

When the habitus of participants is regarded as capital for learning, there is less likelihood that science will be perceived as symbolic violence and coparticipation can become feasible for all. Coparticipation assumes that teachers and learners can negotiate to build a new shared language that becomes a vehicle for communication and legitimate participation in a community (Lave and Wenger, 1991; Roth, 1995). The goal of promoting science achievement through coparticipation is inconsistent with an advocacy for linguistic imperialism (Phillipson, 1992) which proceeds by elevating the status and associated power of a majority language over native languages, dialects, and nonproficient usage of a majority language. Since coparticipation involves the negotiation of a shared language, the focus is on sustaining a dynamic system in which discursive resources are evolving in a direction that is constrained by the values of the majority culture while demonstrating respect for the habitus of participants from minority cultures, all the time guarding against the debilitation of symbolic violence. In the process of negotiating a shared language, it is essential that students use all of their language resources to develop understandings of science.

Chapter 13
Remarks on the education of elementary teachers

HEINRICH BAUERSFELD

The main thesis of this chapter is that the culture of teacher education must share the core characteristics of the desired mathematics classroom culture. In particular, this relationship must hold if teacher education is to exercise a reforming influence on in-service teachers and create a break in the circle of reproduction by which the weaknesses of the existing school system are perpetuated. It follows that more attention should be devoted to the relation between alternative classroom experiences and theoretical instruction, to the fundamental role of everyday language for the understanding of mathematics, the balance of self-directed work and the negotiation of meanings in seminars and tutorials, and to the development of reflection and self-monitoring. Our remarks can be grouped according to five main questions:

- What can learning and teaching mean for students and for teachers?
- What are the relevant effects of current teacher education?
- What does research say about the necessary reforms of teacher education?
- How might we promote necessary changes in teachers' basic orientations and routines?
- Given the necessary changes in teacher education, what are the available options?

Clearly, there are no simple, definite answers. Accordingly, the following comments should be viewed more as suggestions or possible options to be worked out at some time in the future. It is my belief that small-scale reform experiments are more effective than large-scale, top-down reform efforts. In terms of implementation, such experiments offer greater flexibility and a wider range of opportunity for involvement by, and change in, the individual teacher. On the other hand, the more open-ended an approach is, the more it becomes necessary to reflect on the theoretical considerations on which suggestions and options are to be based.

What do learning and teaching mean?

[The] dominant model of teacher education . . . : the university provides the theory, the methods, and skills; schools provide the classroom, curriculum, and students; and the student teacher provides the individual effort. . . . This training model, however, ignores the role of the social and political context of teacher education while emphasizing the individual's effort.

Britzman, 1986, p. 442

From an integrated interactionist-constructivist perspective (Bauersfeld, 1993), the key problem of all organized learning is: what are the conditions which are capable of inciting learners to change their ways, means, and routines of interpreting and acting? Such an effort at definition brings out four key issues:

1. The active, constructive part taken by the learner: change has to be processed by the learner and not by the teacher only; the learner is the main actor in the process, since it is his or her own structuring which is at stake.
2. The impact of the learner's socialization, of that which has been learned previously: the learner constantly acts by means of reactivating expectations, routines, and ways of doing which were formed in the past and which he or she relates to the present situation; there is no "tabula rasa"!
3. The tentative, conjectural nature of teaching: as seriously organized learning processes, teaching can only provide opportunities for learning; there is no reliable "transmitting" or "passing on" of knowledge; the teacher can only foster subjective restructuring on the part of the learner.
4. The social dimension of the teaching-learning process: the notion of "conditions" is generally meant to include not just subject matter but all relevant dimensions such as psychological factors, teaching methods, as well as social interaction and cooperation within the institution, the classroom (sub-)culture, background cultures, and so forth.

Discussions of learning generally dwell on students' learning, but what is said in this case applies equally to the learning process of teachers. We know much more about students' learning than we do about the conditions of the professional learning process of teachers. In particular, prescriptions and models for preservice education underestimate – indeed, ignore – the negative power and impact of student teachers' own classroom experiences as students over a dozen or more years of schooling in most cases (see Pinner and Shuard, 1985). And the very same models overestimate the positive effects of the usual academic training in pure mathematics. From this perspective, teacher education is more like a *re*-education of former students than an introduction into a new profession.

Relevant effects of common teacher education

Psychologists and educators are far short of charting the full extent of children's capacity for understanding.

Siegal, 1991, p. 133

For the understanding of learning and teaching mathematics, the preceding analyses provide a model for participating in a culture rather than a model for transmitting knowledge or introducing students to a body of objective knowledge. Participation in the processes of a mathematics classroom is participation in a culture of using mathematics or, better still, a culture of mathematizing as a practice. In addition to numerous skills, the core of what is learned through participation is when to do what, how to do it, and why. Knowledge (in a narrow sense) will be of no interest whatsoever if the user cannot identify situations in which such knowledge can be put to use. In addition, knowledge will not be of much help if the learner has not the flexibility to relate and transform the necessary elements of knowing into his or her actual situation. In other words, the most powerful, or core, effects which emerge from participation in the culture of a mathematics classroom manifest primarily on the meta level, and are "learned" indirectly, or are "colearned."

What has been described above in the case of students is also valid for teachers and the orientations that their action will take. Teacher education at universities and colleges functions like other institutional subcultures, regardless of the allowances which the institutions make or do not make for such effects. In all countries, the curricula used in educating mathematics teachers place too much emphasis on mathematical understanding, skills, knowledge, and expertise. The usual academic ways of mathematics lecturing and exposing mathematical knowledge are quite different from how mathematics might best be taught at the elementary level, to take a case in point. Accordingly, the mathematical habits developed by student teachers during their preparation at universities do not have much in common with the mathematical habits which will be made use of in a school setting. Furthermore, what is taught at universities about the realities and conditions of teaching is based more on "knowledge" and skills than on the spin-off of participation in a process of teaching which provides for a genuine approximation with the teacher's future practice in a classroom setting.

Surprisingly enough, it is clear that no one has yet discussed whether these methods provide for "enculturation"[1] of a type which is appropriate with respect to the teacher's role in the classroom. A recent review of forty studies of preservice education has led Kagan (1992) to conclude, in short, that: (1) these studies give evidence of "the stability and inflexibility of (the student teachers') prior beliefs and images" (p. 140); (2) "these personal beliefs and images generally remain unchanged by a preservice program and follow candidates into classroom practica and student teaching" (p. 142); and, consequently, (3) "quickly disillusioned and possessing inadequate procedural knowledge, novice teachers tend to grow increasingly authoritarian and custodial" (p. 145).

Neglecting the crucial fit occurring between the *habitus* (about this term, more in the following section) which the teacher takes on over the course of his or her university education and the habitus which is necessary to functioning in a school setting amounts to missing the opportunity of offsetting an average twelve to thirteen years of socialization as pupils among preservice teachers. Once the young teacher enters school again, it will be too late to change much, since the functioning of the school system is clearly weighted in favor of the time-honored, minimum solutions. Under the pressure of everyday duties and difficulties, the opportunities for initiating theoretically informed change and reform will be minimal. Whenever young teachers are confronted with problem situations, it is the old, reliable habitus formed during experiences as a student which will come to the fore. The regressions which typically occur upon reentering the school system entrench habitus which are only too at ease with the "solutions" of yore and which all too easily serve to reproduce the old school.

What kind of professional attitudes and what sort of "metaknowledge" will future mathematics teachers need? To what extent does current teacher education provide for these? And what promise do alternative approaches hold for a reform of the elementary school system? The following two sections will discuss these issues in greater detail.

Recommendations from related research

You don't learn speaking a language by learning a theory that can be formulated explicitly, you learn it be participating in a certain practice – you pick it up. Now picking up a language enables you to do two things. It enables you to understand and to use certain regularities *though without knowing what they are.*

Feyerabend, 1991, pp. 116–17, emphasis in the original

If the reality of the mathematics classroom is understood as constituting an ongoing, interactive development, then simple cause-and-effect rules are inadequate for guiding the teacher's permanent decision-making tasks. What characterizes effective teachers – aside from the quantities of school knowledge they are usually exposed to – is a certain habitus. Pierre Bourdieu (1980) originally defined habitus as a "generative mechanism" enabling a person to act appropriately as a member of his or her social class, even in situations that he or she has never experienced previously. When applied to the teacher's role in classroom culture, the concept of habitus provides an exact description of the individual background which is drawn on in the moment-related genesis of the subjective "definition of the situation" and of the related issues of "when and how" to do something in an "acceptable" manner.

Putnam, Lampert, and Peterson (1990) noted in their summary of an extensive review of teaching and learning mathematics in elementary schools that: "two features of instruction" are of particular importance: (1) "talking about mathematics," and (2) "considering the kinds of mathematical activities in classrooms" (p. 138). This seems to be very close to the notion of culture advocated here, particularly when the authors state: "Verbal discourse . . . constitutes an important means of revealing individual knowledge" and "much of what is learned about mathematics is implicit." According to their recommendations, the teacher "will need to talk with students, challenging them with counterexamples rather than with judgments about the wrongness of their answers" (p. 138).

Reviewing related research work from about 1985 to 1990, Anne Reynolds (1992) has arrived at the following synthesis of expectations for beginning teachers. She asserts, with no small degree of perspicaciousness, that:

Beginning teachers should enter the first year of teaching with: a) knowledge of the subject matter they will teach; b) the disposition to find out about their students and school, and the ethnographic and analytical skills to do so; c) knowledge of strategies, techniques, and tools for creating and sustaining a learning community, and the skills and abilities to employ these strategies, techniques, and tools; d) knowledge of pedagogy appropriate for the content area they will teach; and e) the disposition to reflect on their own actions and students' responses in order to improve their teaching, and the strategies and tools for doing so. (pp. 25–6).

In the next section, these useful recommendations will be fleshed out within a more fully integrated theoretical framework.

How are changes in teachers' habits to be promoted?

The principle "motive" in language acquisition is the better regulation of the underlying social-cultural processes . . . that are shared by prelinguistic and linguistic communication.

Bruner, 1983, p. 128

The basic, thorny difficulty involved with the genesis of the habitus itself is that the transmission of desired characteristics cannot be achieved by lecturing on or teaching them directly. However, exposing students to lectures inevitably contributes to the formation of a habitus, as does all participation in the social interaction of institutions or groups. Developing out of the student teacher's experience of academic education, this habitus is the principal culprit in the reproduction of the widespread custom of lecturing, as has been documented so often in microsociological investigations of regular classrooms (see Edwards, 1997; Hoetker and Ahlbrand, 1969).

If the formation of habitus is derived from participation in a social practice, then we will have to organize preservice education as a culture which itself actualizes the desired characteristics. By referring to the notion of *actualization,* we wish to underscore the necessity of participation in a culture of cooperative mathematizing. In this process, students and preservice educators make a joint attempt at adhering to desired norms and conventions; immediately following class activities, all discuss and reflect on their experiences and use the latter as a basis upon which to negotiate taken-as-shared issues. Reflections and considerations necessarily form an integral part of these model cultures; they will play a key role in breaking with the usual pattern of replacing some original experience by discourse on other people's experiences or lectures on expected outcomes. These considerations have led us to advocate an alternative practice not only of preservice teaching for mathematics teachers but of providing a mathematics education to these same student teachers, who require special courses and seminars in mathematics.

As to prescriptions concerning the "contents" of the subject area of mathematics, the numerous endeavors in problem solving (see Polya's excellent books) may be taken as helpful starting points. According to the constructivist principle, learning develops from subjective constructions; from the interactionist view, it arises from the joint negotiation of social conventions and norms of mathematizing rather than from "reading" or "discovering" objectively given truths or external structures. It follows, then, that teacher education will have to devote much more attention to the negotiation of student teachers' subjective constructions of meaning. The processual nature of such adaptations and personal reconstructions, taken with their genesis through emergence rather than through organized elicitation, will necessitate new forms of encounter in the training setting. The purpose of such encounters should be to provide an experiental foundation that is useful in forming a desired habitus. Groundwork for improved student/teacher interactions at the university level can be laid through experimentation with alternative seminars, presentations, and curricula.

I would also argue for a reformed role of practice teaching in preservice education. The initial encounters with the reality of the mathematics classroom must be devised with a view to different aims and different purposes. Practica should not serve as an introduction into the techniques of teaching nor be used for developing professional skills, as has been attempted in microteaching experiments, for example. Rather, the main purpose of such practice encounters is to be located in their role in: (1) developing both a sufficient, personally experienced framework for the necessary theoretical reflections and the motivation required to engage in such reflections; (2) sensitizing students to the hidden structures of this complex field of activity, dwelling in particular on their own experiences as a school student (in retrospect) and the limitations inherent to these experiences; and (3) indirectly contributing to the development of an alternative school mathematical habitus.

Options for necessary changes in teacher education

The following paragraphs present additional detailed recommendations for innovating in the preservice education of elementary mathematics teachers. (This list makes no claim to being exhaustive; also, the order of the sections does not suggest any particular hierarchy).

The academic teaching of mathematics

> *"Intersubjectivity" is no concept at all, rather a makeshift solution . . . a paradox, which does not denote what it seems to denote. . . . Each subject has his own intersubjectivity.*
>
> *Luhmann, 1986, p. 42, my translation*

Since, in many countries, mathematics departments have made mathematics education a subdivision coming under their control, it may be allowed that the function and importance of pure mathematics have exercised undue influence over teacher education. But the need for complementing and reorienting present teacher education lies not so much in modifying the syllabus of mathematical topics, or the content and scope of these, as in altering how professors actually teach. Where the lack is most keenly felt is in the area of an organized theoretical grappling with the processes occurring in the mathematical classroom. If one of the fundamental goals of elementary education is to help more children develop a stable self-image through the experience of accomplishing things, then obviously the same also applies in the case of an academic education in mathematics.[2]

Of course, we cannot expect university professors in mathematics to act like elementary mathematics teachers. But they must come to see themselves not only as authorities in a particular topic of mathematics but as representatives of a culture which is characterized both by doing mathematics and by teaching and learning mathematics. Through their activities, professors demonstrate their ways of mathematizing, of dealing with mistakes and incorrect inferences, of using mathematical models in other areas, and, last but not least, of using graphic symbols and other means to depict or explicate issues, tasks, outcomes, and so on. In other words, the culture of academic mathematizing during preservice education should not differ too greatly from the culture of the mathematics classroom awaiting future teachers; at the very least, the former should not function at odds with the latter. This makes obvious the need for university professors who specialize in preservice education. It is a widespread if seemingly unnoteworthy phenomenon that many university faculties the world over boast specialized professors in mathematics, in addition to physics, chemistry, psychology, medicine, and so on. Surprisingly enough, however, no thought is given as to whether student teachers really evidence a crying need for such specialized knowledge; in addition, the reasons underlying such a need are likely to be at some variance with the justifications provided in currently adopted approaches.

Fundamental attitudes and the investigations approach

In contrast with learning as internalization, learning as increasing participation in communities of practice concerns the whole person acting in the world.

Lave and Wenger, 1991, p. 49

There is a simple chain of conditions linking desired actions among students to the necessary prerequisites among teachers. As we all well know, the mental development of students at school depends on the quality of the repeated, varied activities which they involve themselves in; it also depends on the teacher's expertise, interaction, and personality. These qualities are intimately bound up with the potential power and richness of the mathematical classroom. A crucial element of this culture is the teacher's continual fostering of an attitude of curiosity and inquisitiveness among students, wherein patterns and regularities are sought out and surprising outcomes are held to be the norm. Since human nature is too complex and has yet to prove amenable to development through simple cause-and-effect models, it follows that this chain offers no one-to-one correspondence between ''input'' and ''output.'' The teacher's role in this interaction represents a necessary, but not sufficient, condition for the development of desired activities.

The aim of these remarks is to emphasize the development of an attitude through participation, rather than the oft-mentioned pedagogical techniques going under the heading of ''motivation'' (as cognitive psychology has termed this) or ''enlivening things'' through so-called applications or relationships to ''everyday realities.'' Wherein lies the difference from earlier ''discovery'' approaches, as favored by Bruner in the early sixties? It is in the shift from casually inserted, exceptional arrangements toward an integrated, ongoing experience in the mathematics classroom (see Table 13.1).

In passing, it should be mentioned that, from a constructivist perspective, serious doubts can be entertained as to what, if anything, the notion of ''discovery'' is able to describe (see Bauersfeld, 1995). The British ''investigations'' approach (e.g., Burton, 1984; Mason, Burton,

Table 13.1. Classical versus integrated approach

Classical Discovery Approach (focus on the single learner)	Integrated (Culture) Approach (focus on style in social interaction)
In explicitly defined situations, the student "researcher" begins with an introduction, then works on prepared material, and proceeds finally to discuss and clarify his or her findings in a session involving the entire class.	In all classroom situations, students are expected to search for pattern, presuppose regularities, and relate developing or contrasting ideas, in addition to providing arguments and justifications for the issues under discussion.

and Stacey, 1982; Mottershead, 1978, 1985) and the many novel approaches advanced by the Freudenthal Institute in Utrecht, Netherlands (formerly the IOWO) are promising. They provide teachers with encouraging starting points in the form of: using open-ended tasks, taking advantage of moment-related, everyday situations, and providing for the (relatively) self-organized processing of ''data'' (often of a self-collected variety) and of questions and solutions (see the numerous contributions on this subject in the Dutch journal *Willem Bartjens*; also de Lange, 1987; Streefland, 1991; Treffers, 1991). The preferred mode of organization makes use of small group activities involving pairs of students (dyadic interactions).

It will be up to preservice teaching programs to introduce student teachers to such practices, since future practice in school settings occurs too long ''after the fact'' of socialization to produce any modification in a teacher's fundamental attitudes. The reproductive power of the classic school system and its ineffective, minimum[3] solutions for everyday activities are too strong and too resistant to change. Why not organize seminars using the book by Brown and Walter (1990), whose focus consists in developing the art of varying the problems at hand and adapting such variations to different individual needs for (1) understanding and (2) strategy development? Why not organize selected teaching practica, in which one student teacher works with two or three schoolchildren in related situations, and is thus exposed to only a limited range of classroom experience? Why not discuss and concomitantly analyze classroom episodes that have been videotaped using conversation analysis methods (Edwards, 1997)?

Mathematical language

It should . . . then be one of the most persistent aims of education to provide for the child such an environment as this. There should be about him con-

stantly a life which can unfailingly supply the unity which the more or less isolated appearance of different powers in the child lacks. It is characteristic of the modern family and school that it fails signally in this function.

Mead, 1896, cited in Rucker, 1968, p. 150

For many teachers, the strength and the generalizability of mathematics is inseparable from the strictness and precision of its underlying representations, be they verbal or otherwise symbol using. Like priests who celebrate the esoteric language game of their caste, many mathematics teachers constantly insist on stating, and having stated to them, subject matter in "true" mathematical language – that is, one which is as "fine-tuned" as possible. An observer may come to the conclusion that this technical language is germane to what the teacher wishes to elaborate on. For students, however, this emphasis prompts them to learn how to "say things exactly the way the teacher said them," with the predictable dire consequences.

One may indeed wonder whether many teachers are actually capable of "mastering" their mathematical concepts in any other way at all. That is to say that these teachers know how to talk about "it" in the terminology of the accepted language game. But what command they may possess does not go far, for it offers little usefulness in other "contexts," is ill suited to the situations for which it is actually drawn on, and bespeaks an incapacity to metaphorize the issues at hand.

To be perfectly honest, I as yet know no one at the university level who encourages preservice teachers to speak about the (mathematical) content conveyed by everyday language, to use metaphors, or to bring out related issues and the like. Cognitivists may prefer expressions like "translating," "saying it in other words," "referring something (back) to other things," "embedding," "visualizing." The upshot of this, however, is to treat the subject matter as a kind of object rather than as something emerging from moment-related, situated processes. Thus, many mathematics teachers are quite rigid in how they express themselves verbally and in how they evaluate their own students' utterances. However, they remain quite permissive with respect to the social organization of their class. From a social interactionist or constructivist perspective, it would appear that the other way around holds out greater promise. In other words, it would be more useful to accept and encourage students' mathematical utterances within very wide limits as to "how it is said" and the use of metaphors, provided that some serious underlying motive (reason, argument, etc.) can be identified; at the same time, it is important to hold firm on the social regulations, insisting that students are attentive to the interaction and explanations of the others, ensuring that everyone waits their turn and that they give serious consideration to other people's bona fide contributions, et cetera.

Analysis of many videotapes from different countries reveals the all-too-widespread poverty of classroom communication from this perspective. If the culture students experience in their classrooms is impoverished in terms of languaging (Bauersfeld, 1995a; Brown, 1997) and presenting models of desired interaction, if it is lacking in incentives and challenges, if it is a nontransparent celebration of technical language rather than an opportunity to participate in a "scaffolding"[4] culture (see Bruner, 1983), and if it offers nothing for the critical mind to grapple with nor anything by which to spur on the keen minded, what then are we to expect from our schools and the school mathematical habitus they give rise to?

The difficulty here – and it is by no means a slight one – involves the negative effects of much of the initial *mathematical* instruction of preservice teachers. "Learning how to use language involves both learning the culture and learning how to express intentions in congruence with the culture" (Bruner and Haste, 1987, p. 89). And "one has to conclude that the subtle and systematic basis upon which linguistic reference itself rests must reflect a natural organization of mind, one into which we *grow* through experience rather than one we achieve by learning" (p. 88, emphasis in the original). This points to the need for thoroughgoing innovation in the initial training received by preservice teachers in terms of language and speaking, particularly with respect to the interrelations occurring between mother tongue, everyday language, figurative speech, and technical (mathematical) language.

Benjamin Lee Whorf (1956), known primarily in connection with the "Whorfian hypothesis" concerning the intimate relation between thinking and language, offered a remarkable example of how precise natural language descriptions can be, even though the speakers use concepts which differ quite widely from one another (i.e., hold a variety of meanings; see Figure 13.1). Paradoxically, the crux of this demonstration hangs on the use of mathematical set language.

Seminars on languaging mathematically, on "how to speak about the issue meant," on presenting given tasks with different words (and different graphical means), using adequate metaphors and so forth may prove useful (see Shuard and Rothery, 1984). In addition to contributing, presumably, to the development of greater empathy with the student teacher, such experiences can provide for a more highly ef-

The intersection of a few extensive concepts can be quite narrow and sharp, permitting many other connections

Whereas the use of just one narrow concept stands to suffer from the poor relationships it entertains with other (narrow) concepts

Figure 13.1. Extensive concepts versus narrow concepts

fective introduction to our knowledge of classroom communication and interaction.

The constructive orientation versus deficit repair

> *People can help each other learn when they use their differences in a joint activity. Much schooling in America has a contrasting focus, namely, finding reasons why each others' contributions are inadequate.*
>
> *Newman, Griffin, and Cole, 1989, cited in Bredo and McDermott, 1992, p. 36*

Since their professionally developed mathematical expectations serve as defining criteria, teachers inevitably perceive and assess the inadequacy of a student's mathematical action in terms of being "wrong." As a result, and despite being pedagogically counterfunctional in most cases, their reaction is aimed at eliminating the gap between a student's actual performance and their own ideal, desired response.

Take, for example, the common pedagogical conviction that students' mathematical errors are most often caused by a strategy or rule. The teacher's efforts at repairing are, as a result, focused on replacing the faulty rule by *the* appropriate one. However, even though a student's response in a specific situation may be perceived by the teacher as being rule guided, it in fact leaves room for widely differing interpretations. For example, such a response can originate in: a ready-made but faulty strategy; a slip in using a correct though rather complicated subjective strategy (as fast learners are prone to do); a passing, merely tentative forming of an answer using poorly developed bases; or spontaneous adoption of a hit-or-miss approach, and so on.

In keeping with the tenets of deficit repair, wherein students are encouraged to produce the correction themselves, teachers lapse into a form of questioning which proceeds step-by-step and in an atmosphere of mounting tension until the correct answer is finally uttered, either by the student or by the teacher him- or herself. This is a widespread, emergent pattern of interaction in the classroom – that is, a "funnel pattern" (Bauersfeld, 1978, 1995) – of which students and teachers alike are unaware. Furthermore, the intensive discussion of "wrong" strategies and conceptualizations runs the risk of stabilizing or hardening a tentative construction, which is all the more reliably stored and activated from memory the greater the emotional load of the situation is, whence the capacity for managing failure the next time around.

If the obvious mistakes are understood as individual constructions which are produced in response to the situation at hand, rather than as the product of something like conscious knowing, selection, and application of rule, then the possibility of devising an alternative strategy emerges. It may be more useful to identify the appropriate parts and steps in the student's faulty procedure and to constructively develop these toward an acceptable solution. Thus, by ignoring the weak points, the teacher can reduce the likelihood of neglecting students' constructions. Students arrive at mental constructions and regularities with widely varying degrees of achievement, stability, and receptiveness to reformulation, depending on their perception of the situation at hand. Accordingly, the alternative strategy appears to be more cautious in most situations.

When, on the other hand, the "funnel" pattern is resorted to, the teacher all too often brings the episode to a close in a way suggesting that successful invention and successful repair have been accomplished. But because the ongoing questioning does not provide the student with a chance to adapt his or her attempts to proposed or sanctioned modeling activity, the impression of accomplishment is but an illusion. Thus, the teacher's "surgery" is damaging for students' tentative efforts at constructing. Furthermore, it is in fact useful on occasion to simply demonstrate the expected solution or strategy and to discuss it so as to avoid lapsing into the funnel pattern.

Why not replace the deficit criterion by a constructive orientation altogether? The teacher would then have to identify the positive or concordant elements in the student's moment-related production and modify the task at hand accordingly. That way, the student could enjoy the opportunity of extending his or her use of positive elements, thereby reinforcing those elements and interactions which function satisfactorily (see, in this connection, Vygotsky's "zone of proximal development": Bruner, 1984; Newman, Griffin, and Cole, 1989). Teachers who engage in a relational negotiation of meaning with students will surely engender less frustration and greater feelings of accomplishment than is customarily the case whenever contradictions are forced out into the open and questioning turns into a continual squeezing process. However, there is no simple verbal transmission of the alternative strategies of which it is a question here, nor of ways of identifying the appropriate moment to act, nor of useful forms of interaction and variations thereon – indeed, these must be learned and developed in action.

In terms of connectionist theory, or neuroscience (see Bauersfeld, 1993), the proposed alternative offers potential for the emergence of stronger (neuronal) connections in the brain by means of the successful accomplishment of desired activities, whereas conventional questioning methods promote the generation of weak connections which can be easily disturbed in situations of confusion or heavy emotional load. Interestingly, recent research on the learning of spelling has arrived at the very same approach, replacing instruction about "mistakes" with the elaboration and orientation of individual constructions (see Brügelmann's contribution in Lorenz, 1991).

If preservice teachers do not learn their mathematics during initial teacher education via a similar mode, how then will they be capable of changing once they have entered the classroom? Again, we arrive at the need for professors in mathematics who themselves have specialized in educating teachers. The more that academic disciplines evolve and undergo differentiation from one another, the more it should be possible to implement such a change in mathematics education and not only in preservice training for mathematics teachers.

Geometry: Arithmetic's missing foundation

In no way do I object to methodology as such . . . but it should be the result of an a posteriori reflecting on one's methods, rather than an a priori doctrine imposed on the learner.

Freudenthal, 1991, p. 150

A key issue in the preservice preparation of teachers for elementary mathematics is that missing field, geometry. Usually, geometry plays a minor role in the elementary mathematics curriculum as well. And whenever time runs short at school, what few geometrical themes feature in that day's plans are the first to be dropped. But all kinds of embodiments – for example, arrangements of counters, rods, and blocks; number strips and number lines; dot cards; hundreds boards, addition and multiplication tables, dominoes, geoboards; the representations used to convey the concept of average; fractions as parts of circles and rectangles, et cetera – involve geometrical structures. In elementary textbooks, there is not a single embodiment or graphics-based representation of numbers and arithmetical operations which does not require geometrical structures to produce the desired interpretation.

It is a terrible misfortune, however, that all these modeling devices are used in the classroom as if the child had a command of the geometrical properties which such representations draw on. As long as these devices seem to function, there is no reason to consider the underlying structures, as weak as the children's related constructions of meaning may be. And even when such devices fail to produce the desired results, the teacher's correction is usually provided from an arithmetical perspective; the fundamental geometrical properties fail to be elucidated. This amounts to placing the cart before the horse. Students are forced to adapt their conceptualizations to the arithmetical results, whereas on the contrary they should use geometrical properties to lay the foundations for addressing arithmetical issues. Thus the function of embodiments is turned on its head.

Since the school does not provide preservice teachers with the necessary experiences, how then are we to bring about change within the mathematics classroom? Clearly, lectures about abstract geometry will be of little help. Students as well as teachers indeed require exercises with materials and geometrical models, cutting paper and cardboard, building solids, and so forth. They also need to rehearse the mental operations involved in the use of images of figures and solids by moving, turning, and cutting images and by demonstrating outcomes not only through language but also through body language (deictics) – fingers, hands, et cetera. Also useful are special exercises in how to speak about such transformations in properties, using everyday language and metaphors – which do not rely exclusively on the technical language of geometry experts. It should be clear that we are not referring here to a mechanistic type of drill. Instead, we mean that explanations and reflections are necessary to working with the issues under discussion.

If future teachers have not been provided preparation of this sort, the effects are easy to predict. Fast learners and children with a positive disposition to learning will learn to get by anyway. The victims will be the disadvantaged children – those, precisely, who need support and "scaffolding" most of all. It is they who are most deeply affected by the counterfunctioning of public school systems. In addition, the deficient preparation of teachers serves, in the social sphere, to operate a negative selection upon students.

Teaching experiments in small groups

The more communication [there is], and the more negotiation and resolution takes place over differences in opinion regarding role delineation or task strategy, the more collaborative are the dyads (teacher/student interaction) – and, as corollary, the more collaborative the dyads, the greater the level of success on the task and the greater the cognitive gains and benefits.

Garton, 1992, p. 119

Early in the seventies, Jack Easley provided convincing demonstration of how useful teaching experiments with small groups of school students could be (see the related dissertations from Driver, 1973; Erlwanger, 1974; Shirk, 1972; also Bauersfeld, 1980). As a complement to, but not a substitute for, initial encounters with the entire complexity of a mathematics classroom, preservice teachers could teach small groups of school children in guided experiments. Preparation should occur in connection with seminars concerning the function of materials and embodiments, about students' learning processes, problem solving, and so on. The advantage of this approach is to provide an initiation into school practice in a situation of reduced complexity, which is supplemented by documentation through video recordings. Repeated reviewing of the tapes, and the application of different analytical perspectives thereto, should also follow suit.

Such teaching experiments are particularly useful when preservice teachers have had prior opportunities to work out their own experiences with the materials and the structures and possible uses of such materials. To overcome preservice teachers' own deficits, rehearsals of the following required tasks should be held: solids and their nets and cuts, straw-models, plane figures and their properties, reflections and rotations, thumb movies (animation of the functional change of figures and their properties), the enlargement and reduction of figures, geoboard activities, Polyominoes, paper folding and cutting, sections of 2-D and 3-D models, and so forth. All too many teachers have difficulties with organizing such experiences for students since they themselves were not exposed to such experiences, and, worse, they consider such exercises as too difficult for schoolchildren. Once teachers venture to use these tasks, they often become aware of the fact that children have much less difficulty accomplishing them than was expected and are able to learn more easily and proceed more quickly. What is more, many children actually enjoy these tasks.

Video recording has made possible a number of new approaches: Classroom episodes can be selected and played back repeatedly, providing opportunities for a whole variety of analyses of the very same episode from different perspectives and theoretical orientations. These documents are more reliable than field notes or reports culled from recollections. (However, they, too, are interpretations and do not represent objective documentation, due to selection, distance, focus, cuts, and so on.) Teachers who try to remember portions of their lessons inevitably blend experiences and intentions together, since their perception of teaching as this action is unfolding is inseparably interwoven with the aims they are pursuing.

To repeat, the problem with academic seminars and teaching experiments is the way in which they are run: in other words, the difficulties lie with the culture in which mathematical action emerges rather than with the materials or the mathematical topics (see Baruk, 1985; Brown and Walter, 1990). How do the educators of preservice teachers bring out not only their own ways of thinking and constructing and, as well, their disappointment and ways of dealing with their own failure so that future teachers might learn from this? How do these same educators assist student teachers in understanding what children do and make attempts at demonstrating? How do preservice teachers learn to vary tasks spontaneously, in ways which are nevertheless commensurate with children's needs, acting neither too soon nor too late? How do student teachers learn to encourage emerging constructions and interaction, neither intervening too hastily nor nipping pending action in the bud through overcriticizing. The problem lies not in *training* in these skills – they can only develop from coherent and long-term practice – but in the basic way attention is kept focused, in overall awareness, and in a condition of preparedness for situations as these arise. Such are the prerequisites which should underlie all theoretical analysis and indeed the kind of outlook which should be developed in future teachers.

Conclusion

Without the constituting role of culture, we are unworkable monstrosities.
Geertz, cited in Bruner, 1990, p. 12

The crux of most school reforms lies in the fundamental changes which must be brought about in teachers' attitudes and beliefs, as well as in classroom culture. Once we begin to understand preservice teacher education, school reality, curriculum, administration, and in-service education as a system in which the modification of a single factor will cause incalculable disturbance and irritation rather than the expected change, things may take a turn for the better. In the future, perhaps, school reforms will be initiated and anchored at earlier stages and over a broader spectrum of interaction, thereby proving to be more effective not only for schools but also in terms of students' mathematical competence. The revamping of preservice teacher education will certainly prove crucial to such reform endeavors.

The radical constructivist principle, according to which every cognitive construction is a person's individual construction, has as corollary that a fundamental condition for students' learning is that situations occur which are conducive to constructions and learning interaction. In addition, such situations should prompt the elaboration of constructions which surpass previously held notions and perceptions. We would apply the concept of *culture* to this position statement. To be more specific, in a mathematics classroom, we find what may be termed a subculture, "a matter less of artifacts and propositions, rules, schematic programs, or beliefs, than of associative chains and images that tell what can be reasonably linked up with what" (Rosaldo, quoted in Bruner and Haste, 1987, p. 90). If the education of mathematics teachers is to become more effective, it will be necessary to organize the related academic culture in such a way as to render it less counterfunctional and to bring it into closer contact with the desired culture of the mathematics classroom.

In keeping with Luria's (1979) notion of "romantic science," I should like to conclude with two stories, both of which relate to concrete classroom experiences:

- Many years ago, the Australian teacher Nancy Shelley wrote a thesis (unpublished) about her work in mathematics with a few dropouts from secondary school in New Guinea. She worked intensively with them in analytic geometry, on parabolas in particular. She taught these students to cup both their hands like a parabola in accordance with her oral presentation of equations such as "y equals three x-square" or "y equals half x-square" and so forth. The students liked these exercises, particularly when she jumped from equation to equation, thus requiring them to adapt their hands accordingly. One day, Nancy started off such an episode by saying to one student: "y equals x-square." He reacted as expected, cupping his hands to form a normal parabola. Then she said: "y equals two x-square." This time he did not react. She repeated the formula, emphasizing the word "two," and looking him in the eye. As many a mathematics student knows, by adding the factor of 2, the parabola was modified. Direct eye contact did not do much to make him budge, however. When Nancy repeated the formula yet another time, now raising her voice, he replied: "I changed the scale!"

- In one of the first-grade classes we observed, perhaps the third month into the school year, the teacher had the children show numbers with their fingers: "Show me 4!" The children raised four fingers. "Now, can you show me 3, using two hands?" The children used one hand to hold out 1 finger and the other hand to hold out 2. "Can you show me 5 with three hands!" The kids laughed, and a few replied: "I only have two hands!" But other children took their neighbor's hand, had him hold out 1 finger, and raised their own hands each with 2 fingers held out. Then the teacher tried to tease them: "Can you show 1 using two hands?" They all laughed again, and appeared at a loss for a solution. One little bright-eyed girl then raised both hands with the thumbs up, each one bent at the knuckle.

I believe that, generally speaking, such cases are classified under the heading of "creative production" – that is, as a mere, if agreeable, stroke of luck, a moment as fleeting as the flight of the butterfly, hence as something essentially different from routines, skills, and everyday operations. But once we identify human interactions in the mathematics classroom with a subculture, a number of helpful questions come to the fore: To what extent do our usual approaches to operations and skills, in classrooms contribute to the development of such events? To what extent does teacher education prepare future teachers to understand, accept, and encourage such events? Is it not the case that every action contributes to the culture and reinforces routines just as much as constructions and interactions of the butterfly variety? How, then, can we aspire to create a culture which, in all the relevant dimensions, is capable of furthering serious and productive mathematizing in schools and universities?

Chapter 14
Constructivism as a referent for reforming science education

MICHAEL L. BENTLEY

Since World War II, mathematics and science education have been high on the educational reform agenda in many countries, including the United States. As the century comes to a close, the dominant approach to reform involves establishing for schools common ''standards'' for subject matter content and teaching practice, even though this kind of top-down approach does not stand up to scrutiny. For example, since the mid-eighties, following publication of *A Nation at Risk* by the National Commission on Excellence in Education (NCEE, 1983), funding for reform initiatives has been increasing. To be sure, commentators have noted ''modest gains'' in student performance on standardized tests, particularly among African-American students (Suter, 1993). Others point out, however, that science still is ''not taught frequently in many schools,'' and ''many children tend to lose interest in science at about the fourth grade'' (Sivertsen, 1993). Overall, researchers continue to paint a fairly dismal picture of the state of science and mathematics teaching in U.S. schools (Roychoudhury, 1994). In the elementary grades particularly, science often is neglected, and when it is taught, the textbook often is the sole source of the curriculum, and ''stand-and-deliver'' teaching methods eclipse all else in classroom practice. Researchers describe typical lessons as dominated by teacher talk, with much emphasis on memorization and (in mathematics) computation (Gallas, 1995; Lemke, 1990).

In other words, despite the gains in standardized test results, few American students attain higher levels of achievement in mathematics or science (National Center for Education Statistics, NCES, 1996). Further, the gap between the achievement (i.e., the test scores) of whites and minority children has persisted. The gap increases through the elementary years and is quite large by the eighth grade (Danek, Calbert, and Chubin, 1994). Haury (1994) pessimistically suggests that this achievement gap is more like a ''wedge that irrevocably separates those who will participate fully and reach their potential in mathematics and science from those who will always be on the margin'' (p. 2). But is it so irrevocable? And, what if the technocratic, top-down approach of reform has something to do with this kind of gap, with the tendency of the teachers to address a lot of content-specific minutia to bolster norm-referenced test scores, while children's interest remains untapped, their motivation sapped, and the world outside continues to go to hell in a handbasket ecologically? And again what if the main outcome of this type of reform is no more than to distract educators from the more intractable problems of schools, as Eisner (1995) emphasized, that is, ''from paying attention to the importance of building a culture of schooling that is genuinely intellectual in character, that values questions and ideas at least as much as getting right answers'' (p. 764). In other words, what is being lost in the standards movement is attention to the central purposes of education, the multiplication of potentialities, the development of children as competent social actors, while what is being perpetuated is the widely held view of the teacher's role, that teachers do not have to enact curriculum but only execute it.

In this chapter, I wish to suggest some ways to reframe this conception of reform in science education. These ways are at one time theoretical and empirical – that is, rooted in the constructivist perspective and in The Professional Practice Community (PPC), a grassroots model for collaboration that may be a constructivist medium to foster educational reform even in the present era of national standards. This model may offer effective structures not only for ''valuing questions and ideas'' in relation to the usual beliefs on cognition, learning, and teaching, but also for providing a network to support risk taking and change. But before that, some comments on the current U.S. reform project.

The sidetracking of school reform in the United States

In 1986, the American Association for the Advancement of Science initiated Project 2061, a major reform effort in science education, which produced *Science for All Americans* and *Benchmarks for Science Literacy* (AAAS, 1989, 1993). The former presented a general science background for teachers while the latter specified what major concepts should be learned at the end of particular grade levels. During the same period, the National Science Teachers Association initiated its own reform project, the *Scope, Sequence, and Coordination of Secondary School Science Project*, which has focused on reorganizing the high school curriculum to eliminate the single-year courses in biology, chemistry, and physics (NSTA, 1992).

By the end of the1980s, a number of states had initiated reform efforts that were centered around producing curriculum frameworks and/or student performance standards. The California Department of Education (CDE, 1990) published several influential documents, one of which addressed science education. At about the same time, the National Council of Teachers of Mathematics (NCTM, 1989) released its K–12 mathematics standards, and that has led to efforts in almost all the states to revise state mathematics frameworks.

With the passage of the Goals 2000 legislation in 1994, requirements for standards are now written into the Elementary and Secondary Education Act (ESEA), elevating the standards movement to national policy. But even while national standards were being written, most states were jumping on the standards bandwagon by publishing their own frameworks (Council of Chief State School Officers, 1995). This reform strategy appears compatible with "state agendas to provide more effective teacher education and steering of classroom processes" (Popkewitz, 1991, p. 168). The *National Science Education Standards* (National Research Council, NRC, 1996) are among the most recently published standards. They include guidelines for content, teaching, assessment, and the overall science program. The document even addresses the reform of the whole educational system as it relates to establishing policies and practices outside the classroom that support science teaching and learning.

While standards are now the policy, the implementation of the various national standards documents themselves is to be voluntary. However, financial considerations are likely to compel states and localities to align their local programs with the national model. Federal funding for science education likely will depend on state compliance with the standards (Alberts, 1994). As Klapper (1994, p. 4) noted, "it is necessary to acknowledge that standards as played out in assessments will become mandatory at some level in the educational system. . . . In all likelihood, standards will not be voluntary for teachers whose curriculum offerings will still be mandated by others."

While the standards-based reform approach has generated a higher profile for science in the curriculum, basing school improvement on standards is of questionable value. For one thing, national standards represent a policy shift in the direction of establishing a uniform national curriculum. A consequence may be to constrain local program innovations and to reduce diversity in practice. Further, as I mentioned earlier, the standards also represent a top-down curriculum development model, thus, implicitly, a way of conceiving of the work of the teacher. Many science educators have severely criticized this view of the work of the teacher, since, among other things, it promotes prescription rather than negotiation and, therefore, ignores the reality that teaching practices are notably embedded in the assumptions and professional motivations of the teacher. As Jenkins (1995) notes: ''Standards in science teaching ultimately reside in the practice, discourse, assumption and aspirations of science teachers. They derive from shared experience and properly grounded professional judgments, allied with a commitment to bringing the best out of all one's students'' (p. 448).

Yet another objection to standards-based reform relates to the stated purpose of education. According to the U.S. science education standards, ''scientific literacy'' is the overarching aim, and this is defined as including, for the first time, a goal for science education to ''increase their [students'] economic productivity through the use of the knowledge, understanding, and skills of the scientifically literate person in their careers'' (NRC, 1996, p. 13). Relating the purpose of science in the curriculum – both for the child and for the society, to economic productivity, is a confusing message at best, as many of the country's most pressing environmental problems relate directly to the overconsumption of resources fostered by a growth-dependent economic system. Moreover, this stated goal also conveys an interpretation of the purpose of education that renders it more like a training focused on the student's performance instead of on the ''multiplication of potentialities,'' as expressed by von Foerster (1992). In other words, whereas one of the most fruitful directions in research on teaching recognizes the importance of context, then, of diversity, the standards-based reform project emphasizes conformity. The agenda of standards-based reform includes giving status to expert knowledge and narrowing the decision-making processes within teachers' work (Popkewitz, 1991). One only has to think of the big issue of assessment. If assessment is tied to the standards, which seems likely, more ''teaching to the test'' may be the unfortunate result, whereas in my view, as well as the views of many educators, the purpose of education should emphasize diversity, creativity, social responsibility, empowerment to think and, more particularly, to act (DeBoer, 1991, p. 240).

Given this background on the U.S. reform situation, constructivism and its varieties seems to me to be a fruitful referent for rethinking science education as an empowering sociocognitive process for students as well as for teachers.

The relevance of constructivism as a referent for science education

Concurrent with the ascendancy of the standards-based reform movement, U.S. science educators have been grappling with decades-old developments in the foundational areas: educational psychology, philosophy of education, and philosophy of science. Within the science education community, traditional beliefs about teaching and learning are under assault while *constructivism* has become almost a household word (Shamos, 1989).

The source of the label *constructivism* is the idea that we build or *construct* our meanings. Involved is "a conception of the knower, a conception of the known, and a conception of the relation of knower-known" (Bettencourt, 1993, p. 39). As a form of pragmatism, constructivism centers on how people arrive at the knowledge that enables them to cope with the world (Good, Wandersee, and St. Julien, 1993). Thus, constructivism is a theory of knowledge-in-the-making or, more precisely, a theory of how individuals and communities of individuals (e.g., scientists) make sense of the world.

Constructivism offers a view of learning that is quite different from the *conduit*, or "jug-and-mug" view which has dominated American education for the past fifty years. This "sender-receiver" view, as expressed by Phelan (1994), "posits classroom communication as an exchange of factual information rather than as a meaning-making activity by participants" (p. 103), while, according to the constructivist view, children are not "repositories for adult knowledge, but organisms which, like all of us, are constantly trying to make sense of, and to understand their experience" (von Glasersfeld, 1989a, p. 12). Moreover, this phenomenon of meaning making is not limited to simply saying that we construct our meanings. Indeed, cognition must be considered an *adaptive* function, since it refers to the conceptual structures "that turn out to be . . . viable within the knowing subject's range of experiences" (von Glasersfeld, 1989, p. 125).

While constructivism has become a major philosophical referent for the reform of science education, it is an umbrella term covering diverse interpretations, as Larochelle, Bednarz, and Garrison point out (in this book). Indeed, over the years, the constructivist label has been used by different writers in different ways, so that various versions have evolved. Good et al. (1993) identified fifteen different descriptive adjectives used by various workers to modify constructivism, such as radical, pragmatic, contextual, Piagetian, social, et cetera. Kelly (1955) used the term in his work in ways that are not fully consistent with those of Piaget or those of Piaget's chief contemporary proponent, Ernst von Glasersfeld (Gergen, 1995). John Dewey did not describe his own position with the constructivist label (he eschewed labels), but his epistemological work certainly is consistent with much of constructivist thought (Garrison, 1994, and in this book). At any rate, as Good et al. conclude, ''A rich stew of approaches seems to be cooking in the field'' (p. 76).

Von Glasersfeld's *radical* constructivism currently is the point of departure for much debate over epistemological-pedagogical issues. A key idea in von Glasersfeld's position is that an external reality may exist, but direct access to it is not possible (von Glasersfeld, 1996). A corollary is that the orderliness perceived by the knowing subject is due at least as much to the conceptual structure of his or her theories as to the data considered relevant. As von Glasersfeld (1996, pp. 3–4) puts it:

> The leading scientists themselves have, I believe without exception, come to share the view that Einstein expressed by a brilliant metaphor. He compared the scientist to a man who, faced with a clock he cannot possibly open, invents mechanisms that might explain the movements of the hands and the ticking he perceives – knowing full well that he will never be able to check his model against what ''really'' goes on inside the clock.

In short, as von Foerster put it in a nutshell, ''The logic of the world is the logic of the description of the world'' (in Segal, 1986, p. 4).

In a certain sense, radical constructivism, in the Piagetian tradition, looks like a ''personal'' constructivism, since it adopts the metaphor of the individual placed at the center of meaning making. Many interpret Piaget to hold cognitive development as a natural process that is primary to learning: the development of logical classes or mental structures comes first, thereby allowing the child to systematically develop concepts. Piaget's individual would be ''a self-regulating autonomous organism, making sense and meaning from sensorimotor, social, and textual experiences'' (Lerman, 1996, p. 147).

In contrast, there are constructivist positions that opt for metaphors that are more socially and contextually oriented. For instance, Vygotsky (1978), who is a seminal theorist for most social constructivists, often is cited for holding that learning is primary to development and that the development of systematic concepts is not dependent on prior logical structures; it is "supported by social experience in the context relevant to the domain of knowledge" (Panofsky, John-Steiner, and Blackwell, 1990, p. 253). However, Cole and Wertsch (1996) argue that too much has been made of this personal-social dimension in comparing the epistemologies of Piaget and Vygotsky. They point out that "Piaget did not deny the co-equal role of the social world in the construction of knowledge" (p. 251) and Vygotsky recognized that active construction was the central process in coming to know.[1]

Constructivist positions of the contextual flavor also differ from radical constructivism in considering the accessibility of external reality. Schlagel (1986), for example, argues for a position he calls "contextual realism" in which reality is not considered completely out of human reach. Most scientists are realists in believing the world exists and that patterns in nature can be discovered, and this position is the view of science presented in *Science for all Americans* (AAAS, 1989). However, Schlagel holds that scientific knowledge is context bound: "Truth or reality is restricted to the context applicable to the event under consideration, recognizing that no theory or knowledge of nature should be understood as final" (p. 80).

Gergen (1995), to contrast his position from that of the radical constructivists, speaks of social *constructionism.* In his view, community has priority over the individual and one's personal rationality is considered a by-product of communication and social life. Gergen also distinguishes his position from that of Vygotsky. In social constructionism, human relationship is placed in the foreground, while the foreground for Vygotsky was occupied by a mental space, the "zone of proximal development." This zone is the space between one's actual and potential cognitive functioning. According to Gergen (1995), Vygotsky and his followers concern themselves primarily with "mental processes of abstraction, generalization, comparison, differentiation, volition, consciousness, maturation, association, attention, representation, judgement, sign-mediated operations, and so on," while the constructionist focuses on "such matters as negotiation, cooperation, conflict, rhetoric, ritual, roles, social scenarios, and the like, but avoids psychological explanations for microsocial process" (p. 25).

The mathematics educator Stephen Lerman (1996) also aligns himself with the Vygotskian tradition but nevertheless recommends that both radical and social constructivism be rejected as theoretical foundations for mathematics education. Lerman advocates a fully sociocultural epistemology and cites Vygotsky's view that the social plane is primary and that meaning is first sociocultural, "to be internalized by the subject's regulation within discursive practices" (1996, p. 147). To Lerman, the key issue between constructivism and a sociocultural theory is intersubjectivity – that is, the fact that people achieve at least temporary states of shared knowledge. He claims that in principle, constructivists would have to hold that each person has a different type of knowledge and thus intersubjectivity would not be possible, and he also argues that mentalism lies at the heart of Piaget and therefore all constructivisms. I think constructivisms are conceivable, however, that recognize the possibility of shared knowledge and that are not mentalistic – see, for example, Garrison's description of the pragmatic social constructivism of Dewey and George Herbert Mead (in this book). However, I can agree with Lerman's conclusion emphasizing the value of shifting our pedagogical theorizing "from a view of the autonomous cognizing subject constructing her or his subjectivity and knowing to one of the construction of human consciousness in and through communication. . . . It is in discourses, subjectivities, significations, and positionings that psychological phenomena actually exist" (p. 136).

Finally, one can also consider constructivism as a postmodern epistemology, in the sense that, as the latter, constructivism could be seen as a reflective way to deconstruct aspects of widely held beliefs and to transcend the modern mechanicist worldview which developed out of seventeenth century Galilean-Cartesian-Baconian-Newtonian science. This association between constructivism and the simultaneously deconstructive and constructive postmodernist way of seeing[2] constitutes for me a powerful framework to provide meaning and appropriateness to the integration of such a perspective within science education. Indeed, it permits me to reconcile my deep concern about the actual dominant worldview that imperils humanity's long-term ecological well-being with my intuition that a form of ongoing reflective conversation should be fostered within the teaching community about the beliefs taken for granted. On the other hand, the constructivism-postmodernism association also permits me to call into question the ideology of self-contained individualism that is promoted in the hidden curriculum of most schools, according to Bigelow (1996, p. 15):

> The hidden ecological curriculum . . . encouraged students to *not-think* about the earth, to *not-question* the system of commodification that turns the world,

> including the land, into things to be bought and sold. . . . When the curriculum is silent about aspects of life – racism, sexism, global inequality, or the degradation of the earth – that silence normalizes these patterns. . . . And that's the lie.

Constructivism and teaching

It is worth noting that, in my understanding, constructivism is not a pedagogical theory and, therefore, it cannot state what education should be without simultaneously running the risk of lapsing into the critical top-down approach I alluded to above. Though constructivism can serve as a useful referent for education, no straightforward recipe for teaching practice can be derived from constructivism, as Bettencourt (1993) also points out: "Practice is never a simple application of general rules to concrete situations, and theory is never the simple abstraction-generalization from practical situations to general schemes. Practice and theory, like knowledge and experience, stand in a relation of mutual adaptation, of mutual questioning, and of mutual illumination" (p. 47).

Figure 14.1 represents my own distillation of teaching practices frequently associated with constructivism in the literature. For example, Bettencourt (1993), a radical constructivist, recommends that "discussions, images, time for reflection, and opportunities to use the ideas in different situations are needed" (p. 47). He also supports hands-on investigations but cautions that "unless hands-on science is embedded in a structure of questioning, reflecting, and requestioning, probably very little will be learned" (p. 48). Saul, Reardon, Schmidt, Pearce, Blackwood, and Bird (1993) cite constructivism as well as whole language as referents for their workshop model for instruction, while Daniels (1996, p. 1) calls the classroom workshop "the pedagogical embodiment of constructivist learning theory":

> One of the most powerful instructional metaphors to emerge in recent years is the idea of the classroom as workshop. Under this model, elementary and secondary classrooms are no longer merely locations where information is transmitted. Instead, they become working laboratories or studios, where genuine knowledge is created, real products are developed, and authentic inquiry pursued. . . . [In] a workshop, students and teachers together reinvent whatever field of study they are engaged in.

Constructivism also has served as a referent for the creation of teaching models, an important element in an educational theory. For example, various *learning cycle* models have been used in science

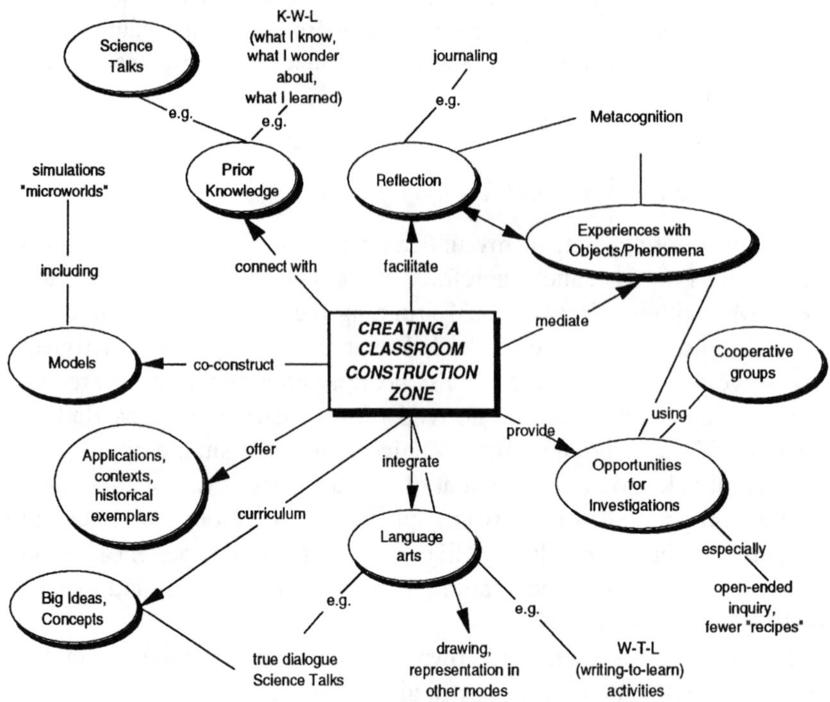

Figure 14.1. Teaching practices associated with constructivism in the literature

education since the sixties as well as in social studies education (Needham, Powell, and Bentley, 1994).[3] But, the most popular and widespread interpretation of constructivism for practice in science education has been the conceptual change teaching model, which interprets learning as a process of deconstructing misconceptions and reconstructing in their place valid scientific conceptions (Hewson and Hewson, 1988; Posner, Strike, Hewson, and Gertzog, 1982; Strike and Posner, 1992).

For the researchers who see science as a culture with a special language and learning science as a process of induction into the disciplinary discourse, the conceptual change model is too restrictive (Driver, Asoko, Leach, Mortimer, and Scott, 1994; Solomon, 1987).[4] For example, Tobin (1989) relates constructivism to a model for teaching science that is broader than the conceptual change model and which implies a constant negotiation process as a key to sense making and favors "minds-on" activities and sharing in the classroom. Driver and Oldham (1986) also present a teaching model derived from constructivist thought. Whereas Tobin's model comes from a radical constructivist perspective, Driver's Constructivist Teaching Sequence (CTS) assumes a sociocultural construction of knowledge. In the CTS, children's ideas are elicited and children are invited to examine their understandings against the scientists' concepts. In the CTS, the teacher does not seek to replace children's ideas but rather seeks to introduce children to "the concepts, symbols, and conventions of the scientific community" (Driver et al., 1994, p. 8).

Cobern (1993) also is critical of the conceptual change model and points out that it "only works when students share the plausibility structure of the science teacher and the science textbook" (p. 58), that is, when science for students is not a second culture. In his contextual constructivism, teaching is essentially seen as mediation, meaning that the teacher "works as the interface between curriculum and student to bring the two together in a way that is meaningful for the learner" (p. 51). Further, Cobern calls attention to the important role children's worldviews play in learning. A worldview represents an epistemological level antecedent to any particular concept about physical phenomena and can be thought of as "culturally organized macrothought . . . the culturally dependent, generally subconscious, fundamental organization of the mind" (p. 58). To Cobern, a truly liberating education must address beliefs at the worldview level.

One educator whose work does just that is Gallas. Indeed, her constructivist/ socioculturally based pedagogy follows Bakhtin (1986) and Lemke (1990) and constitutes an example of a teaching practice using situated cognition, that is, "of situating science instruction in the student's 'frame of reference,' (personal experiences, of events in literature, and hands-on activities)" (Kumar and Voldrich, 1994, p. 8). Gallas (1995) refers to children's "Stories about Science" instead of their misconceptions and uses a method she calls "Science Talks" to engage them in dialogue that gets at deep questions and issues in their lives.[5]

Constructivism and the nature of science

Constructivism has implications for science teaching from yet another angle. Indeed, as an epistemology, constructivism speaks to the nature of science, and the nature of science is part of the content of the curriculum. Over the past several decades, postmodern concepts of the nature of science have gained widespread acceptance among scholars in the fields of philosophy, history, and sociology of science (Garrison and Bentley, 1990). While many scholars and educational reformers recognize that the nineteenth-century positivistic philosophy of science is an inadequate foundation for the science curriculum, postmodern concepts of the nature of science have yet to make a significant impact on the content of science textbooks or on the methods texts used in science teacher preparation. Very different views of science from those which are typically communicated in science classrooms emerge from the work of Kuhn, Lakatos, Toulmin, Feyerabend, Laudan, Quine, Hanson, Rorty, Maturana, Bateson, and others.

From such scholarship, many assumptions underlying positivism have been found to be untenable: for example, that knower and known are clearly separated, that objective knowledge is the product of scientific methods, and that theories are sharply distinct from facts, and facts from values. Now rejected is the positivist view that "scientific knowledge is essentially a [logical] codification of sense data" (Bohm and Peat, 1987, p. 55). On the contrary, an element of subjectivity now is acknowledged to be involved in all "objective" statements because perceptions only become meaningful through theory; experience is *theory-laden* and *value-laden* (Hanson, 1958). Further, science is no longer considered the search for truth, nor is it considered a body of knowledge "out there" (as in a library or in an encyclopedia). To the constructivist, scientific knowledge is a complex of meanings continually negotiated in a community of knowledge workers and does not exist outside of minds. Science also "is a process that assists us to make sense of our world" (Lorsbach and Tobin, 1992, pp. 1–2).

Unfortunately, these kinds of assumptions are rarely considered in textbooks or discussed in classrooms. For example, in many classrooms, "the scientific method" is still taught as a singular, linear process, often described as a stepwise procedure of experimentation beginning with either a question or a hypothesis and ending with a conclusion, verified new knowledge. The "hidden curriculum" is that valid conclusions are reached by a cookbook procedure, which is straightforward nineteenth-century inductivism (Garrison and Bentley, 1990). Thus, as a view of the nature of science, constructivism has yet another role to play as a referent for reform in science education.

Constructivism and teacher education

My final observations regarding constructivism and educational reform have to do with teacher education. For several years now, across the country, preservice and in-service teachers have been considering constructivism as a referent for their philosophies of education and for classroom practice. Further, I have seen my own colleagues reorienting their teaching away from stand-and-deliver methods toward more emphasis on cooperative learning, problem solving, critical thinking, and reflective practice. Worthwhile experimentation with program structures is also occurring. At my university, Virginia Tech, new models of teacher education have been created and are currently undergoing trial.

Before moving to Virginia Tech in 1996, I worked for eight years in the Chicago area with a group of faculty at National-Louis University who founded the Chicago Project on Teaching and Learning (Daniels, 1996a).[6] The project worked by connecting small clusters of schools, primarily elementary and middle schools, into networks that involved parents and community resources (Schnobrich and Bentley, 1997). The project developed independently of, but in many ways was similar to, the Professional Practice Communities (PPCs) discussed by Tippins, Nichols, and Tobin (1993). The 1988 Chicago School Reform Act provided an impetus for reform. With this act, the centralized bureaucracy was drastically reduced and the citywide curriculum abandoned. Local School Councils were given authority over the school curriculum.

Several PPCs were initiated and developed in Illinois between 1990 and 1996. In the collaborative situations with which I worked, the teachers, parents, and administrators began with the aim to improve curriculum and instruction in science, which sometimes was coupled with mathematics, social studies, or technology. Grant funding enabled adjacent urban schools to form working relationships not only with each other, but with other community institutions and resources. The collaborative included all stakeholders – parents, teachers, principals, teacher educators, community members, and educators from informal educational institutions. The Chicago PPCs began with four West Chicago elementary schools linked to resources provided by National-Louis University (NLU), Malcolm X College of the Chicago Community College system, and the Chicago Academy of Sciences.[7] Community building, reflective practice, and locally produced curriculum were important aspects of this work. For example, a cadre of students from Malcolm X learned mentoring and tutoring skills to enable them to work with small groups of children from the neighboring elementary schools, and every Chicago PPC involved "family night" events designed to engage children with family members in investigations.

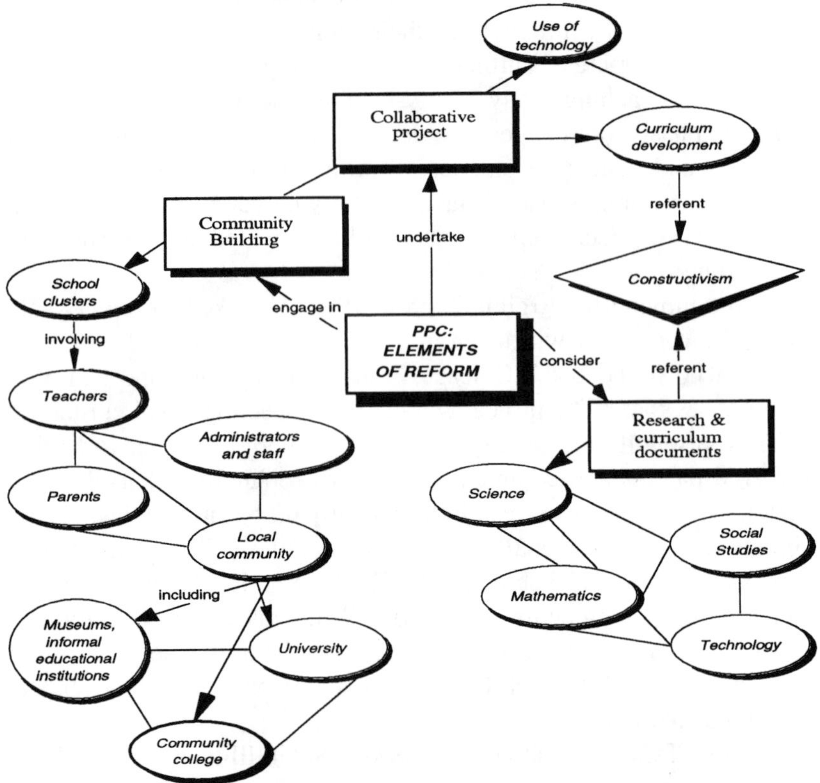

Figure 14.2. Elements involved in Chicago-area educational reform projects

Later a similar network was formed from a coalition of Waukegan elementary schools, NLU, the College of Lake County (also a community college), the Chicago Botanic Gardens, and Powerhouse (a science museum).[8] Like the Chicago projects, the Waukegan–Lake County coalition focused on creating a Professional Practice Community involving reflective practice, community building for support, and learner-centered curriculum development. The elements involved in these reform projects are diagrammed in Figure 14.2.

The participants involved in the PPC alliance work embraced a number of fundamental propositions regarding educational reform. First, they agreed that practitioners need time and incentives to reconceptualize their teaching roles and the outcomes of practice, and to engage in activities and processes in which they are both learners and teachers (Darling-Hammond and McLaughlin, 1995). Teachers need time also to interact collegially with one another and to build teams (Isaacson and Bamburg, 1992). Team building is important because it is empowering and promotes enduring intra- and intergroup communication networks. Teachers also need time for other worthwhile purposes, including time to connect the written curriculum to children's lives and needs, time to come to consensus, time to share visions of purpose, and time to work toward the implementation of a plan for change (Garmston and Wellman, 1995).

A second proposition about educational reform that we embraced was that curricula and instruction need to be tied to the cultural experiences and values of the urban student – that is, to the child's world (Gardner, 1993). A third was that classroom environments conducive to learning are more likely to develop when teachers are engaged in activities such as integrating the subjects, connecting content to applications outside the classroom, using technologies in meaningful ways for significant amounts of time, applying ideas to different situations, thinking critically and creatively about practice, reflecting on experiences, sharing ideas and experiences with others, and working collaboratively in groups (Fort, 1993; Peck and Dorricott, 1994; Villasenor and Kepner, 1993). We believed that if teachers became active learners themselves, a spin-off of excitement and curiosity would contribute to a richer learning environment for children, and there would be more opportunities for learning to become integrated into children's lives outside the classroom (Sagor, 1995).

A fourth proposition about educational reform held by the participants was that parents, community members, and community resources all must be incorporated into the learning framework (Department of Education, 1994; Henderson and Berla, 1994). We believed that less emphasis should be placed on what families lack, and more on how parents and community members can become empowered through communication, working partnerships, and active networking systems (Finders and Lewis, 1994; Hargreaves, 1995). Working together is a way of building relationships and collective resolve. Collaboration turns individual learning into shared learning and becomes a catalyst for change in education (Fullan, 1993).

Constructivism was a major referent for the educational process utilized in the Chicago-area PPC projects. Indeed, the PPC model shares the underlying assumption of constructivism which postulates that understanding results from the operations of the knower as he or she enacts his or her world, as well as the assumption of social constructivism which emphasizes the negotiation process as the key to sense making. For instance, university faculty, museum educators, and classroom teachers in the PPC projects worked together in groups as peers to address curriculum renewal by reading and critiquing research on teaching and learning and the relevant national standards and other curriculum reform documents. Participants worked together within and across school boundaries to study and discuss issues of curriculum and instruction, such as how to facilitate student understanding, how to integrate subjects, how to use technology appropriately, and how to embed assessment into instruction. Several groups collaboratively developed curriculum units addressing local needs that had been identified (Bentley and Nalbandian, 1994).[9] The aim of the curriculum work was to move away from a pedagogy of imposition or transmission to a pedagogy of negotiation and construction in which the development needs of the children and the total community of learners at large are recognized. Thus, parent and community education was part of these projects.

A by-product of the PPC projects has been a higher profile for science education throughout the communities involved. Further, parents, principals, and teachers have recognized the value of enlisting external support on a continuing basis for their local educational program. In the process of identifying and addressing local needs, teachers have examined, discussed, and often utilized national standards, reform reports, state curriculum guides, and published research, as well as new curriculum materials and electronic media and technology. These grassroots projects illustrate that the PPC model may be a constructivist medium to foster educational reform even in the present era of national standards.

Conclusion

Standards and constructivism are strange bedfellows, but both factor in the changes in curriculum and instruction now occurring in U.S. schools. To be sure, many issues and challenges remain, including the following:

- What assessment strings will be attached to state and national standards? Will standards lead to more teaching-to-the-test?
- How can curriculum resources – print materials, electronic media, and the community – be made more accessible to teachers? How can such resources be used to optimize learning opportunities?

- How can science in the curriculum be of more service to female students, Latino and African-American students, and economically disadvantaged students?
- What level of funding and what kind of teacher support structures are necessary to initiate and sustain reform?
- Can schools become agencies of intellectual liberation, enabling children to become competent social actors and citizens of an ecologically stressed planet?

Despite the unresolved questions, my experience with the Chicago-area PPCs has strengthened my belief that enduring reform in education requires at the very least the recognition that teachers inevitably act according to their values and frameworks, which become evident and may be challenged through a shared experience rather than through a top-down model. In this sense, as teaching and learning are not trivial but complex processes, involving so many types of contexts and issues, teachers should have time and authentic opportunities for reflective practice, collaboration, networking, and community building. That is why the Professional Practice Community is a promising model for teacher professional development, notably because it is "accompanied by a vision of lifelong teaching and learning in an atmosphere of equity and collaboration" (Tippins, Nichols, and Tobin, 1993). Indeed, the collegial forums underlying structures such as the PPC can provide a comfort zone for teacher experimentation and personal theorizing. Further, according to my understanding of constructivism as a postmodern epistemology, these forums also can provide a comfort zone for "valuing questions and ideas" regarding the dominant worldview which seems too often to pervade science education, a worldview that favors competition rather than solidarity, and therefore the ideology of self-contained individualism.

Part V
Conclusion

Chapter 15
Critical-constructivism and the sociopolitical agenda

JACQUES DÉSAUTELS, JIM GARRISON, AND STEPHEN C. FLEURY

In reading over the different chapters in this book, one cannot but acknowledge that they constitute a convincing illustration of the theoretical and practical educational pertinence of constructivism conceived as a theory of cognition. In adopting a constructivist stance toward the individual and collective production of knowledge in different contexts, educators have been able to elaborate and test sound and promising pedagogical practices, thereby showing how it is possible to initiate significant transformations at different educational levels.

In another sense, these chapters also constitute a well-articulated response to some of the criticism constructivism has been subject to lately, in particular for supposedly favoring student-centered pedagogies in line with the dominant individualistic ideology in Western societies (Muller and Taylor, 1995). As one may notice in this book, constructivists do not picture the student as an isolated, almost schizophrenic subject, alone in face-to-face interaction with the world. The intrinsic social character of the educational process is taken into account in numerous ways. For instance, different authors posit that, in the process of the construction of the subject, the alter ego, the other, is constitutive of the self and not an indifferent thing-in-the-world. To be sure, this does not mean that the theoretical discussion about the social or psychological nature of learning has undergone closure in the educational field. However, as Cole and Wertsch (1996) argue, in respect of the debate which has most often crystallized around Piaget and Vygotsky, too much emphasis is put on the opposition between psychogenesis and sociogenesis. Both authors insisted on the necessity of simultaneously integrating the social and the psychological in order to understand development and learning. For example, while Piaget persisted methodologically in developing a theory of the universal epistemic subject, he was well aware that the concrete and embodied subject is for all matters a cultural being, a social subject. He reiterated this preoccupation quite often in his numerous publications. The following excerpt (quoted in Doise, 1985, p. 45) exemplifies his position on the subject: "Cooperation opposes both autism and constraint. It progressively reduces autistic or egocentric processes of thought. . . . Discussion generates inner reflection. Mutual control generates the need for proof and objectivity. The exchange of thought implies adopting the principles of contradiction and identity as discourse regulators. As regards constraint, cooperation destroys it whenever differentiation and free discussion between individuals develop."

The sociality of the educational process is also given due consideration in many chapters by means of the importance assigned to the interactions among the actors of the educational situation in the very definition of what it means to learn. Accordingly, it is in the context of classroom cultures which legitimate a plurality of possible answers to significant problems through rational debates that the best type of learning occurs, individually and collectively. In other chapters, the concept of re-production of social patterns and power structures through schooling is proposed as a means to criticizing existing pedagogical practices, followed by suggestions or descriptions of alternative practices aiming at the reconstruction of the habitus which orient those processes. Finally, the concept of paradigm is helpful in making sense of a constructivist position about the ethical dimension of life in society and of educational practices. We may then safely conclude that the constructivist thesis is far from conveying an "unthinking image of society" (to paraphrase Billig, 1993).

Nevertheless, the possibility of coopting constructivism as a mere educational slogan by the now dominant technicist ideology in education is quite possible. For instance, Zeichner (1993) has shown how the concept of reflective practice has been stripped of its social emancipatory potential to become an end in itself in preservice and inservice teacher professional development. In analyzing different teacher preparation programs advocating teacher reflexivity and empowerment, Zeichner concludes with the following:

> Closely related to this persistence of technical rationality under the banner of reflective teaching, is the limitation of the reflective process to consideration of teaching skills and strategies (the means of instruction), and the exclusion from the process of defining the ends of teaching, of the ethical and philosophical realms of teaching from the teachers' purview. Here again

teachers are denied the opportunity to do anything other than fine-tune and adjust the means for accomplishing ends determined by others. Teaching becomes merely a technical activity. Important questions related to values such as what should be taught to whom and why are defined independently and relegated to others removed from the classroom. (p. 10)

In a paradox of sorts, considering the origins of the concept of reflective teaching, the integration of this concept within a context from which social reflectivity is absent can in fact contribute to the disempowerment of teachers. Hence, we must keep in mind that the enactment of any curriculum is, in all of its dimensions, a sociopolitical project which can be more or less emancipatory for people and the community. Ignoring this idea can easily lead constructivism to become just a better way to sustain social injustice in furthering particular social interests through our educational practices.

In this chapter we would like to stress the contingency of the socially constructed world along with the social and political consequences of reifying and decontextualizing knowledge so as to make it appear necessary, indubitable, and unalterable. We want to develop a critical-constructivist stance toward the production and ownership of knowledge, in particular scientific knowledge, in society at large. We will examine some of the issues of power and social regulation involved in the social production of knowledge.

About the "*rapport au savoir*" and its transformation

Through its contribution to dismantling truth as a form of correspondence to reality (Lawson and Appignanesi, 1989), and the recognition of the impossibility of specifying an ultimate foundation of knowledge, constructivism can have a potential emancipatory effect in education. Indeed, if one accepts these premises, a critical-constructivist must endorse the ethical necessity of applying the principle of epistemological symmetry – that is, symmetry of a type which considers the knowledge developed by students in the context of their local culture as viable and genuine (Larochelle and Bednarz in this book). Taking account of what the student already knows in teaching goes well beyond the instrumental goals associated, for instance, with the "conceptual change" approaches to learning advocated by numerous constructivist scholars. It literally means that the sociocultural voice of the students is recognized as such and that school knowledge is considered as but one of the instruments in helping them emancipate themselves from their own biographies, admittedly a time-consuming but potentially powerful process. This position has been vividly described by Aikenhead (1996) in an article about the ins and outs of a cultural perspective in science education:

> [Science education as cultural border crossing] may be facilitated in classrooms by studying the subcultures of students' life-worlds and by contrasting them with a critical analysis of the subculture of science (its norms, values, beliefs, expectations, and conventional actions), *consciously* moving back and forth between life-worlds and the science-world, switching language conventions explicitly, switching conceptualizations explicitly, switching values explicitly, switching epistemologies explicitly, but never requiring students to adopt a scientific way of knowing as their personal way. This "no assimilation" rule does not preclude teachers from capturing student interest and curiosity in science and then doing a good job at a rite of passage into the subculture of science. (pp. 41–2)

The consequences of adopting such a stance toward students' knowledge are far-reaching for them, if only by helping them transform radically their *rapport au savoir*, understood as "a relation of meaning, and thus of value, between an individual (or a group) and the processes or products of knowledge production" (Charlot, Bautier, and Rochex, 1992, p. 29). But in order to anchor the discussion, we will exemplify the type of unreflective *rapport* to knowledge usually developed by students in the context of present-day schooling through the analysis of a student's discourse.

In a study of high school students' representation of scientific knowledge, a student made the following comment:

> I have a lot of difficulty seeing how scientists can deal [with things we cannot see]. They [the teachers] explain it to us and we understand how [the scientists] could see that. They say: "The distance from the moon to the earth is such and such. . . ." I don't know it by heart. But how did they measure that? They don't have a measuring tape that long! I have a lot of difficulty with that. . . . And the guy who discovered it: How did he do it? It happened just like that one morning? I don't get it. I understand when it has been explained, but this guy nobody ever gave an explanation to, how did he do it? He must have been really gifted. One must necessarily be gifted, interested, intelligent. Some are more intelligent than others. It is like the law of nature we were talking about: some trees grow while others will always stay small. (Désautels and Larochelle, 1989, p. 155)

This student is struggling to make sense of what scientific knowledge is all about and assimilates it to a familiar process of literally describing what can be seen, thus ignoring its essentially relational, constructed, and contingent character. We can then reasonably argue that, like the majority of his schoolmates, he will come to think that scientific knowledge is equivalent to the revelation of the true nature of reality or the world. If this is the case, in the face of "truth," there is only one possible intellectual attitude he may adopt in the long run, submission, which leads to the depreciation of other forms of knowledge including the one he has constructed through living in a specific culture. It is no wonder, then, that the measurement of the distance between the earth and the moon is conceived as a feat performed by especially gifted and intelligent people called "scientists." And, in reifying intelligence as he does and assuming its unequal distribution among the people to be a lawful fact, he has elaborated a fatalist and depreciative image of his own intellectual capacities (a small tree). Finally, the spontaneous portrayal of the person of the scientist as a man (the guy) can be interpreted in this context as manifesting an inherited sexist attitude. In brief, he has constructed a disempowering and alienating rapport to scientific knowledge. This can have considerable personal and social stakes.

It is quite difficult to anticipate that this student will ever imagine that he can participate in the production of scientific knowledge. Not that choosing to do so is important in itself, since it is just as legitimate to want to become an artist or a journalist. What is important to consider however is that the type of inhibition resulting from the symbolic violence (Bourdieu's expression) exerted through classroom practices reduces his field of possibilities as he forbids himself access to a scientific career. Moreover, he will probably develop a feeling of inferiority toward those who eventually ply the knowledge trade. This feeling of inferiority will condition the type of social relations he will establish with them. Will he not, like a majority of his schoolmates, tend to naively trust those who possess this type of knowledge as they make social decisions about sensitive issues arising in connection with energy production, biotechnology, environmental control, and so on. (Driver, Leach, Millar, and Scott, 1996)? Also, in expressing this particular belief about the nature of intelligence, does it not become "natural" or "normal" that only certain persons and not everyone in our society are given privileges (honors, money, power, etc.), since inequality between human beings seems inevitable, as the metaphor of the differential growth of trees serves to suggest? In short, the rapport to scientific knowledge constructed by students has much to do with the production and reproduction of the social power structures in a society. How does a constructivist pedagogy initiate a transformation in the rapport to knowledge which students inevitably build in learning situations? The apparently simple activity of classifying living beings by students serves as an illustration.

In just about every primary school, children are taught that all living beings can be subsumed under two categories, namely, plants and animals. But Hills (1989) reports that children do not necessarily agree that this is the case; many of them think that persons cannot be classified as animals. Most of the time, after a few minutes of discussion the teacher states that persons are animals – but animals who stand high in this category. In other words, the institutional authority of the teacher is the warrant used to impose the right answer without any further arguments! The next step is to have the children give examples belonging to each category.

In a critical-constructivist perspective this strategy cannot be qualified as acceptable pedagogical practice. Instead, if we suppose there is consensus in the class about the distinction between living and nonliving beings, the teacher would suggest to the children working in small groups to classify living beings and to write down a list of the criteria or reasons they use for making their judgments. Following this exercise, they would be invited to discuss these matters with other people in their social environment (parents, friends, and others) and report the results of their investigation to the class. A certain number of parents could even be invited to participate in the discussion. Some of the groups may have retained the three-category system while others may have concluded that two categories are enough to operate the distinctions. What is important is that the students are now ready to participate in an open discussion about this delicate subject. A good number of significant problems and paths of investigations can be defined: Does the three-category classification work well in everyday life? What are the reasons supporting this classification? Are there other classifications based on different criteria in use in other cultural contexts? On what grounds can a two-category classification be useful? Why do biologists prefer a two-category classification? In terms of an evolutionary scheme, how do we determine the advent of what we call people? If persons are classified as animals, why do we have a human rights charter? The questions can go on, but whatever happens next, the teacher should help the students become aware that they knew how to classify living beings and that their particular knowledge not only works well but is also supported by a number of good reasons by the people in their community. He or she should also help them understand that for other reasons there are many ways of classifying living beings – that is, classifications used by biologists or by people from other cultures. In other words, this type of exercise will have the children reflexively understand that the activity of classification is contingent and entails making decisions about the criteria used to make distinctions – and that there is always more than one way to do it.

Becoming reflexively aware of the pervasive effects of reifying the contingent categories we use to make sense of our experiences is a necessary condition for considering alternative ways of "seeing" and critically examining their foundations. A critical-constructivist pedagogy does not rank forms of knowledge, but rather promotes a pluralistic epistemological democracy which favors the enrichment of the field of possibilities for the students through their participation in different knowledge games. In a similar line of thinking, The New London Group (1996) advocates the following: "The role of pedagogy is to develop an epistemology of pluralism that provides access [to social power] without people having to erase or leave behind different subjectivities. This has to be the basis of a new norm" (p. 72). In the case of the classification of living beings, children could realize that there is no Great Divide between us and those from other cultures who, as Latour (1989) ironically points out, have only an ethnozoology and not a zoology. They could also, with a certain dose of humor, ask the biologists to explain why they enter into places even though there are signs indicating that animals are not allowed to go in. More seriously, they could develop an understanding of the origins of racist or sexist categorizations, which is no small educational accomplishment.

The construction of knowledge and personal identity

Critical-constructivism does not seek clues for understanding human cognitive activity (including the construction of the identities, concepts, and categories of thought) in the deep inner workings of the brain or spirit, but rather in the social and historical forms of life. Meanings in the intersubjective world are objectified, but this does not mean they are fixed, final, or perfectly pellucid. Often they remain hidden under layers of historically sedimented social practices that conceal the context of their origin or the powers they now serve. We will illustrate this concealment by an example of a familiar social practice borrowed from Wertsch (1991, pp. 35–7) before exploring parallel examples in education.

We composed this chapter on the keyboard of a personal computer. Christopher Latham Sholes designed the configuration of this keyboard in 1872 to cope with certain mechanical limitations of his typewriter machines; they were "slower" than the typists' fingers. Sholes solved the problem by slowing down the typist. The most common letters (E, T, O, A, N, I) were distributed, frequent combinations such as ED were arranged so that they had to be struck by the same finger, and the typist was required to use the left hand 57 percent of the time. The result is the familiar QWERTY keyboard. In 1936, August Dvǒrák, using time and motion studies, created a more efficient keyboard that put all five vowels and the five most common consonants (D, H, T, N, S) on the "home row." Seventy percent of typing can be done on the home row in this system.

Several inferences may be drawn from this example. First, historical context is powerful in shaping familiar social practices. Second, see how the meaning of historically entrenched social practices may become lost or concealed. Third, the QWERTY system empowered its designer and not its users; indeed, users were disempowered. Fourth, most participants in the common social practice of typing probably assume that the QWERTY system is the most efficient, although it was deliberately designed for inefficiency. In fact, there is a long-standing, more efficient alternative. Nevertheless, the inefficient system remains entrenched. Fifth, there is a tendency to reify these historically entrenched social practices as "natural," necessary, and not subject to change. This leads to the conclusion that it is senseless to seek alternative possibilities, thus leaving one enslaved to the existing practice.

We believe that these inferences apply to the entrenched social practices of schooling. Mehan (cited in Wertsch, 1991, pp. 36–8) has studied bureaucratic problem solving in schools. Mehan discloses how school systems excogitate "clarity from ambiguity." The crucial idea is realizing that "events in the world are ambiguous. We struggle to understand these events, to imbue them with meaning. The choice of a particular way of representing events gives them a particular meaning" (in Wertsch, 1991, p. 36). Mehan examines the event of students being sorted by schools into "normal," "special needs," or "learning disabled.'' These institutionally defined categories construct the student's identity within the sociocultural context of the school system. These constructions will significantly orient the schooling history of these students, what they experience, and what they will learn. For the students sorted, these determinations may well become their destiny; they will experience the consequences of their assignment to an institutionally constructed (hence contingent) classification as an objectively real and harsh necessity. It rarely occurs to a student's parents or teachers to challenge the categories or tests used, much less the efficiency of the placement. The correctness of established cultural, historical, and institutional power is rarely questioned.

In making their determinations, school systems rely on supposedly objective standardized tests derived from psychological research and administered by educational experts. These tests purport to represent the real, intrinsic essence of every individual in spite of their unique particularities. Such intrinsic essences are highly abstract and completely decontextualized from all material conditions including the child's home life, classroom context, personal history, diet, personal needs, and interests. Experts assume the student's essential self is a logical universal that does not vary across context, time, or place. These same experts do, however, often consider the context and material conditions of the school system.

Mehan found that special education placements sometimes seemed defined in terms of an aggregate of financial incentives determined by the institutional context. The U.S. federal government provided supplementary funding to support special education for a fixed percentage of the student body. Those selected were placed in ''pullout'' and ''whole day'' special education programs in the school district; funding was not provided for students sent outside the district. Mehan concluded that ''the fact that there were *no* out of district placements during the year we studied the Coast district makes sense when placed against this background'' (in Wertsch, 1991, p. 37). Regarding this contextual conclusion Wertsch (1991) observes: ''Such facts do not indicate some kind of conspiracy or even a conscious decision; they derive from the institutionally situated categories [e.g., intelligence] and the patterns of speaking and thinking employed by the teachers, psychologists, administrators, and parents'' (p. 37). Almost everyone, including the empowered designers and disempowered ''users'' of such systems, forget the power of historical context and entrenched social practices. Many also assume that the system is the most efficient, with the result that the system is reified and assumed to be efficient at assigning students to the appropriate educational category. The inferences drawn from reflecting on the QWERTY system apply to special education placements and, we believe, the entire educational bureaucracy.

Technocracy arises when bureaucracy is baptized in the waters of science. Scientific categories, such as those guiding special education placements and tracking, are assumed to be especially objective, necessary, fixed, and final. What happens when a single person sets out to challenge these supposedly indubitable structures? Let us look at the special education placement of Tony Mitchell and the alternative assessment of Pam Simpson, an experienced teacher conducting qualitative research in Tony's school.[1]

Tony had spent much of his life traveling with a small carnival-type circus and very little time in school. Prior to enrolling at Thurber, Tony had previously had only two weeks of formal schooling. Eleven-year-old Tony was placed in Judith Samuelson's self-contained fourth-grade class. Students in Judith's class were required to take two state-mandated tests, the Literacy Passport Test (LPT) in February and the IOWA Test of Basic Skills (IOWA) in March, and the district-mandated Survey of Basic Skills (SBS) achievement test in early May. Judith felt responsible for teaching students what they needed to know for the tests. As dates for administrating the IOWA and SBS achievement tests approached, Judith assigned more and more worksheets. To familiarize students with the content and multiple-choice, bubble-in format of the standardized tests, she also made assignments from a test preparation workbook. Tony received all of these materials but did not take the three tests that spring because those participating in the decision process felt that it would be too stressful for him.

Judith was concerned about Tony's developmental stage and therefore initiated the special education evaluation cycle. Ironically, though Tony did not take the LPT, IOWA, or SBS with his class, the SBS as well as eight other assessments were administered to him individually as part of his special education evaluation during the last three weeks of the school year. The results were placed in Tony's Confidential Category II file.

This testing process permanently constructed Tony's institutional identity and defined the way the institution would perceive and respond to Tony in the future. The school's guidance counselor also used the classroom Observational Checklist required by the district's special education office. The counselor observed that Tony was frequently off task and failed to follow directions. These results went into his Category II file as well. Neither the observational checklist nor the counselor's written summary depicted Tony's behavior in the context of Judith's classroom or his instructional and curricular program. Often the lesson was not keyed to the lower grade texts that Tony had been assigned by Judith, nor was it noted that when he was "off task" it was because there was no work for him to do at the time. Tony was not participating because his unique needs were not being addressed at the time.

What follows are some of the results of the seven tests administered by the school psychologist:

> *Results and Impressions* – Cognitively, Tony appears to be functioning within the borderline range of overall ability according to the WISC-III. His Full Scale IQ of 75 reflects the 5th percentile by normative comparison. According to this assessment Tony demonstrates a mental age of approximately 9 years.
>
> Another measure of intelligence was administered. The TONI is a language-free measure of mental ability. The TONI relies on nonverbal problem solving skill. Tony's responses earned him a TONI quotient of 74, which reflects the 4th percentile and the borderline range. This estimate is quite consistent with the scores of the WISC-III.
>
> Tony's responses to the PPVT-R suggest receptive language skills in the borderline range. His standard score of 78 reflects the 7th percentile by normative comparison. This indicates an understanding of the spoken word at an 8 year 11 month level.
>
> *Summary and Recommendations* – At this, the conclusion of Tony's one year of formal education he is achieving at a first to second grade level.

This "technical" report did not consider the effects of the testing environment or the short time frame during which the tests were administered. It did not acknowledge that Tony had not met the psychologist prior to the first day of testing or that he had never before taken a standardized test. Furthermore, while other students enjoyed the end-of-school-year activities, Tony was pulled out of class and placed in an unfamiliar setting. Tony's assessment was based on his ability to reproduce right answers to totally decontextualized questions.

Educators are systematically blinded from seeing a student's unique and particular strengths and potential by the abstract, universalized, and decontextualized instruments used to measure the social construct called "intelligence." The text of Tony's Confidential Category II file became the context for constructing Tony's essential self. Such recontextualization is a common practice in educational technocracies such as schools. We believe that Tony was the victim of assault by a battery of tests that, once they became a part of his permanent record, turned Tony's contingent potential self into a cipher (75, 74, 78). Many educational technocrats affirm the Thorndike principle, that is, the idea that everything exists in some quantity and can be measured. Mere numbers reduce the meaning of Tony's life to those things that can be calculated. It is assumed that the only appropriate ethical system is utilitarianism and the only rational response is one based on calculative rationality. John Dewey (1932) states, "It is sympathy which saves consideration of consequences from degenerating into mere calculation, by rendering vivid the interests of others" (p. 270). Abstract, decontextualized universals are often unable to render a sympathetic assessment of a student's possibilities. We would like to suggest a more sympathetic alternative construction.

Pam Simpson had been an observer at Thurber for several weeks as part of the collaborative research project before she met Tony one Wednesday when she offered to teach his fourth-grade class while Judith conferred with individual students. In the course of the lesson she was surprised at Tony's ability to explain a complex passage that the class was reading. This was, as Pam put it, "my ah-ha experience" with Tony; afterwards she was unable to perceive him as a nonreader and nonwriter. She decided to work more with Tony one-on-one using a blank book that Tony titled and in which he composed his own stories beginning with one about people being shot out of a cannon. On this and many other topics relating to circus events, Tony was the expert. As the result of many such interactions in their own private space as well as in the larger classroom, Pam prepared a document that countered Judith's description of Tony as well as the psychologist's report. She believed that continuing to define Tony's instructional and curricular program in terms of individualized and decontextualized drills on skills limited his opportunities to read and write. She recommended Tony be placed in Ann McMann's fifth-grade class. Pam felt it offered an environment in which he could learn through the kind of social interaction and engagement of individual interests that she had documented as working best for him.

As a result of Pam's efforts, Tony was placed in Ann's class. In the spring of his fifth-grade year Ann talked about Tony and his progress in her class: "Tony's a reader and a writer. He's not afraid [to try]. I hope I've created a classroom where he can take risks." Pam believes that Ann created a classroom context where Tony was willing and able to become an active part of a community of readers and writers that stimulates his growth.

Who is Tony and what is he capable of learning? What do the standardized tests tell us? We do not know for certain. Why? Because we are dealing with the contingencies of human social construction. We do believe there is a tragic flaw in the abstract, decontextualized, hypostatized, and hyperrationalized technocratic concepts and categories when they are used to construct student's personal identities and perceive the future of their best possibilities.

Teacher education as the difference that makes a difference

In the first section of this chapter, we demonstrate the emancipatory possibilities of critical-constructivism in understanding the contingent nature of scientific categories and constructs. Our example is from science education – the classification of living forms – but examples can be drawn equally as well from every other school subject. Swartz (1996) illustrates the emancipatory possibilities for social studies teachers by attending to the accuracy of historical information, inclusion of indigenous voices, and promotion of critical thinking. She makes her point by showing how a typical textbook passage can be reworked by teachers to reposition the "historical voice."

> Anger over the soldiers finally exploded in violence. On March 5, 1770, about 100 Bostonians moved toward some soldiers guarding the customs house. One of the Bostonians' leaders was a black man named Crispus Attucks. The crowd yelled, then threw some rocks and snowballs. Fearing for their safety, the soldiers opened fire. They killed Attucks and four other colonists.
>
> Crispus Attucks was a runaway slave who worked on the docks in Boston. He was about 50 years old when he was killed in the Boston Massacre. (p. 405)

In dissecting this passage, one cannot help but note how a series of events has been reified as "The Boston Massacre." The beliefs, passions, and reasons for the involvement of any of the five patriots who were killed are subsumed in a seemingly objective description. And an omission technique (McNeil, 1986) is used in organizing this account that conceptually reduces Attucks's leadership role by representing him "uncritically through his enslavement." Attucks had freed himself twenty years earlier from the bonds of slavery, yet the textual passage will likely lead students to construct an image of Attucks as someone "on the run" who is already breaking civil laws. Swartz illustrates how this passage could suggest a different representation, once reworked by teachers:

> Crispus Attucks was a sailor and dock worker in Boston who believed deeply in freedom. In 1750, he took his own freedom by escaping from the system of slavery. In 1770, at the age of almost 50 years, he showed how much he still believed in freedom when he led Bostonians in a demonstration against British soldiers. Attucks was one of the five men to be killed when these soldiers opened fire on the revolutionaries. This event was later called the Boston Massacre. (p. 405)

Note the changes. The Boston Massacre is now a contingent category, one that was constructed later. Attucks is no longer merely "added" to the description of the Boston Massacre, a marginal and relatively replaceable figure. Instead, he becomes for the reader a central figure with beliefs and passions giving life to this account. He is an admirable human being, with patriotic beliefs and interests relating to, but transcending his own struggle for personal freedom. He is part of a bigger cause, a cause to which more students can relate, both students traditionally marginalized as well as students from predominantly Eurocentric backgrounds. Swartz's reconstruction shows that with the addition of small amounts of information, the representations of Attucks and the Boston Massacre not only become more accurate, but increasingly provide opportunities for teachers and students to pursue critical questions that have an emancipatory effect by encouraging multiple constructions of the event. For example, was Crispus Attucks's presence in Boston in 1770 "unusual, or were other people of African descent living in Boston . . . and involved in the struggle for freedom from England?" (p. 405). What were their relationships to white patriots? And so forth. The point is similar to what we saw earlier in the deconstruction of school science; what we notice here is the same possibility in the social sciences for reworking historical accounts, thereby allowing students to gain a plurality of perspectives.

In the second part of this chapter, we have shown how the reified and decontexualized scientific categories that organize the schooling experience for students (and the work expectations for teachers) can ultimately harm a student's education. Pam's opposition to the technocratic rationality of schooling prevents Tony from being discarded in the educational process as a "low score." Pam was an astute observer, who through serendipitous circumstances noticed how Tony's experiential responses contradicted the way he was classified. But the important questions for the last section of this chapter concern what the emancipatory possibilities are for teachers and how these can be brought about.

A relatively recent occurrence within the paradigm of teacher professionalization has been the turn taken by educational research toward studying the process of teachers' thinking (Popkewitz, 1991). Within this paradigm, teachers supposedly become the source of their own knowledge base, which seems like an inherently empowering idea. Research into the individual and collective thinking of teachers in practice presumably informs a new construction of expert knowledge about pedagogy. In this scheme of things, the basis of educational expertise is rooted in the teachers themselves. Using teacher thinking as the source of a knowledge base about teaching, it is claimed, places educational research in a more valid position among school practitioners, who have traditionally perceived research as irrelevant for teaching practices.

A fundamental and fatal flaw in this research paradigm, however, is that it ignores the fact that teachers themselves are entangled to a great extent in the technical rationality of schooling, with its reified constructs about student learning, academic content, and school organization. Through their experiences as students in the formal educational system for a minimum of sixteen years, a static, nonproblematic image of formal knowledge has been imprinted through taxonomies, discrete codifications, and implicit and explicit hierarchical organizational forms. Their educational experience has been a continual process of repeated instances of reification and normalization of the contingent categories making up school knowledge. An example of this is provided by a preservice science teacher's point of view about science teaching:

> I am visual, very visual. Science that is put into words . . . that is all very nice. In books too. *But we have to have concepts, even a reality, so that they [teachers] show us something*. I loved that. I've had teachers that showed me, as simple as that. I was in biology. Well, if there is one thing that it's important to see, it is to try to conceptualize something, to get a handle on something, to put it under your eyes and simply enable someone to see. . . . What I like is to show that science is not something up there in the clouds, it is concrete, we can visualize it. . . . That is what I liked about the way I was taught science. It's putting it in front of us, so we could touch it, so that we could see it and look at it, that's good. (Ruel, 1994, p. 277, emphasis added)

For this college-educated student of science and soon-to-be teacher, things appear as they are. The reification process is complete, neither concepts nor reality are problematic. In fact, there is clearly no distinction between concepts and reality for this student.

Powerful structural forces are also at work in the socialization process of learning to think as a teacher (Zeichner and Gore, 1990). The "student-teacher" induction model of preparing teachers – the predominant model – perpetuates habits of thinking that are resilient and difficult to change. Consider the proportionally few courses occurring within a future teacher's college experience in which the educational process is deliberately studied in its fullest extent – that is, in which questions are raised about the sociopolitical nature of knowledge and knowing. A comparison to medical education is always a treacherous one, but should we not be asking this question before allowing incisions on the minds and spirits of youngsters? Much of the time spent in "studying" teaching occurs in the form of acquiring techniques in actual classroom settings, but without systematic reflection. Without the benefit of this kind of reflection, the contingent nature of knowledge and of the techniques acquired through these activities is not exposed. One result is that the language of teaching is imbued with metaphors that separate content from method, feelings from thoughts, objectivity from subjectivity, teaching from learning, and – ultimately – teachers from students.

Regarding the possibilities for "reinventing teaching," Meier (1992) posits that conditions need to be created for teachers to change how they view teaching and learning, to develop new practices consistent with these new understandings, and develop collegial work habits to replace the overly private and individualistic work culture which presently defines their activities. She places the onus of making these structural changes on the teachers themselves: "Teachers must lead the way to their own liberation" (p. 599). To us this means that teachers must be able to deconstruct and reconstruct the contingent categories that have been continually reified through their educational biography.

We agree that teachers are the agents with the greatest potential for transforming how teaching and learning occur. They are the only ones that can make "a difference that makes a difference" (Bateson's expression, 1981). But considering the overpowering grip that technocratic rationality holds over the socialization of students and teachers, it seems unrealistic to expect teachers to collectively reinvent ideas about teaching and learning on their own. Meier (and others) seems to hold little hope for formal teacher education programs to bring about this change, and perhaps for good reason if one investigates the historical track record of most programs. But one has to ask where else in the socialization of a teacher's knowledge will they be exposed to questions about epistemology and ontology that go to the very heart of the political nature of formal knowledge? It is this question which leads us to believe that a heavy burden for bringing about transformative teaching practices should be placed on teacher educators and teacher preparation programs to put critical-constructivism at the center of discussions about the nature of learning, teaching, content, and schooling as a sociopolitical process.

Short of traumatic or perturbing personal or academic experiences in a person's life, there are relatively few situations in formal education, kindergarten through university, that allow one's conceptions to go on a radically different trajectory from the predominant paradigm of official knowledge. The disciplinary requirements and political pressures in academia often issue in a college experience for preservice teachers that can hardly be labeled liberating (and may more appropriately be considered an experience in the "conservative arts"). A college education in a particular discipline seldom involves concerted study of the conflicts and contradictions within the discipline itself. How commonly are undergraduate students required to study the history and philosophy of their own major academic content field? Without this kind of experience, potential teachers begin teacher preparation programs with a firm ontological view informed by their major discipline, but are rarely perplexed by socioepistemological considerations or made aware of the political consequences of such a view. The implications for any possibility of emancipation for teachers, and therefore students, directly follow. If teachers are not posed with problematic situations that challenge their epistemologies and ontologies, in all likelihood their students will not be aware of these either.

The absence of experiencing perplexities about the nature of knowledge and knowing may account for both the complacency and the unwillingness of many educators to respond to important educational issues. For example, given all the important problems in the world (hunger, poverty, AIDS, etc.) educators conspicuously embrace answers to problems that really are relatively insignifiant, that is, merit pay, competency testing, and vouchers, et cetera. The logic of ontological reification emphasized in our educational experience makes it natural for educators to identify as problematic only those things fitting the technical solutions already existing. Again, reified and decontextualized knowledge normalizes a nonproblematic approach for identifying and responding to educational problems.

There is another reason why teacher preparation programs must carry the banner for creating the conditions that facilitate the emancipation of teachers' thinking. Teaching is an ethical act. Teaching is also a sociopolitical endeavor. Teachers and teacher educators have the best opportunities for ''orienting'' students' conversations about their constructions of their worlds. One of the primary moral, social, and political questions of teaching involves whether or not to let students in on the knowledge game. But in order to even ask this question teachers themselves must have the opportunity to become well versed in how knowledge is constructed in multiple ways. Borrowing Swartz's (1996) phrase (who borrows it from Toni Morrison), teachers are the leverage point for making students ''response-able'' (p. 397). Epistemological, ontological, and social response-ability is the endless task of critical-constructivism, as has been illustrated many times in this book.

Notes

1. Constructivism and education: beyond epistemological correctness

1. The shift from one linguistic and cultural repertory to another is no simple matter. As Sjøberg so justly remarked (1996), "This is not only a matter of differences of terminology, but rather of deep-rooted differences in how problems are conceived, conceptualized and approached" (p. 401). The concept of didactics is no exception to the rule. Little esteemed in English because of its moralizing connotations, it has been used here within a meaning more frequently encountered on the Continent. It is intended to convey something more specific than the art or science of teaching, implying in particular a set of problematics, concepts, and methodologies for use in analyzing a given educational situation. The educational situation per se does not militate in favor of a psychological perspective centering on interpersonal relationships over and above the development of an informed relationship toward formal knowledge among students. Accordingly, the student appropriation of the elements typifying a given field becomes the affair of representations, such as modes of argumentation or validation. It goes without saying, however, that such representations exist in the eye of the beholder – in this case, the "didactician" – whose own epistemological and ideological options and, indeed, relationship to knowledge and teaching color the focus and perceptions of the said educational situation. Thus, the semantic field of didactics proves to be every bit as heterogeneous as that of constructivism itself!
2. Quite obviously, any answer made to this or a similar question comes down to making a decision as to the object of constructivism and its limits. That is how our comments on this subject should be construed. It follows that an attempt in that direction constitutes a normal (i.e., to be expected) caveat which, from the perspective in question, can and should not be avoided.
3. This paraphrase somewhat alters the meaning of the original quotation which is to be found in a commentary on Wittgenstein's *Tractatus* and

which reads as follows: "The miracle may be suggested, but it cannot be *expressed*" (p. 15, emphasis added).

4. The concept of actor applies equally to human beings, instruments, and things. Thus, textbooks, curricula, personal computers, or a chemical reaction (spectacular or otherwise) are all part of a category of actors, inasmuch as they cannot be mobilized in any way whatsoever and can impose types of interaction on other actors. They are the mouthpieces of those who have invented them (Callon, 1989).
5. On the subject of sensory receptors and their "blindness" with respect to the "quality" of stimulations, see von Foerster (1988).
6. For example, see Bakhurst and Sypnowich (1995).
7. Indeed, the situation, particularly in France, appears somewhat different if one refers to the numerous publications of the Institut National de la Recherche Pédagogique (INRP) devoted to the teaching of history, geography, economics, and other social sciences within a constructivist mode.

2. Why constructivism must be radical

1. This definition, however, poses yet another problem: The work that combines and transforms elements of sensation and, as a result, creates objects of perception, processes, and events is work of which we are usually not conscious. Thus, each time a cognitive organism accomplishes this work in the face of its environment, I consider this as coming within the realm of experience.
2. For a constructivist, this "intersubjectivity" is obviously devoid of objectivity or absoluteness. It is again the construction of an observer, which is based on the personal observations which he or she has made within the world of his or her own experience. In my opinion, this is what constitutes the major difference between radical constructivism and the recent current that goes under the name of "social constructionism."
3. I borrowed the term *orientation* from Humberto Maturana, who was the first to introduce the notion of orientation in his analysis of linguistic interaction (see, in particular, Maturana and Varela, 1980).

4. Toward a pragmatic social constructivism

1. I would like to acknowledge many helpful discussions with Gert Biesta.
2. Elsewhere Dewey (1896) wrote "stimulus and response are functional divisions of labor" (p. 99).

5. Individual construction, mathematical acculturation, and the classroom community

1. The research reported in this paper was supported by the National Science Foundation (under grant No. MDR 885–0560) and by the Spencer Founda-

tion. The opinions expressed do not necessarily reflect the views of these foundations. Several notions central to this paper were elaborated in the course of discussions with Heinrich Bauersfeld, Götz Krummheuer, and Jörg Voigt at the University of Bielefeld, Germany, and with Koeno Gravemeijer at the Freudenthal Institute, State University of Utrecht, Netherlands.

6. The construction of answers to insoluble problems

1. This project was made possible by a grant from the Fonds National Suisse de la Recherche Scientifique (FNRS contract no. 1372–0.86, Perret-Clermont and Schubauer-Leoni), to whom we wish to express our thanks.
2. The principle of relevance assumes that the actors see themselves as legitimate interlocutors, who enjoy linguistic, pragmatic, and social competence. The principle of coherence refers to the existence of worlds which are taken-as-shared. The principle of reciprocity presupposes the possibility which each actor has of collaborating on the construction of the (pole of) reference. The principle of influence refers to play with and upon the issues arising in connection with the situation.
3. We are referring here to a research experiment involving the conservation of discrete quantities by a group of schoolchildren. The experimenter presented herself to the group first as a schoolteacher and then as a lady who wanted to play a game with the schoolchildren. For analysis and interpretation of the results, see Schubauer-Leoni et al., 1992.
4. This class was made up of ten girls and twelve boys. Children came from the following social strata: upper (18%), middle (46%), and lower (36%). The proportion of each socioprofessional group is close to the average for the Canton of Geneva.
5. In the French version of this chapter, four case interviews were described, thus providing for a more subtle analysis. However, the three cases which have been kept for the purposes of this presentation suitably portray the essentials of the private/public dynamic used to characterize students' answering activity.
6. The grading scale currently in effect in Geneva goes from 0 to 6. In this class, 18% obtained the highest score; 59% obtained 5; 14% obtained 4; and 9% obtained 3. The teacher considered this class a good class.

8. Constructivism-in-action: students examine their idea of science

1. This research provided the basis of a book, a number of excerpts from which have been included here with the permission of the publisher (see Larochelle and Désautels, 1992).
2. The term *spontaneous* underscores the notion that the contents of this

knowledge (or conception) differ from that of scientific knowledge on the subject (for a listing of studies on the subject, see Pfundt and Duit, 1994).

3. This "looping back" of thought upon itself may give rise to intellectual vertigo of a kind which might provoke anxiety among some. There is always a blind spot in a conceptual structure, which makes searching for an absolute basis to knowledge an absurdity. As von Foerster (1990) has shown, however, the reiteration of an operation does not necessarily lead to an instance of infinite regression.

9. Constructivism and ethical justification

1. This is what Isabelle Stengers has called practicing the epistemology or history of science from an agnostic point of view with respect to the ultimate nature of scientific knowledge. On this subject, see Fourez (1996).
2. This method was used by Latour and Woolgar (1988), and by Callon (1976) as well, to study scientific practices. In so doing, they imitate anthropologists who, in their studies of sorcery, do not necessarily ascribe the same meanings to sorcery that sorcerers do. Thus, it is possible to study the ways by which people justify their ethical positions without necessarily subscribing to such ways.
3. Similar to the spheres of justice of Walzer (1983).
4. Although occasionally there may be "arrangements," that is, situations in which the parties merely "halt the disagreement without exhausting it, without getting to the bottom of the matter," and without "reaching back to some principle of justice" (Boltanski and Thévenot, 1991, p. 163).
5. Likewise: "To evaluate greatness in the domestic sphere, reference is not made to codes and criteria as is the case in the industrial world, but instead to the outstanding deeds of the great, and to the life of the illustrious" (Boltanski and Thévenot, 1991, p. 167). "In a domestic situation, lesser individuals are as important as the great . . . whereas a public collectivity (civic order) or a technician (industrial order) go unidentified" (ibid., p. 169) (actually, either entity does not exist in these worlds). Everywhere, "the forms of knowledge are adapted to the evaluation of states of greatness" (ibid., p. 167).
6. According to Latour and Woolgar (1988), a laboratory is a place where objects are defined in and by the paradigm of a discipline. See also Fourez (1996, pp. 97–9).
7. To pursue the parallel with epistemology, a "world" can, according to Boltanski and Thévenot, be compared to the reality perceived by a particular discipline – e.g., the world of physics, the world of biology, of economics, etc. In either case, an instituting structure (paradigm or city) structures the real in the form of objects which have meaning in this context.
8. In the case of some worlds at least, these criticisms do not always appear in a rational light of the sort generally associated with a city, but are not

irrational for all that. Consider, for example, certain forms of workers' resistance, "which appear to be implacably opposed to a specifically industrial state of greatness and which are expressed in a coup brought off by the rank and file or in bodily violence and hence constitute to the same degree as exercises of mortification in classic ascetism, ways of increasing one's greatness which relate to the inspirational order" (Boltanski and Thévenot, 1991, p. 267).

9. In the same way that interdisciplinary work presupposes the search for a type of discourse or truth which reaches beyond discipline-bound representations.
10. On the subject of the hardening or entrenching of scientific concepts, see Stengers (1987) and Fourez (1996).
11. In the same way that new disciplines are, generally speaking, interdisciplinary approaches that have "solidified" and become socially stabilized (see Fourez, 1996, p. 107).
12. A relativistic metaphysics would purport, generally speaking, that everything is equivalent, whereas a metaphysics of relativization would state merely that a point of view may be shown to be relative to a context and a project. For example, an engineer is quite capable of "relativizing" the worth of each technique, but would not be of the opinion, however, that all techniques work fairly much the same way or are of equal worth.
13. Are Boltanski and Thévenot correct in speaking of pardon as a type of forgetting? It is possible to pardon by deciding to forego measuring the totalization of past actions without, by the same token forgetting. On the contrary, when a person pardons without forgetting, the interpersonal link which was a source of hurt and which has not been forgotten also becomes a part of the new relationship. In other words, as Lavelle (1957) has brought out, the very offense which was committed against us by others creates a bodily relationship between ourselves and them, which pardon thus spiritualizes.

11. Practical knowledge and school knowledge: a constructivist representation of education

1. The phenomenon of self-fulfilling prophecies in knowledge of the self, of others, and of the world, is one of the problems, if it is not indeed *the* problem, confronting constructivist counseling and psychotherapy today. Although this phenomenon offers a productive angle with which to view a major portion of what goes under the heading of "learning difficulties," it has, to my knowledge, been neglected or more or less underestimated in constructivist-type approaches to educational psychology or didactics.
2. It is only too often assumed that students share, or ought to share, our obsession with knowledge that has been institutionally ratified.

3. These observations do not apply to the supposedly more exact disciplines alone. In terms of moral education, for example, knowledge of good and evil by a subject is the practical knowledge of what does the person good and what does him or her harm. It is not some abstract, transcendental entity which is exhibited to the subject and to which conformity is required. Likewise, in terms of personal and social education, a subject's practical knowledge consists in whatever enables him or her to manage on a daily basis. It is not some sort of universal ideal of psychological or social development which is proposed to the subject as offering a greater degree of adaptation, in disregard of concrete contexts and problems.
4. That is why, also, the pedagogical power of work on the metaphors synchronically underlying several sectors of practical knowledge (Lakoff and Johnson, 1980; Ortony, 1984) cannot be underestimated. It may be hypothesized that school knowledge deals with practical problems of a kind which frequently present analogies with the various sectors of the subject's experience and practical knowledge, and which could be mobilized and utilized to make this same school knowledge tangible.
5. This is understandable since the institutional raison d'être which prefigures and justifies this type of research and practice is the problem of teaching specific discipline-based knowledge (e.g., mathematics, language, physics, biology, the social sciences, philosophy, personal and social development – in short, anything that can be made into a school subject) that has been developed ''elsewhere'' and not the problem of human adaptation in general. Whence the difficulty for didacticians of looking into the impact of didactics-in-action on the construction which a student fabricates of him- or herself, knowledge, and educators.
6. Often it is over such ethical questions of the value of goals that disagreements and criticisms arise. But even constructivists frequently forget that this value is itself constructed.

12. Sociocultural perspectives on the teaching and learning of science

1. However, we have noticed that teachers sometimes have a limited language to describe what happens in their classroom and what they believe about such issues as student learning and the nature of science (Tobin and McRobbie, 1996).

13. Remarks on the education of elementary teachers

1. The notion of ''enculturation'' is used here in a metaphorical sense. I do not use it elsewhere because of the related connotation of becoming *en-*

culturated into something like an already existing and objectively given culture. The culture of a classroom is an emergent social system and is not pregiven.

2. In Germany, an average of only approximately 20% of students who matriculate in mathematics actually graduate in their field. This is not because they fail the final examination, but because they drop out along the way.
3. Indeed, these are classical maximum-minimum solutions: they produce maximum smoothness in regular classroom processes and require a minimum of effort on the part of the teacher.
4. Due to possible mechanistic connotations, Bruner's notion of ''scaffolding'' may be misleading, but this metaphor clearly denotes a genuine interactionist and constructivist orientation.

14. Constructivism as a referent for reforming science education

1. To Cole and Wertsch, the more interesting difference between Piaget and Vygotsky has to do with the role of cultural artifacts in relation to the individual-social spectrum.
2. Philosophical postmodernism has grown from the work of Friedrich Nietzsche and Martin Heidegger, especially as expressed by Jacques Derrida, Michel Foucault, and other French thinkers. Some postmodernist philosophy is considered *deconstructive*. It addresses the modern worldview through criticism that eliminates the ingredients of a worldview – e.g., purpose, self, a real world, truth as correspondence. Other postmodernist philosophy is constructive, representing a project to revise the premises and concepts of modernism so as to create a postmodern worldview (Orr, 1992).
3. Learning cycle models generally have an exploratory phase that involves tapping prior knowledge, followed by a concept introduction phase, then by a phase that emphasizes application and extension.
4. Garrison and I have expressed a similar view (Garrison and Bentley, 1990). We noted that the conceptual change model is guilty of what William James called the *intellectualistic fallacy*, the assumption that a complete account of a psychological phenomenon – i.e., science learning, can be given in terms of concepts and their relations.
5. An example cited by Kumar and Voldrich (1994) involved using relevant fiction to connect science content to simulated real life situations, which is what I also had in mind with the book *Astronomy Smart, Jr.*, a novel with science woven throughout for young teens (Bentley, 1996).
6. Faculty associated with projects linked through NLU's Center for City Schools included Harvey Daniels, Arthur Hyde, Stephen Bloom, Marilyn Bizar, Janet Schnobrich, and others.

7. Taken together, the five schools in the Chicago Public Schools (CPS) that have been involved in PPC projects portray the ethnic and social-economic diversity of Chicago's public schools. As a group, the four elementary schools have a composite ethnic makeup which is 83% minority and 73% economically depressed (based on free and reduced lunch data). The range of educational achievement among the parents is equally diverse, ranging from those with less than a high school education to some with graduate degrees.
8. The initial PPC project in 1994 involved culturally diverse schools. A second project was begun in 1995 involving four other equally diverse Waukegan schools.
9. The locally developed curriculum units are available from the ERIC Document Reproduction Service (nos: 394 829, 394 830, 394 831).

15. Critical-constructivism and the sociopolitical agenda

1. Except for Pam Simpson, all names, including that of the school, have been changed. Tony's story and the lessons drawn from it rely heavily on Simpson and Garrison (1995).

References

Agger, B. (1992). *The discourse of domination: From the Frankfurt school to postmodernism.* Evanston, Ill.: Northwestern University Press.

Aikenhead, G. S. (1996). Science education: Border crossings into the subculture of science. *Studies in Science Education, 27,* 1–52.

Alberts, B. M. (1994, October 26). *A foundation for science in the twenty-first century: Researchers and physicians as science educators.* Evanston, Ill: Annual Klopsteg Lecture, Northwestern University.

Alves Martin, M., and Carvalho Neto, F. (1990). A influência dos factores sociais contextuais na resoluçao de problemas. *Anàlise Psicològica, VIII,* 265–74.

American Association for the Advancement of Science. (1989). *Science for all Americans (Project 2061).* Washington, D.C.: Author.

(1993). *Benchmarks for science literacy: Project 2061.* New York: Oxford University Press.

Amerio, P. (1991). Idées, sujets et conditions d'existence. In V. Aebischer, J.-P. Deconchy, and E. M. Lipiansky, eds., *Idéologies et représentations sociales* (pp. 99–116). Fribourg, Switzerland: Delval.

Apple, M. W. (1990). *Ideology and curriculum.* New York: Routledge.

Ashby, R., Lee, P., and Dickinson, A. (1997). How children explain the "why" of history: The Chata research project on teaching history. *Social Education, 61,* 17–21.

Ashton-Warner, S. (1963). *Teacher.* New York: Simon and Schuster.

Bakhtin, M. M. (1986). *Speech genres and other late essays.* Austin: University of Texas Press.

Bakhurst, D., and Sypnowich, C., eds. (1995). *The social self.* London: Sage.

Balacheff, N. (1991). Treatment of refutations: Aspects of the complexity of a constructivist approach to mathematics learning. In E. von Glasersfeld, ed., *Radical constructivism in mathematics education* (pp. 89–110). Dordrecht, Netherlands: Kluwer.

Banks, J. A. (1995). Transformative challenges to the social science disciplines: Implications for social studies teaching and learning. *Theory and Research in Social Education, 23*, 2–20.

Barbin, E. (1988). La démonstration mathématique: significations épistémologiques et questions didactiques. *Bulletin de l'association des professeurs de mathématiques de l'enseignement public* (APMEP), December, 591–620.

Barnes, B. (1982). *T. S. Kuhn and social science.* New York: Columbia University Press.

Barton, K. C. (1997). History – it can be elementary: An overview of elementary students' understanding of history. *Social Education, 61*, 13–16.

Barton, K. C., and Levstik, L. S. (1996). ''Back when God was around and everything'': Elementary students understanding of historical time. *American Educational Research Journal, 33*, 419–54.

Baruk, S. (1985). *L'âge du capitaine: De l'erreur en mathématiques.* Paris: Seuil.

Bateson, G. (1981). *Steps to an ecology of mind* (9th ed.). New York: Ballantine.

Bauersfeld, H. (1978). Kommunikationsmuster im Mathematikunterricht – Eine Analyse am Beispiel der Hand lungsverengung durch Antworterwartung. In H. Bauersfeld, ed., *Fallstudien und Analysen zum Mathematikunterricht* (pp. 158–70). Auswahl, Reihe B, *95*, Hannover: H. Schroedel Verlag.

(1980). Hidden dimensions in the so-called reality of a mathematics classroom. *Educational Studies in Mathematics, 11*, 23–41.

(1988). Interaction, construction, and knowledge: Alternative perspectives for mathematics education. In D. A. Grouws, T. J. Cooney, and D. Jones, eds., *Effective mathematics teaching* (Vol. 1, pp. 27–46). Reston, Va.: Erlbaum and National Council of Teachers of Mathematics.

(1993). Theoretical perspectives on interaction in the mathematical classroom. In R. Biehler, R. W. Scholz, R. Sträber, and B. Winkelmann, eds., *Didactics of mathematics as a scientific discipline* (pp. 133–46). Dordrecht, Netherlands: Kluwer.

(1995). The structuring of the structures: Development and function of mathematizing as a social practice. In L. P. Steffe and J. Gale, eds., *Constructivism and Education* (pp. 137–58). Hillsdale, N.J.: Erlbaum (Abridged version, cf. Occasional paper *122*, IDM, Universität Bielefeld, October 1990).

(1995a). 'Language games' in the mathematics classroom – Their function and their effects. In H. Bauersfeld and P. Cobb, eds., *The emergence of mathematical meaning: Interaction in classroom cultures* (pp. 440–75). Hillsdale, N.J.: Erlbaum.

Bauersfeld, H., Krummheuer, G., and Voigt, J. (1988). Interactional theory of learning and teaching mathematics and related microethnographical studies. In H. G. Steiner and A. Vermandel, eds., *Foundations and meth-*

odology of the discipline of mathematics education (pp. 174–88). Antwerp, Belgium: Proceedings of the Second Theory of Mathematics Education Conference.

Bentley, M. L. (1996). *Astronomy Smart, Jr.* New York: The Princeton Review.

Bentley, M. L., and Nalbandian, M. (1994). *Community resource curriculum development: A cooperative effort project.* Chicago, Ill.: The Chicago Academy of Sciences (ERIC Document Reproduction Service Nos. 394 829, 394 830, 394 831).

Benyamna, S. (1987). *La prégnance du modèle particulaire dans les représentations d'étudiants en science à l'égard de phénomènes naturels.* Doctoral thesis, Université Laval, Québec.

Benyamna, S., Désautels, J., and Larochelle, M. (1993). Du concept à la chose: la notion de particule dans les propos d'étudiants à l'égard de phénomènes physiques. *Revue canadienne de l'éducation, 18,* 62–78.

Berger, P. L., and Luckmann, T. (1967). *The social construction of reality.* New York: Doubleday.

Berliner, D. C., and Biddle, B. J. (1995). *The manufactured crisis: Myths, fraud, and attack on America's public schools.* New York: Addison-Wesley-Longman.

Bernstein, B. (1977). *Class, codes, and control* (Vol. 3: *Toward a theory of educational transmissions).* London: Routledge and Kegan Paul.

Bernstein, R. J. (1983). *Beyond objectivism and relativism: Science, hermeneutics, and praxis.* Philadelphia: University of Pennsylvania Press.

Bettencourt, A. (1993). The construction of knowledge: A radical constructivist view. In K. Tobin, ed., *The practice of constructivism in science education* (pp. 39–50). Hillsdale, N.J.: Erlbaum.

Bigelow, B. (1996, Fall). How my schooling taught me contempt for the Earth. *Rethinking Schools*, 14–17.

Billig, M. (1993). Studying the thinking society: Social representations, rhetoric, and attitudes. In G. M. Breakwell and D. Canter, eds., *Empirical approaches to social representations* (pp. 39–62). Oxford: Oxford University Press.

Blanchet, A. (1987). Interviewer. In A. Blanchet, R. Ghiglione, J. Massonnat, and A. Trognon, eds., *Les techniques d'enquête en sciences sociales* (pp. 82–126). Paris: Dunod.

Bohm, D., and Peat, F. D. (1987). *Science, order, and creativity.* New York: Bantam Books.

Boltanski, L., and Thévenot, L. (1991). *De la justification, les économies de la grandeur.* Paris: Gallimard.

Bourdieu, P. (1980). *Le sens pratique.* Paris: Les Éditions de Minuit.

(1991). *Language and symbolic power* (G. Raymond and M. Adamson, trans.). Cambridge, Mass.: Harvard University Press.

(1994). *Raisons pratiques.* Paris: Seuil.

Bourdieu, P., and Passeron, J. C. (1977). *Reproduction in education, society, and culture* (R. Nice, trans.). London: Sage.

Bowers, C. (1993). *Critical essays on education, modernity, and the recovery of the ecological imperative*. New York: Teachers College Press.

Bracey, G. W. (1996). International comparisons and the condition of American education. *Educational Researcher, 25*, 5–11.

Bredo, E., and McDermott, R. P. (1992). Teaching, relating, and learning. *Educational Researcher, 21*, 31–5.

Brissiaud, R. (1988). De l'âge du capitaine à l'âge du berger. Quel est le contrôle de la validité d'un énoncé de problème au CE2? *Revue française de pédagogie, 82*, 23–31.

Britzman, D. P. (1986). Cultural myths in the making of a teacher: Biography and social structure in teacher education. *Harvard Educational Review, 56*, 442–72.

Bronowski, J. (1965). *Science and human values*. New York: Harper and Row.

Brophy, J., VanSledright, B., and Bredin, N. (1992). Fifth-graders' ideas about history expressed before and after their introduction to the subject. *Theory and Research in Social Education, 20*, 440–89.

Brossard, M. (1994). *École et adaptation*. Bordeaux: Stablon.

Brousseau, G. (1984). The crucial role of the didactical contract in the analysis and construction of situations in teaching and learning mathematics. In H. G. Steiner, ed., *Theory of mathematics education* (pp. 110–19). Occasional paper 54. Bielefeld: Institut für Didaktik der Mathematik.

(1986). *Théorisation des phénomènes d'enseignement des mathématiques*. Doctoral thesis, Université de Bordeaux I, France.

(1988). Le contrat didactique: le milieu. *Recherches en didactique des mathématiques, 9*, 309–36.

(1996). Fondements et méthodes de la didactique des mathématiques. In J. Brun, ed., *Didactique des mathématiques* (pp. 45–143). Lausanne: Delachaux and Niestlé.

Brown, S. I., and Walter, M. I. (1990). *The art of problem posing*. Hillsdale, N.J.: Erlbaum.

Brown, T. (1997). *Mathematics and language*. Dordrecht, Netherlands: Kluwer.

Brun, J., and Conne, F. (1990). Analyses didactiques de protocoles d'observations du déroulement de situations. *Éducation et recherche, 3*, 261–86.

Bruner, J. S. (1983). *Child's talk – learning to use language*. Oxford: Oxford University Press.

(1984). Vygotsky's zone of proximal development: The hidden agenda. In B. Rogoff and J. V. Wertsch, eds., *Children's learning in the "zone of proximal development"* (pp. 93–7). San Francisco, Calif.: Jossey-Bass.

(1990). *Acts of meaning*. Cambridge, Mass.: Harvard University Press.

(1996). *The culture of education*. Cambridge, Mass.: Harvard University Press.

Bruner, J. S., and Haste, H. (1987). *Making sense: The child's construction of the world*. London: Methuen.

Burton, L. (1984). *Thinking things through: Problem solving in mathematics*. Oxford: Basil Blackwell.

Butler, J. (1990). *Gender trouble: Feminism and the subversion of identity*. New York: Routledge.

Byrnes, J. P., and Torney-Purta, J. V. (1995). Naive theories and decision making as part of higher order thinking in social studies. *Theory and Research in Social Education*, *23*, 260–77.

California Department of Education. (1990). *Science framework for California public schools: Kindergarten through grade twelve*. Sacramento: Author.

Callon, M. (1976). L'opération de traduction comme relation symbolique. In C. Gruson, P. Roqueplo, and P. Thuillier, eds., *Incidence des rapports sociaux sur le développement scientifique et technique* (pp. 105–42). Paris: Cordes-CNRS.

Callon, M., ed. (1989). *La science et ses réseaux*. Paris: La Découverte/Conseil de l'Europe/Unesco.

Callon, M., and Latour, B., eds. (1991). *La science telle qu'elle se fait*. Paris: La Découverte.

Carraher, T. N., Carraher, D. W., and Schliemann, A. D. (1985). Mathematics in the street and in schools. *British Journal of Developmental Psychology*, *3*, 21–9.

Carson, R. C. (1982). Self-fulfilling prophecy, maladaptive behavior, and psychotherapy. In J. C. Anchin and D. J. Kiesler, eds., *Handbook of interpersonal psychotherapy* (pp. 64–77). New York: Pergamon.

Carugati, F. (1991). Interazioni, conflitti, conoscenze. In G. Gilli and A. Marchetti, eds., *Prospettive sociogenetiche e sviluppo cognitivo* (pp. 65–86). Milan: Raffaello Cortina.

Chaiklin, S., and Lave, J., eds. (1996). *Understanding practice. Perspectives on activity and context*. New York: Cambridge University Press.

Charlot, B., Bautier, E., and Rochex, J.-Y. (1992). *École et savoir dans les banlieues . . . et ailleurs*. Paris: Armand Colin.

Chevallard, Y. (1988). *Sur l'analyse didactique. Deux études sur les notions de contrat et de situation*. Marseille: Institut de recherche sur l'enseignement des mathématiques d'Aix-Marseille, *14*.

(1991). *La transposition didactique – Du savoir savant au savoir enseigné* (2nd ed.). Grenoble: La pensée sauvage.

(1992). Concepts fondamentaux de la didactique: perspectives apportées par une approche anthropologique. *Recherches en didactique des mathématiques*, *12*, 73–112.

Clark, D. L., and Astuto, T. A. (1986). The significance and permanence of changes in federal education policy. *Educational Researcher*, *15*, 4–13.

Cobb, P., and Steffe, L. P. (1983). The constructivist researcher as teacher and model builder. *Journal for Research in Mathematics Education*, *14*, 83–94.

Cobb, P., Wood, T., and Yackel, E. (1991). Analogies from the philosophy and sociology of science for understanding classroom life. *Science Education, 75*, 23–44.

(1991a). A constructivist approach to second grade mathematics. In E. von Glasersfeld, ed., *Radical constructivism in mathematics education* (pp. 157–76). Dordrecht, Netherlands: Kluwer.

Cobb, P., Wood, T., Yackel, E., and McNeal, B. (1992). Characteristics of classroom mathematics traditions: An interactional analysis. *American Educational Research Journal*, *29*, 573–602.

Cobb, P., Yackel, E., and Wood, T. (1989). Young children's emotional acts while doing mathematical problem solving. In D. B. McLeod and V. M. Adams, eds., *Affect and mathematical problem solving: A new perspective* (pp. 117–48). New York: Springer-Verlag.

Cobern, W.W. (1993). Contextual constructivism: The impact of culture on the learning and teaching of science. In K. Tobin, ed., *The practice of constructivism in science education* (pp. 51–69). Hillsdale, N.J.: Erlbaum.

(1996). Worldview theory and conceptual change in science education. *Science Education*, *80*, 579–610.

Cole, M., and Wertsch, J. V. (1996). Beyond individual-social antimony in discussions of Piaget and Vygotsky. *Human Development*, *39*, 250–6.

Collins, H. M. (1990). *Artificial experts: Social knowledge and intelligent machines*. Cambridge, Mass.: MIT Press.

Confrey, J. (1980). *Conceptual change, number concepts, and the introduction to calculus*. Doctoral dissertation, Cornell University, Ithaca, N.Y.

(1991). The concept of exponential functions: A student's perspective. In L. P. Steffe, ed., *Epistemological foundations of mathematical experience* (pp. 124–59). New York: Springer-Verlag.

(1993). Learning to see children's mathematics crucial challenges in constructivist reform. In K. Tobin, ed., *The practice of constructivism in science education* (pp. 299–321). Hillsdale, N.J.: Erlbaum.

(1994). A theory of intellectual development, Part I. *For the Learning of Mathematics*, *14*, 2–8.

(1995). Student voice in examining "splitting" as an approach to ratio, proportion, and fractions. In L. Meira and D. Carraher, eds., *Proceedings of the Nineteenth International Conference for the Psychology of Mathematics Education* (Vol. 1, pp. 3–29). Recife, Brazil: Universidade Federal de Pernambuco.

Confrey, J., and Scarano, G. H. (1997). Constructivism for the practicing teacher. In Eisenhower National Clearinghouse, ed., *In support of excellence: Views from the field* (CD-ROM). Columbus, Ohio: Ohio State University.

Confrey, J., and Smith, E. (1994). Exponential functions, rates of change, and the multiplicative unit. *Educational Studies in Mathematics, 26*, 135–64.

(1995). Splitting, covariation, and their role in the development of exponential functions. *Journal for Research in Mathematics Education, 26* , 66–86.

Cornbleth, C., and Waugh, D. (1995). *The great speckled bird: Multicultural politics and education policymaking*. New York: St. Martin's Press.

Council of Chief State School Officers. (1995). *State curriculum frameworks in mathematics and science: How are they changing across the states.* Washington, D.C.: Author.

Daignault, J. (1985). *Pour une esthétique de la pédagogie*. Chicoutimi, Québec: Éditions N.H.P.

Danek, J. G., Calbert, R., and Chubin, D. E. (1994, February). *NSF's programmatic reform: The catalyst for systemic change*. Paper presented at an invitational conference sponsored by the National Science Foundation, ''Building the System: Making Science Education Work,'' Washington, D.C.

Daniels, H. (1996). The classroom as workshop. *Best Practice, 10*, 1.

(1996a). The Best Practice Project: Building parent partnerships in Chicago. *Educational Leadership, 53*, 38–43.

Darling-Hammond, L., and McLaughlin, M. W. (1995). Policies that support professional development in an era of reform. *Phi Delta Kappan, 76*, 597–604.

Davis, P. J., and Hersh, R. (1981). *The mathematical experience.* Boston, Mass.: Birkhäuser.

Davydov, V. V. (1988). Problems of developmental teaching (Part II). *Soviet Education, 30*, 3–83.

DeBoer, G. E. (1991). *A history of ideas in science education: Implications for practice*. New York: Teachers College Press.

De Corte, E., and Verschaffel, L. (1983, April). *Beginning first graders' initial representation of arithmetic problems*. Paper presented at the annual conference of the American Educational Research Association, Montréal.

Department of Education. (1994). *Strong families, strong schools: Building community partnerships for learning*. Washington, D.C.: Author.

Désautels, J., and Larochelle, M. (1989). *Qu'est-ce que le savoir scientifique? Points de vue d'adolescents et d'adolescentes.* Québec: Presses de l'Université Laval.

Désautels, J., Lauzon, B., and Larochelle, M. (1987). *L'énigmatique, un log-*

iciel pour l'enseignement des sciences. Québec: Centre d'enseignement et de recherche en informatique Clément Lockquell.

Dewey, J. (1895, 1971). The theory of emotion. In J. A. Boydston, ed., *John Dewey: The early works* (Vol. 4, pp. 152–88). Carbondale: Southern Illinois University Press.

(1896, 1972). The reflex arc concept in psychology. In J. A. Boydston, ed., *John Dewey: The early works* (Vol. 5, pp. 96–109). Carbondale: Southern Illinois University Press.

(1922, 1983). Human nature and conduct. In J. A. Boydston, ed., *John Dewey: The middle works* (Vol. 14). Carbondale: Southern Illinois University Press.

(1925, 1981). Experience and nature. In J. A. Boydston, ed., *John Dewey: The later works* (Vol. 1). Carbondale: Southern Illinois University Press.

(1932, 1985). Ethics. In J. A. Boydston, ed., *John Dewey: The later works, 1925–1953* (Vol. 7). Carbondale: Southern Illinois Press.

Dionne, P., and Ouellet, G. (1990). *La communication interpersonnelle et organisationnelle: l'effet Palo-Alto*. Boucherville, Québec: Gaëtan Morin.

Doise, W. (1985). Piaget and the social development of intelligence. In L. Camaioni and G. de Lemos, eds., *Questions on social explanation: Piagetian themes reconsidered* (pp. 43–54). Amsterdam/Philadelphia: John Benjamins.

Driver, R. (1973). *The representation of conceptual frameworks in young adolescent science students*. Doctoral thesis, University of Illinois, Urbana/Champaign, Illinois.

(1989). Student's conceptions and the learning of science. *International Journal of Science Education, 2*, 481–90.

Driver, R., Asoko, H., Leach, J., Mortimer, E., and Scott, P. (1994). Constructing scientific knowledge in the classroom. *Educational Researcher, 23*, 5–12.

Driver, R., and Easley, J. (1978). Pupils and paradigms: A review of literature related to concept development in adolescent science students. *Studies in Science Education, 5*, 61–84.

Driver, R., Leach, J., Millar, R., and Scott, P. (1996). *Young people's images of science*. Buckingham, U.K.: Open University Press.

Driver, R., and Oldham, V. (1986). A constructivist approach to curriculum development in science. *Studies in Science Education, 13*, 105–22.

Duschl, R. A. (1988). Abandoning the scientistic legacy of science education. *Science Education, 72*, 51–62.

Edwards, D. (1997). *Discourse and cognition*. London: Sage.

Egan, K. (1983). *Education and psychology: Plato, Piaget, and scientific psychology*. New York: Teachers College Press.

Eisner, E. W. (1995). Standards for American schools: Help or hindrance? *Phi Delta Kappan, 76*, 758–64.

Elbers, E. (1986). Interaction and instruction in the conservation experiment. *European Journal of Psychology of Education, 1*, 77–89.

Erlwanger, S. H. (1974). *Case studies of children's conceptions of mathematics*. Doctoral thesis, University of Illinois, Urbana/Champaign, Illinois.

Feyerabend, P. (1979). *Against method* (2nd ed.). London: Verso.

(1991). *Three dialogues on knowledge*. Oxford: Basil Blackwell.

Finders, M., and Lewis, C. (1994). Why some parents don't come to school. *Educational Leadership, 52*, 50–4.

Fleury, S. C. (1989). Redefining the social studies, absolutely. *Social Science Record, 26*, 7–9.

Fort, D. C. (1993). Science shy, science savvy, science smart. *Phi Delta Kappan, 74*, 674–82.

Foucault, M. (1975). *Surveiller et punir. Naissance de la prison*. Paris: Gallimard.

Fourez, G. (1996). *La construction des sciences* (3rd ed.). Brussels: De Boeck.

Fourez, G., Englebert-Lecomte, V., and Mathy, P. (1997). *Nos savoirs sur nos savoirs. Un lexique d'épistémologie pour l'enseignement*. Brussels/Paris: De Boeck Université.

Freudenthal, H. (1991). *Revisiting mathematics education. China lectures*. Dordrecht, Netherlands: Kluwer.

Fullan, M. (1993). *Change forces*. New York: Falmer Press.

Gadotti, M. (1979). *L'éducation contre l'éducation*. Lausanne: L'Âge d'homme.

Gallagher, J. J. (1993). Secondary science teachers and constructivist practice. In K. Tobin, ed., *The practice of constructivism in science education* (pp. 181–91). Hillsdale, N.J.: Erlbaum.

Gallas, K. (1995). *Talking their way into science: Hearing children's questions and theories, responding with curricula*. New York: Teachers College Press.

Gardner, H. (1993). *Multiple intelligences: The theory in practice*. New York: Basic Books.

Garmston, R., and Wellman, B. (1995). Adaptive schools in a quantum universe. *Educational Leadership, 52*, 6–12.

Garnier, C., Bednarz, N., and Ulanovskaya, I., eds. (1991). *Après Vygotski et Piaget. Perspectives sociale et constructiviste. Écoles russe et occidentale*. Brussels: De Boeck.

Garrison, J. (1994). Realism, Deweyan pragmatism, and educational research. *Educational Researcher, 23*, 5–14.

Garrison, J., and Bentley, M. L. (1990). Teaching scientific method: The logic of confirmation and falsification. *School Science and Mathematics, 90*, 188–97.

Garton, A. F. (1992). *Social interaction and the development of language and cognition*. Hillsdale, N.J.: Erlbaum.

Gergen, K. J. (1985). The social constructivist movement in modern psychology. *American Psychologist, 40,* 266–75.

(1995). Social construction and the educational process. In L. P. Steffe and J. Gale, eds., *Constructivism in education* (pp. 17–39). Hillsdale, N.J.: Erlbaum.

Ghiglione, R. (1987). Questionner. In A. Blanchet, R. Ghiglione, J. Massonnat, and A. Trognon, eds., *Les techniques d'enquête en sciences sociales* (pp. 127–82). Paris: Dunod.

Gilly, M. (1991). Psicologia sociale delle costruzioni cognitive. In G. Gilli and A. Marchetti, eds., *Prospettive sociogenetiche e sviluppo cognitivo* (pp. 21–45). Milan: Raffaello Cortina.

Good, R. G., Wandersee, J. H., and St. Julien, J. (1993). Cautionary notes on the appeal of the new ''ism'' (constructivism) in science education. In K. Tobin, ed., *The practice of constructivism in science education* (pp. 71–87). Hillsdale, N.J.: Erlbaum.

Good, T. L. (1996). Educational researchers comment on the education summit and other policy proclamations from 1983–1996. *Educational Researcher, 25,* 4–6.

Gravemeijer, K. P. E. (1991). An instruction-theoretic reflection on the use of manipulatives. In L. Streefland, ed., *Realistic mathematics education in primary school* (pp. 57–76). Utrecht, Netherlands: CD-B Press.

Grossen, M. (1988). *L'intersubjectivité en situation de test.* Cousset, Switzerland: DelVal.

(1993). Conséquences théoriques et méthodologiques d'un changement d'unité d'analyse pour l'étude des interactions entre enfants en situation de corésolution de problème. *Cahiers de psychologie, 30,* 17–37.

Grossman, P. L., and Stodolsky, S. S. (1995). Content as context: The role of school subjects in secondary school teaching. *Educational Researcher, 24,* 5–11.

Handlin, O. (1979). *Truth in history.* Cambridge, Mass.: Harvard University Press.

Hanson, N. R. (1958). *Patterns of discovery.* Cambridge, U.K.: Cambridge University Press.

Hargreaves, A. (1995). Renewal in the age of paradox. *Educational Leadership, 52,* 14–19.

Harrison, A. G., and Treagust, D. F. (1996). Secondary students' mental models of atoms and molecules: Implications for teaching chemistry. *Science Education, 80,* 509–34.

Haury, D. L. (1994). From the Director . . . Cultivating human potential in science and mathematics. *CSMEE Horizon, 2,* 1–2.

Henderson, A. T., and Berla, N., eds. (1994). *A new generation of evidence: The family is critical to student achievement.* Washington, D.C.: Center for Law and Education.

Hendry, G. D., and King, R. C. (1994). On theory of learning and knowledge:

Educational implications of advances in neuroscience. *Science Education, 78*, 223–53.

Herman, W. L., Jr. (1977). How intermediate children rank the subjects. *Journal of Education Research, 56*, 435–6.

Hestenes, D. (1992). Modeling games in the Newtonian world. *American Journal of Physics, 60*, 732–48.

Hewson, P. W., and Hewson, M. G. (1988). An appropriate conception of teaching science: A view from studies of science learning. *Science Education, 72*, 597–614.

Hills, G. S. (1989). Students' ''untutored'' beliefs about natural phenomena: Primitive science or commonsense? *Science Education, 73*, 155–86.

Hirsch, E. D., Jr. (1987). *Cultural literacy: What every American needs to know*. Boston: Houghton Mifflin.

Hoetker, J., and Ahlbrand, W. P. (1969). The persistence of the recitation. *American Educational Research Journal, 6*, 145–67.

Hume, D. (1758, 1963). *An enquiry concerning human understanding*. New York: Washington Square Press (originally published in 1742 and entitled *Philosophical essays concerning human understanding*. London: Millar).

Hurd, P. D. (1994). New minds for a new age: Prologue to modernizing the science curriculum. *Science Education, 78*, 102–16.

Iannaccone, A., and Perret-Clermont, A.-N. (1990, September). *Qu'est-ce qui s'apprend? Qu'est-ce qui se développe?* Paper presented at the conference ''Les savoirs quotidiens. Les approches cognitives dans le dialogue interculturel,'' Académie suisse des sciences humaines, Sigristwil, Switzerland.

Ihde, D. (1993). *Postphenomenology: Essays in the postmodern context*. Evanston, Ill.: Northwestern University Press.

Institut de recherche sur l'enseignement des mathématiques de Grenoble (Elementary-level research team). (1980). Quel est l'âge du capitaine? *Bulletin de l'association des professeurs de mathématiques de l'enseignement public* (APMEP), *323*, 235–43.

Isaacson, N., and Bamburg, J. (1992). Can schools become learning organizations? *Educational Leadership, 50*, 42–4.

Jenkins, E. W. (1992). HPS and school science education: Remediation or reconstruction? In S. Hills, ed., *Proceedings of the second international conference on the history and philosophy of science in science education* (Vol. 1, pp. 559–69). Kingston, Ontario: Queen's University.

(1995). Benchmarks for science literacy: A review symposium. *Journal of Curriculum Studies, 27*, 445–61.

Kagan, D. M. (1992). Professional growth among preservice and beginning teachers. *Review of Educational Research, 62*, 129–69.

Kant, I. (1787). *Kritik der reinen Vernunft* (Vol. III, 2nd ed. – Werke, Ko-

enigliche Preussische Akademie der Wissenschaften). Berlin: Reimer (2nd ed., 1911).
(1881–84). Opus postumum. (R. Reicke, ed.). In *Altpreussische Monatsschrift, XIX* (quoted by H. Vaihinger in *Die Philosophie des Als Ob,* Aalen: Scientia Verlag, 1986).
Kelly, G. A. (1955). *The psychology of personal constructs.* New York: Norton.
Klapper, M. H. (1994). Education standards: A conference issue. *Cognosos, 3*, 1–4.
Kliebard, H. M. (1987). *The struggle for the American curriculum: 1893–1958.* New York: Routledge and Kegan Paul.
Kawasaki, K. (1996). The concepts of science in Japanese and Western education. *Science & Education, 5*, 1–20.
Kuhn, D. (1993). Science as argument: Implications for teaching and learning scientific thinking. *Science Education, 77*, 319–37.
Kuhn, T. S. (1970). *The structure of scientific revolutions* (2nd ed.). Chicago: University of Chicago Press.
(1983). *La structure des révolutions scientifiques* (L. Meyer, trans.). Paris: Flammarion.
Kumar, D., and Voldrich, J. F. (1994). Situated cognition in second grade science: Literature books for authentic contexts. *Journal of Elementary Science Education, 6*, 1–10.
Lakoff, G., and Johnson, M. (1980). *Metaphors we live by.* Chicago: University of Chicago Press.
Lampert, M. L. (1985). How do teachers manage to teach? Perspectives on the problems of practice. *Harvard Educational Review, 55*, 178–94.
(1990). When the problem is not the question and the solution is not the answer: Mathematical knowing and teaching. *American Educational Research Journal, 27*, 29–63.
Lange, J. de (1987). *Mathematics insight and meaning.* Doctoral thesis, OW et OC, Rijksuniversiteit, Utrecht, Netherlands.
Larochelle, M., and Désautels, J. (1991). "Of course, it's just obvious!" Adolescents' ideas of scientific knowledge. *International Journal of Science Education, 14*, 373–89.
(1992). *Autour de l'idée de science. Itinéraires cognitifs d'étudiants et d'étudiantes.* Québec/Brussels: Presses de l'Université Laval and De Boeck-Wesmaël.
Larochelle, M., Désautels, J., and Ruel, F. (1995). Les sciences à l'école: portrait d'une fiction. *Recherches Sociographiques, 36*, 527–55.
Latour, B. (1987). *Science in action.* Cambridge, Mass.: Harvard University Press.
(1989). *La science en action* (M. Biezunski, trans.). Paris: La Découverte.
Latour, B., and Woolgar, S. (1988). *La vie en laboratoire* (M. Biezunski, trans.). Paris: La Découverte.

Lave, J. (1988). *Cognition in practice: Mind, mathematics, and culture in everyday life*. Cambridge, U.K.: Cambridge University Press.

Lave, J., and Wenger, E. (1991). *Situated learning: Legitimate peripheral participation*. New York: Cambridge University Press.

Lavelle, L. (1957). *Conduite à l'égard d'autrui*. Paris: Albin Michel.

Lawson, H., and Appignanesi, L., eds. (1989). *Dismantling truth. Reality in the post-modern world*. New York: St. Martin's Press.

Leming, J. S. (1989). The two cultures of social studies education. *Social Education, 53*, 404–8.

(1992). Ideological perspectives within the social studies profession: An empirical examination of the two cultures thesis. *Theory and Research in Social Education, 20*, 293–312.

Lemke, J. L. (1990). *Talking science: Language, learning, and values*. Norwood, N.J.: Ablex.

Lemke, J. L. (1995). *Textual politics: Discourse and social dynamics*. London: Taylor and Francis.

Lerman, S. (1996). Intersubjectivity in mathematics learning: A challenge to the radical constructivist paradigm? *Journal for Research in Mathematics Education, 27*, 133–50.

Levstik, L. S., and Pappas, C. C. (1992). New directions for studying historical understanding. *Theory and Research in Social Education, 20*, 369–85.

Loewen, J. W. (1995). *Lies my teacher told me: Everything your American history textbook got wrong*. New York: The New Press.

Lorenz, J.-H. (1991). *Stoerungen beim mathematiklernen*. Untersuchungen zum Mathematikunterricht, Band 16, IDM Universität Bielefeld, Koeln: Aulis Verlag, Deubner.

Lorsbach, A., and Tobin, K. (1992). Constructivism as a referent for science teaching. *NARST: Research matters to the science teacher, 30*, 1–3.

Luhmann, N. (1986). Intersubjektivität oder kommunikation: Unterschiedliche ausgangspunkte soziologischer theoriebildung. *Archivio di Filosofia, 54*, 41–60.

Lunetta, V. N. (1998). The high school science laboratory: Historical perspectives and contexts for contemporary teaching. In B. J. Fraser and K. Tobin, eds., *International handbook of science education* (pp. 249–62). Dordrecht, Netherlands: Kluwer.

Luria, A. R. (1979). *The making of the mind: A personal account of Soviet psychology*. Cambridge, Mass.: Harvard University Press.

Lyons, N. (1990). Dilemmas of knowing: Ethical and epistemological dimensions of teachers' work and development. *Harvard Educational Review, 60*, 159–80.

Mahoney, M. J., and Lyddon, W. J. (1988). Recent developments in cognitive approaches to counseling and psychotherapy. *The Counseling Psychologist, 16*, 190–234.

Marcuse, H. (1969). *Eros and civilisation*. London: Allen Lane and Penguin.

Mason, J., Burton, L., and Stacey, K. (1982). *Thinking mathematically*. London: Addison-Wesley.

Maturana, H., and Varela, F. J. (1980). *Autopoiesis and cognition*. Dordrecht, Netherlands: Reidel.

(1987). *The tree of knowledge. The biological roots of human understanding*. Boston: Shambhala.

May, W. T. (1992). What are the subjects of STS – really? *Theory into Practice*, *31*, 73–83.

McGinn, M. K., Roth, W. M., Boutonné, S., and Woszczyna, C. (1995). The transformation of individual and collective knowledge in elementary science classrooms that are organized as knowledge-building communities. *Research in Science Education*, *25*, 163–89.

McNeil, L. M. (1986). *Contradictions of control: School structure and school knowledge*. New York: Routledge.

Mead, G. H. (1903). The definition of the psychical. In A. J. Reck, ed. (1964), *Selected writings: George Herbert Mead* (pp. 25–59). Chicago: University of Chicago Press.

(1909). Social psychology as counterpart to physiological psychology. In A. J. Reck, ed. (1964), *Selected writings: George Herbert Mead* (pp. 94–104). Chicago: University of Chicago Press.

(1910). Social consciousness and the consciousness of meaning. In A. J. Reck, ed. (1964), *Selected writings: George Herbert Mead* (pp. 123–33). Chicago: University of Chicago Press.

(1912). The mechanism of social consciousness. In A. J. Reck, ed. (1964), *Selected writings: George Herbert Mead* (pp. 134–41). Chicago: University of Chicago Press.

(1913). The social self. In A. J. Reck, ed. (1964), *Selected writings: George Herbert Mead* (pp. 142–9). Chicago: University of Chicago Press.

(1922). A behaviorist account of the significant symbol. In A. J. Reck, ed. (1964), *Selected writings: George Herbert Mead* (pp. 240–7). Chicago: University of Chicago Press.

(1924). The genesis of self and social control. In A. J. Reck, ed. (1964), *Selected writings: George Herbert Mead* (pp. 267–93). Chicago: University of Chicago Press.

(1927). The objective reality of perspectives. In A. J. Reck, ed. (1964), *Selected writings: George Herbert Mead* (pp. 306–19). Chicago: University of Chicago Press.

Mehan, H. (1979). *Learning lessons: Social organization in the classroom*. Cambridge, Mass.: Harvard University Press.

(1996). Beneath the skin and between the ears: A case study in the politics of representation. In S. Chaiklin and J. Lave, eds., *Understanding practice: Perspectives on activity and context* (pp. 241–68). New York: Cambridge University Press.

Meier, D. (1992). Reinventing teaching. *Teachers College Record, 4*, 594–609.

Meyer, M. (1979). *Découverte et justification en science*. Paris: Klincksieck.

Mills, C. W. (1959). *The sociological imagination*. New York: Oxford University Press.

Moscovici, S., and Hewstone, M. (1984). De la science au sens commun. In S. Moscovici, ed., *Psychologie sociale* (pp. 539–66). Paris: Presses universitaires de France.

Mottershead, L. (1978). *Sources of mathematical discovery*. Oxford: Basil Blackwell.

(1985). *Investigations in mathematics*. Oxford: Basil Blackwell.

Moyer, R., and Bishop, J. (1986). *General science*. Columbus, Ohio: Merrill.

Much, N. C., and Shweder, R. A. (1979). Speaking of rules: The analysis of culture in breach. *New Directions for Child Development, 2*, 19–39.

Muller, J., and Taylor, N. (1995). Schooling and everyday life: Knowledges sacred and profane. *Social Epistemology, 9*, 257–75.

National Center for Education Statistics. (1996, December). *TIMSS United States: Initial findings from the Third International Mathematics and Science Study* [Online]. Available HTTP: http://www.ed.gov/NCES/timss/.

National Commission on Excellence in Education. (1983). *A nation at risk: The imperative for educational reform*. Washington, D.C.: U.S. Government Printing Office.

National Council of Teachers of Mathematics. (1989). *Curriculum and evaluation standards for school mathematics*. Reston, Va.: Author.

National Research Council. (1996). *National science education standards*. Washington, D.C.: National Academy Press.

National Science Teachers Association. (1992). *The content core: A guide for curriculum designers (Scope, Sequence, and Coordination of Secondary School Science Project)*. Washington, D.C.: Author.

Needham, R. A., Powell, D., and Bentley, M. L. (1994, April). *Using "Big Books" in science and social studies*. Paper presented at the annual meeting of the International Reading Association, Toronto, Canada.

Newman, D., Griffin, P., and Cole, M. (1989). *The construction zone: Working for cognitive change in schools*. New York: Cambridge University Press.

Newmann, F. M. (1991). Promoting higher order thinking in social studies: Overview of a study of 16 high school departments. *Theory and Research in Social Education, 19*, 324–40.

Novak, J. D. (1977). *A theory of education*. Ithaca, N.Y.: Cornell University Press.

Nunes, T. (1992). Cognitive invariants and cultural variation in mathematical concepts. *International Journal of Behavioral Development, 15*, 433–53.

Orr, D. (1992). *Education and the transition to a postmodern world.* Ithaca, N.Y.: State University of New York Press.

Ortony, A., ed. (1984). *Metaphor and thought.* Cambridge, Mass.: Cambridge University Press.

Panofsky, C. P., John-Steiner, V., and Blackwell, P. J. (1990). The development of scientific concepts and discourse. In L. C. Moll, ed., *Vygotsky and education* (pp. 251–67). New York: Cambridge University Press.

Parenti, M. (1991). *Democracy for the few.* New York: St. Martin's Press.

Peck, K. L., and Dorricott, D. (1994). Why use technology. *Educational Leadership, 50,* 11–14.

Peirce, C. S. (1935). *Collected papers of Charles Sanders Peirce* (Vol. 5, C. Hartshorne and P. Weise, eds). Cambridge, Mass.: Harvard University Press.

Perret-Clermont, A. N., and Nicolet, M., eds. (1988). *Interagir et connaître.* Cousset, Switzerland: DelVal.

Perret-Clermont, A. N., Perret, J. F., and Bell, N. (1991). The social construction of meaning and cognitive activity in elementary school. In L. B. Resnick, J. M. Levine, and S. D. Teasley, eds., *Perspectives on socially shared cognition* (pp. 41–62). Washington, D.C.: American Psychological Association.

Perret-Clermont, A. N., Schubauer-Leoni, M. L., and Grossen, M. (1996). Interactions sociales dans le développement cognitif: nouvelles directions de recherche. In A. N. Perret-Clermont, ed., *La construction de l'intelligence dans l'interaction sociale* (pp. 261–84). Berne: Peter Lang.

Perret-Clermont, A. N., Schubauer-Leoni, M. L., and Trognon, A. (1992). L'extorsion des réponses en situation asymétrique. *Verbum, 1–2,* 3–32.

Pfundt, J., and Duit, R. (1994). *Bibliography: Students' alternative frameworks and science education* (4th ed.). Kiel, Germany: Institute for Science Education.

Phelan, A. M. (1994). Unmasking metaphors of management: A pedagogy of collaborative deconstruction. *Teaching Education, 6,* 101–11.

Phillipson, R. (1992). *Linguistic imperialism.* Oxford: Oxford University Press.

Piaget, J. (1950). *The psychology of intelligence* (M. Piercy, trans.). London: Routledge and Kegan Paul (originally published 1947).

(1961). The genetic approach to the psychology of thought. *Journal of Educational Psychology, 52,* 275–81.

(1967). *Biologie et connaissance.* Paris: Gallimard.

(1970). Piaget's theory (G. Gellerier and J. Langer, trans.). In P. H. Mussen, ed., *Carmichael's manual of child psychology* (Vol. 1, pp. 703–32) (3rd ed.). New York: Wiley.

(1971). *Structuralism* (C. Maschler, trans.). London: Routledge and Kegan Paul (originally published 1968).

(1971a). *La construction du réel chez l'enfant*. Neuchâtel: Delachaux and Niestlé.

(1972). *Psychology and epistemology* (P. A. Wells, trans.). Harmondsworth: Penguin Books (originally published 1970).

(1980). *Adaptation and intelligence: Organic selection and phenocopy* (S. Eames, trans.). Chicago, Ill.: University of Chicago Press (originally published 1974).

(1983). *The origin of intelligence in the child* (M. Cook, trans.). Harmondsworth: Penguin (originally published 1936).

Piaget, J., and Garcia, R. (1983). *Psychogenèse et histoire des sciences*. Paris: Flammarion.

Piaget, J., and Garcia, R. (1989). *Psychogenesis and the history of science* (H. Feider, trans.). New York: Columbia University Press.

Pickering, A., ed. (1992). *Science as practice and culture*. Chicago: Chicago University Press.

Pinner, M. T., and Shuard, H. (1985). *In-service education in primary mathematics*. Milton Keynes, U.K.: Open University Press.

Popkewitz, T. S. (1991). *A political sociology of educational reform: Power/knowledge in teaching, teacher education, and research*. New York: Teachers College Press.

Popper, K. R. (1968). *The logic of scientific discovery*. New York: Harper and Row.

Posner, G. J., Strike, K. A., Hewson, P. W., and Gertzog, W. A. (1982). Accommodation of a scientific conception: Toward a theory of conceptual change. *Science Education*, *66*, 211–27.

Purpel, D. E. (1989). *The moral and spiritual crisis in education: A curriculum for justice and compassion in education*. New York: Bergin and Garvey.

Putnam, R. T., Lampert, M., and Peterson, P. L. (1990). Alternative perspectives on knowing mathematics in elementary schools. In C. B. Cazden, ed., *Review of Research in Education* (Vol. 16, pp. 57–150). Washington, D.C.: American Research Association.

Ravitch, D., and Finn, C. E., Jr. (1987). *What do our seventeen-year-olds know? A report on the first national assessment of history and literature*. New York: Harper and Row.

Reichenbach, H. (1951). *The rise of scientific philosophy*. Berkeley, Calif.: University of California Press.

Restivo, S. (1988). Modern science as a social problem. *Social Problems, 3*, 206–25.

Reynolds, A. (1992). What is competent beginning teaching? A review of the literature. *Review of Educational Research*, *62*, 1–35.

Richards, J. (1991). Mathematical discussions. In E. von Glasersfeld, ed., *Radical constructivism in mathematics education* (pp. 13–52). Dordrecht, Netherlands: Kluwer.

Ricœur, P. (1979). La raison pratique. In T. Geraets, ed., *La rationalité aujourd'hui.* (pp. 225–41). Ottawa, Ontario: Université d'Ottawa (also in P. Ricœur (1989), *Du texte à l'action. Essais d'herméneutique II.* Paris: Seuil).

Rogalski, J. (1982). Acquisition de notions relatives à la dimensionalité des mesures spatiales (longueur, surface). *Recherches en didactique des mathématiques, 3*, 343–96.

Rogoff, B. (1995). Observing sociocultural activity on three planes: Participatory appropriation, guided participation, and apprenticeship. In J. V. Wertsch, P. Del Río, and A. Alvarez, eds., *Sociocultural studies of mind* (pp. 139–64). New York: Cambridge University Press.

Rommeiveit, R. (1974). *On message structure*. London: Wiley.

Rorty, R. (1978). *Philosophy and the mirror of nature.* Princeton, N.J.: Princeton University Press.

Ross, D. (1991). *Origins of American social science*. Cambridge, Mass.: Cambridge University Press.

Roth, W-M. (1995). *Authentic school science: Knowing and learning in open-inquiry science laboratories*. Dordrecht, Netherlands: Kluwer.

(1996). Teacher questioning in an open-inquiry learning environment: Interactions of context, content, and student responses. *Journal of Research in Science Teaching, 33*, 709–36.

Roth, W-M., McRobbie, C. J., Lucas, K. B., and Boutonné, S. (1997). The local production of order in science laboratories: A phenomenological analysis. *Learning and Instruction, 7*, 137–59.

Roychoudhury, A. (1994). Is it minds-off science? A concern for the elementary grades. *Journal of Science Teacher Education, 5*, 87–96.

Rucker, D. (1968). An unpublished paper by George Herbert Mead. *School and Society, 96*, 148–52.

Ruel, F. (1994). *La complexification conceptuelle des représentations sociales discursives à l'égard de l'enseignement et de l'apprentissage chez de futurs enseignants et enseignantes de sciences*. Doctoral thesis, Université Laval, Québec.

Ryan, A. G., and Aikenhead, G. S. (1992). Students' preconception about the epistemology of science. *Science Education, 76*, 559–80.

Sagor, R. (1995). Overcoming the one-solution syndrome. *Educational Leadership, 52*, 24–7.

Säljö, R., and Wyndhamn, J. (1987). The formal setting as context for cognitive activities: An empirical study of arithmetic operations under conflicting premises for communication. *European Journal of Psychology of Education, 2*, 233–45.

Saul, W., Reardon, J., Schmidt, A., Pearce, C., Blackwood, D., and Bird, M. D. (1993). *Science workshop: A whole language approach*. Portsmouth, N.H.: Heinemann.

Schlagel, R. (1986). *Contextual realism: A meta-physical framework for modern science*. New York: Paragon House.

Schnobrich, J., and Bentley, M. L. (1997). Quality education is a family affair: Elementary school reform based upon collaboration, community building, and national standards. *Illinois Schools Journal, 76*, 20–30.

Schön, D. (1985). *The design studio*. London: RIBA Publications.

Schubauer-Leoni, M. L. (1986). Le contrat didactique: un cadre interprétatif pour comprendre les savoirs manifestés par les élèves en mathématiques. *Journal Européen de Psychologie de l'Éducation, 1–2*, 139–53.

(1988). L'interaction expérimentateur-sujet à propos d'un savoir mathématique: la situation de test revisitée. In A. N. Perret-Clermont and M. Nicolet, eds., *Interagir et connaître* (pp. 251–64). Cousset, Switzerland: DelVal.

Schubauer-Leoni, M. L., Bell, N., Grossen, M., and Perret-Clermont, A. N. (1989). Problems in assessment of learning: The social construction of questions and answers in the scholastic context. *International Journal of Educational Research, 13*, 671–84.

Schubauer-Leoni, M. L., and Grossen, M. (1993). Negotiating the meaning of questions in didactic and experimental contracts. *European Journal of Psychology of Education, 4*, 451–71.

Schubauer-Leoni, M. L., Perret-Clermont, A. N., and Grossen, M. (1992). The construction of adult child intersubjectivity in psychological research and in school. In M. von Cranach, W. Doise, and G. Mugny, eds., *Social representations and the social bases of knowledge* (pp. 69–77). Lewiston, N.Y.: Hogrefe and Huber.

Segal, L. (1986). *The dream of reality: Heinz von Foerster's Constructivism*. New York: Norton.

Seixas, P. (1994). Students' understanding of historical significance. *Theory and Research in Social Education, 22*, 281–304.

(1997). Mapping the terrain of historical significance. *Social Education, 61*, 22–7.

Serres, M., ed. (1989). *Éléments d'histoire des sciences*. Paris: Bordas.

Shamos, M. H. (1989). Views of scientific literacy in elementary school science programs: Past, present, and future. In A. B. Champagne, B. E. Lovitts, and B. J. Calinger, eds., *Scientific literacy* (pp. 109–27). Washington, D.C.: American Association for the Advancement of Science.

Shapin, S., and Schaffer, S. (1989). *Leviathan and the air-pump: Hobbes, Boyle, and the politics of experiment*. Princeton, N.J.: Princeton University Press.

Shaver, J. P. (1982). Reappraising the theoretical goals of research in social education. *Theory and Research in Social Education, 9*, 1–16.

Shirk, G. B. (1972). *An examination of conceptual frameworks of beginning mathematics teachers*. Doctoral thesis, University of Illinois, Urbana/Champaign, Illinois.

Shuard, H., and Rothery, A. (1984). *Children reading mathematics*. London: John Murray.

Siegal, M. (1991). *Knowing children: Experiments in conversation and cognition*. Hove, Sussex: Erlbaum.

Simpson, P. J., and Garrison, J. (1995). Teaching and moral perception. *Teachers College Record*, *97*, 252–78.

Sivertsen, M. L. (1993). *Transforming ideas for teaching and learning science: A guide for elementary science education.* Washington, D.C.: U.S. Department of Education.

Sjøberg, S. (1996). Science education research in Europe: Some reflections for the future association. In G. Welford, J. Osborne, and P. Scott, eds., *Research in science education in Europe* (pp. 399–404). London: Falmer Press.

Smith, E., and Confrey, J. (1994). Multiplicative structures and the development of logarithms: What was lost by the invention of function. In G. Harel and J. Confrey, eds., *The development of multiplicative reasoning in the learning of mathematics* (pp. 333–64). Albany, N.Y.: State University of New York Press.

Smylie, M. A. (1996). From bureaucratic control to building human capital: The importance of teacher learning in education reform. *Educational Researcher*, *25*, 9–11.

Solomon, J. (1987). Social influences on the construction of pupils' understanding of science. *Studies in Science Education*, *14*, 63–82.

Solomon, Y. (1989). *The practice of mathematics.* London: Routledge.

Stake, R., and Easley, J. (1978). *Case studies in science education*. Urbana, Ill.: Center for Instructional Research and Curriculum Evaluation, University of Illinois.

Stanley, W. B., and Brickhouse, N. W. (1994). Multiculturalism, universalism, and science education. *Science Education*, *78*, 387–98.

Steffe, L. P., Cobb, P., and von Glasersfeld, E. (1988). *Construction of arithmetical meanings and strategies.* New York: Springer-Verlag.

Steffe, L. P., and Gale, J., eds. (1995). *Constructivism in education*. Hillsdale, N.J.: Erlbaum.

Steffe, L. P., von Glasersfeld, E., Richards, J., and Cobb, P. (1983). *Children's counting types: Philosophy, theory, and application.* New York: Praeger Scientific.

Stengers, I., ed. (1987). *D'une science à l'autre: des concepts nomades*. Paris: Seuil.

Streefland, L. (1991). *Fractions in realistic mathematics education: A paradigm of developmental research.* Dordrecht, Netherlands: Kluwer.

Strike, K. A., and Posner, G. (1992). A revisionist theory of conceptual change. In R. A. Duschl and R. J. Hamilton, eds., *Philosophy of science, cognitive psychology, and educational theory and practice* (pp. 147–76). Albany: State University of New York Press.

Suter, L. E., ed. (1993). *Indicators of science and mathematics education 1992*. Washington, D.C.: National Science Foundation.

Sutton, C. (1996). Beliefs about science and beliefs about language. *International Journal of Science Education, 18*, 1–18.

Swartz, E. (1996). Emancipatory pedagogy: A postcritical response to ''standard'' school knowledge. *Journal of Curriculum Studies, 28*, 397–418.

Terhart, E. (1988). Philosophy of science and school science teaching. *International Journal of Science Education, 10*, 11–16.

The New London Group. (1996). A pedagogy of multiliteracies: Designing social futures. *Harvard Educational Review, 66*, 60–92.

Thornton, S. J. (1990). Should we be teaching more history? *Theory and Research in Social Education, 18*, 53–60.

(1997). First-hand study: Teaching history for understanding. *Social Education, 61*, 11–12.

Tiberghien, A. (1989). Phénomènes et situations matérielles: quelles interprétations pour l'élève et le physicien? In N. Bednarz and C. Garnier, eds., *Construction des savoirs. Obstacles et conflits* (pp. 93–102). Montréal: Agence d'Arc.

Tippins, D. J., Nichols, S., and Tobin, K. (1993, January). *Reconstructing science teacher education within communities of learners*. Paper presented at the first international Conference of the Association for the Education of Teachers in Science, Charleston, S.C.

Tobin, K. (1987). The role of wait time in higher cognitive level learning. *Review of Educational Research, 57*, 69–95.

(1989, October). *Radical constructivism.* An invited lecture presented at Florida State University, Panama City.

(1990). Research on science laboratory activities: In pursuit of better questions and answers to improve learning. *School Science and Mathematics, 90*, 403–18.

(1997). The teaching and learning of elementary science. In G. D. Phye, ed., *A handbook of classroom learning: The construction of academic knowledge* (pp. 369–403). Orlando, Fla.: Academic Press.

(1997a). Authentic practice of elementary science. *International Journal of Educational Research, 27.*

Tobin, K., and Gallagher, J. J. (1987). What happens in high school science classrooms? *Journal of Curriculum Studies, 19*, 549–60.

Tobin, K., and McRobbie, C. J. (1996). Cultural myths as restraints to the enacted science curriculum. *Science Education, 80*, 223–41.

Tobin, K., Tippins, D. J., and Gallard, A. J. (1994). Teachers as learners in the reform of science education. In D. Gabel, ed., *Handbook for research on science teaching* (pp. 45–93). New York: Macmillan.

Torney-Purta, J. (1991). Schema theory and cognitive psychology: Implication for social studies. *Theory and Research in Social Education, 19,* 189–210.

Treffers, A. (1987). *Three dimensions: A model of goal and theory description in mathematics instruction – The Wiskobas Project.* Dordrecht, Netherlands: Reidel.

(1991). Meeting innumeracy at primary school. *Educational Studies in Mathematics, 22,* 333–52.

U.S. Department of Education. (1987). *What works: Research about teaching and learning.* Washington, D.C.

VanSickle, R. L., and Hoge, J. D. (1991). Higher cognitive psychology: Implication for social studies. *Theory and Research in Social Education, 19,* 152–72.

Varela, F. J. (1988). Le cercle créatif. In P. Watzlawick, ed., *L'invention de la réalité* (pp. 329–45) (A. L. Hacker, trans.). Paris: Seuil.

(1989). *Autonomie et connaissance.* Paris: Seuil.

Vergnaud, G. (1983). Didactique et acquisition du concept de volume. Introduction. *Recherches en didactique des mathématiques, 4,* 9–25.

(1983a). Multiplicative structures. In R. Lesh and M. Landau, eds., *Acquisition of mathematical concepts and processes* (pp. 127–73). New York: Academic Press.

Vico, G. (1710). *De antiquissima Italorum sapientia* (Pomodoro, trans., 1858). Naples: Stamperia de Classici Latini.

Villasenor, A., and Kepner, H. S. (1993). Arithmetic from a problem-solving perspective: An urban implementation. *Journal for Research in Mathematics Education, 24,* 62–9.

Vinh-Bang and Lunzer, E. (1965). *Conservations spatiales. Études d'épistémologie génétique, XIX.* Paris: Presses universitaires de France.

Voigt, J. (1985). Patterns and routines in classroom interaction. *Recherches en didactique des mathématiques, 6,* 69–118.

von Foerster, H. (1988). La construction d'une réalité. In P. Watzlawick, ed., *L'invention de la réalité* (pp. 45–69) (A. L. Hacker, trans.). Paris: Seuil.

(1990). Understanding understanding. *Methodologia, 7,* 7–22.

(1992). Ethics and second-order cybernetics. *Cybernetics & Human Knowing, 1,* 9–18.

von Glasersfeld, E. (1978). Radical constructivism and Piaget's concept of knowledge. In F. B. Murray, ed., *The impact of Piagetian theory* (pp. 109–122). Baltimore, Md.: University Park Press.

(1979). Cybernetics, experience, and the concept of self. In M. N. Ozer, ed., *A cybernetic approach to the assessment of children: Toward a more humane use of human beings* (pp. 67–113). Boulder, Col.: Westview Press.

(1981). Feedback, induction, and epistemology. In G. E. Lasker, ed., *Applied systems and cybernetics* (Vol. 22, pp. 712–19). New York: Pergamon Press.

(1982). An interpretation of Piaget's constructivism. *Revue internationale de philosophie*, *36*, 612–35.

(1983). On the concept of interpretation. *Poetics, 12*, 207–18.

(1984). An introduction to radical constructivism. In P. Watzlawick, ed., *The invented reality* (pp. 17–40). New York: Norton.

(1985). Reconstructing the concept of knowledge. *Archives de Psychologie, 53*, 91–101.

(1987). *The construction of knowledge. Contributions to conceptual semantics*. Seaside, Calif.: Intersystems Publications.

(1987a). Learning as a constructive activity. In C. Janvier, ed., *Problems of representation in the teaching and learning of mathematics* (pp. 3–18). Hillsdale, N.J.: Erlbaum.

(1988). Introduction à un constructivisme radical. In P. Watzlawick, ed., *L'invention de la réalité* (pp. 19–43) (A. L. Hacker, trans.). Paris: Seuil.

(1989). Cognition, construction of knowledge, and teaching. *Synthese*, *80*, 121–40.

(1989a). Constructivism in education. In T. Husen and N. Postlethwaite, eds., *International encyclopedia of education* (Suppl., pp. 11–12). Oxford: Pergamon Press.

(1990). Environment and communication. In L. P. Steffe and T. Wood, eds., *Transforming children's mathematics education* (pp. 30–8). Hillsdale, N.J.: Erlbaum.

(1991). Abstraction, representation, and reflection. In L. P. Steffe, ed., *Epistemological foundations of mathematical experience* (pp. 45–67). New York: Springer Verlag.

(1995). *Constructivism: A way of knowing and learning*. London: Falmer Press.

(1996). The limits of science [Letter to the editor]. *Academe*, *82*, 3–4.

Vosniadou, S. (1994). Capturing and modeling the process of conceptual change. *Learning and Instruction*, *4*, 45–69.

Vygotsky, L. S. (1962). *Thought and language* (E. Hamfnann and G. Vakar, trans.). Cambridge, Mass.: MIT Press and Wiley.

(1978). *Mind in society: The development of higher psychological processes* (M. Cole, V. John-Steiner, S. Scribner, and E. Souberman, eds.). Cambridge, Mass.: Harvard University Press.

(1985). *Pensée et langage* (F. Sève, trans.). Paris: Messidor and Éditions sociales.

Walkerdine, V. (1988). *The mastery of reason: Cognitive development and the production of rationality.* London: Routledge.

Walzer, M. (1983). *Spheres of justice: A defence of pluralism and equity.* New York: Basic Books.

Watzlawick, P. (1988). *Les cheveux du baron de Münchhausen. Psychothérapie et ''réalité''* (A. L. Hacker and M. Daltzer, trans.). Paris: Seuil.

(1988a). Les prédictions qui se vérifient d'elles-mêmes. In P. Watzlawick, ed., *L'invention de la réalité* (pp. 109–30) (A. L. Hacker, trans.). Paris: Seuil.

Wertsch, J. V. (1991). *Voices of the mind: A sociocultural approach to mediated action*. Cambridge, Mass.: Harvard University Press.

Whelan, M. (1992). History and the social studies: A response to the critics. *Theory and Research in Social Education*, *20*, 2–16.

Whorf, B. L. (1956). Language, thought, and reality. In J. B. Carroll, ed., *Selected writings from Benjamin Lee Whorf*. New York/London: M.I.T. Press and Wiley.

Young, M. F. D. (1971). Knowledge and control. In M. F. D. Young, ed., *Knowledge and Control* (pp. 1–17). London: Collier-Macmillan.

Zeichner, K. M. (1993). Connecting genuine teacher development to the struggle for social justice. *Journal of Education for Teaching*, *19*, 5–20.

Zeichner, K. M., and Gore, J. (1990). Teacher socialization. In R. W. Houston, ed., *Handbook of research on teacher education* (pp. 329–48). New York: Macmillan.

Index

MODERN TRENDS IN HINDUISM

LECTURES ON THE HISTORY OF RELIGIONS
SPONSORED BY THE
American Council of Learned Societies
NEW SERIES, NUMBER TEN